Musical Renderings of the Philippine Nation

THE NEW CULTURAL HISTORY OF MUSIC

SERIES EDITOR **Jane F. Fulcher**

SERIES BOARD Celia Applegate
Philip Bohlman
Kate Van Orden
Michael P. Steinberg

*Enlightenment Orpheus: The Power of Music
in Other Worlds*
Vanessa Agnew

Voice Lessons: French Mélodie in the Belle Epoque
Katherine Bergeron

*Songs, Scribes, and Societies: The History
and Reception of the Loire Valley Chansonniers*
Jane Alden

*Harmony and Discord: Music and the Transformation
of Russian Cultural Life*
Lynn M. Sargeant

Musical Renderings of the Philippine Nation
Christi-Anne Castro

CHRISTI-ANNE
CASTRO

Musical Renderings of the Philippine Nation

OXFORD
UNIVERSITY PRESS

OXFORD
UNIVERSITY PRESS

Oxford University Press, Inc., publishes works that further
Oxford University's objective of excellence
in research, scholarship, and education.

Oxford   New York
Auckland   Cape Town   Dar es Salaam   Hong Kong   Karachi
Kuala Lumpur   Madrid   Melbourne   Mexico City   Nairobi
New Delhi   Shanghai   Taipei   Toronto

With offices in
Argentina   Austria   Brazil   Chile   Czech Republic   France   Greece
Guatemala   Hungary   Italy   Japan   Poland   Portugal   Singapore
South Korea   Switzerland   Thailand   Turkey   Ukraine   Vietnam

Copyright © 2011 by Oxford University Press, Inc.

Published by Oxford University Press, Inc.
198 Madison Avenue, New York, New York 10016

www.oup.com

Oxford is a registered trademark of Oxford University Press.

Library of Congress Cataloging-in-Publication Data
Castro, Christi-Anne.
Musical renderings of the Philippine nation / Christi-Anne Castro.
    p.   cm.   (The new cultural history of music series)
Includes bibliographical references and index.
ISBN 978-0-19-974640-8
1. Music—Political aspects—Philippines—History—20th century.   2. Nationalism in music.
3. Music and state.   4. Music—Philippines—20th century—History and criticism.   I. Title.
ML3917.P55C37 2011
781.5'9909599—dc22   2010015955

9 8 7 6 5 4 3 2 1

Printed in the United States of America
on acid-free paper

This book is for my parents, Cristina and Mabini Castro,
from whom inspirations great and small ripple forth like laughter and song.

ACKNOWLEDGMENTS

The consultants featured in this book are responsible for the best insights and none of the flaws found in the text. For their time and thoughts, I owe my gratitude to Leonilo Angos, Josephine Barrios, Michael Dadap, Lois Espinosa, Marijo Castro Fadrigalan, Regalado T. Jose, Lucrecia Kasilag, Zen Lopez, Leo Mascarinas, Elena Rivera Mirano, Ramón Obusan, Ding Pajaron, Jim Paredes, Teresa Rances, Andrea Veneracion, Paz Villanueva, and Patricia Yusah. There are many others not directly quoted in this text but without whom my ideas would not have formed in the same ways. Thanks also to Suzie Benitez and Marton Benitez for the beautiful photographs of Bayanihan, and to Alice Esteves for her help in the library of the Cultural Center of the Philippines.

My research also benefitted from a Rackham Faculty Research Grant from the University of Michigan and from time off given to me by the Musicology Department and the School of Music, Theatre & Dance.

I am indebted to Judith Becker, Heidi Feldman, Francis Gealogo, Katherine Hagedorn, Kathleen Hood, and the anonymous readers for their comments on earlier portions of the book.

For their support and help throughout the publishing process, without which this book would not have made it into its final form, I especially thank series editor Jane Fulcher, Suzanne Ryan, and the capable editorial staff at Oxford Press.

Finally, great thanks go out to my "everyday people," my family and friends. My family is my touchstone. And to Constance Olson, who visions while I tinker and whose faith in me even I cannot assail.

CONTENTS

Musical Renderings of the Philippine Nation

The official culture of the public world is western. It is constitutional, democratic, Roman Catholic. Its legal system is in English. So is the serious press. Public school is bilingual. Global fads and fancies are easily—often eagerly—adopted. The appearance of things is western indeed. Some of this is real, some of it is make-believe, some of it is mere veneer. The point of it is, of course, that it all is Filipino, and that we have to take in how people live with it, how they interpret and understand it themselves.

Niels Mulder (1997)

Music and Self

The group I traveled with had been in the Philippines less than a day, transferring from plane to shuttle to bus to reach the site of the First International Rondalla Festival in 2004. Near the end of the nine-hour drive from Manila to Naga City in the Bikol region, somebody yelled, "Wake up, there are American flags!" Faintly, over the rumbling engine, I heard the sound of brass and drums. Indeed, a small marching band of schoolchildren in full regalia had inserted itself directly in front of the flat snout of our bus, mere footsteps from the exhaust tail of the bus ahead. Additionally, a long ribbon of children stood poised on the lip of the sidewalk, hesitating with homemade paper flags on sticks while they waited for the buses that carried local and international delegates to pass them. Buttoned up smartly in school uniforms on this relentlessly hot Sunday—likely with instructions from civic leaders and teachers at their elementary schools—the children unleashed their ebullient cheers, stiff flags swatting the air, as the wheeled procession finally reached them. From our slowly rolling perch many feet above them, we could make out the multitude of small crayon-colored Mexican, Israeli, Russian, Australian, and U.S. flags clutched by each child. In response to their infectious energy, we dotted the glass windows with our fingertips, pointing and smiling with sleepy enthusiasm. A few of us looked fruitlessly among our belongings for an American flag or some other symbol to let them know where we hailed from, since our faces alone held no easily discernable distinction. We looked, at least at first glance, as if we were Filipinos too.

Our group, the Iskwelahang Pilipino (IP) Rondalla of Boston, had flown to the Philippines for the week as one of two representatives from the United States for *Cuerdas nin Kagabsan* (Strings of Unity), the First International Rondalla Festival.[1] As a group, we had last been there in 1998, during the Philippine Centennial celebrations, and the veteran and new members were equally excited for this trip (see figure 0.1). Along with twelve or so of the most accomplished *rondallas* in the Philippines, artists from Mexico (*Rondalla Motivos de Guadalajara*), Israel (Three Plucked Strings), and Russia (Quartette Phoenix) represented a small sampling of the diversity of plucked string music ensembles found the world over. In contrast to those international groups, the IP Rondalla, the Fil-Am Veterans Rondalla of San José, California, and Rondanihan of Australia, appeared to be local Filipino ensembles in costume, instrumentation, and ethnic makeup. It was if we were sojourners from the motherland returned—the very embodiments of the Filipino diaspora. Throughout the festival I was aware of this in-between state, expected somehow to be able to negotiate the local idiosyncrasies of transportation and decorum, though we were only slightly better equipped to do so than other foreign tourists. Our guide disappeared at inopportune moments, hinting that other foreign groups might need more help. In this small example and in others, questions involving the nuances of national identity became increasingly apparent as the week progressed.

The festival brought together the local, the diasporic, and the international. It created ties through performance between the Filipino *rondalla*, the Mexican guitar *rondalla*, the Russian *balalaika*, and the classical and avant-garde European tradition, thrusting forth competing but complementary understandings of difference and sameness. Identities and boundaries were eminently clear when the ensembles performed individually in formal

FIGURE O.I. The Iskwelahang Pilipino Rondalla of Boston in the Philippines in 1998 (photo from author's collection)

settings, but the symbolic act of playing together in the final concert trumped all of these as emblematic of the festival. Moreover, this national and international festival also revealed a menagerie of ideologies about music, the arts, and the place of the Philippines in the global community. By far, the strongest applause from the Filipino audiences was reserved for the foreign groups—deserved because of their virtuosity and charismatic stage presence, but also spurred on by the desire to welcome them to the islands. The greatest show of appreciation erupted in the middle of the recital by the Israeli group Three Plucked Strings—consisting of harpsichord, mandolin, and guitar— that gamely played through a light drizzle during an outdoor concert. They artfully traced the melody of "Sarungbanggi," the most well known folk song from the Bicol region in which the festival took place, to the unfettered delight of those assembled. The Filipino audience was proud that a foreign group would add a beloved hometown song to the evening's repertoire, perhaps in the same way that many people appreciate tourists who have bothered to learn something of the local language.[2]

Music, in fact, is often compared with language for its ability to communicate on multiple levels. At the same time, ethnomusicologists are quick to point out that while music is a universal practice of all humankind, no single music is itself universal. It is, rather, a product and process of people in particular places and times and, as such, bears the evidence of context as much as it exhibits the ability to generate context. Music is, to be obvious, very meaningful. In the specific case of the First International Rondalla Festival, musical sound and musical performance were very much about identity and place, and not just in regard to the individual groups. On a larger level, the festival was the declaration by a small nation that it belongs to the international community for its contributions to the world of performing arts (through local and diasporic groups), its musical commonalities with other nations, and its ability to attract foreign artists. The local, read first as the Philippine nation, then as the various towns represented by the Filipino groups, and even the site of the festival itself, is elevated conceptually by the performance event into a transnational hub through which both foreign and local cosmopolitans may pass. And the excuse for the commotion, the reason for the temporarily vitalized local economy, and the force guiding every participant, was music. Further, the musical performance at the festival was inextricable from and fully implicated in acts of identity expression ranging from the personal to the national, leading to the subject matter of this book.

This book is a cultural history of the Philippines that outlines the role of music and performance in defining nation and, in its interrelated converse, the influence of national-level politics on shaping musical expression. The genres of music covered range from 1898 to 1998, but the book places added emphasis on the postcolonial era that begins in 1946. These latter decades of nation-building are intensely interesting to consider, arising from the apocalyptic destruction wrought by World War II and ending with the ensconcing of an action movie hero in the presidential palace. During these fifty-some-odd years, the government was charged with defining national culture—and it is the relationship between musical-cultural production and the representation of a national self that is my primary concern. The place is also a fascinating research site, for the Philippines has undergone multiple colonizations, and its self-image as a meeting point between East and West differentiates it from other Asian countries. The United States was the most recent colonizer, and among Filipinos, there is still a close identification with American culture. Though often overlooked by Americans, colonial rule over the Philippines serves as an important part of the rise of U.S. international power and an early case study of U.S. influence on nation-building in other countries.[3] As the book traces the decades of U.S. colonization of the Philippines and then self-rule, three themes crystallize as integral facets of music and national development in the Philippines.

The first is a broad concern with modernism as an impulse in the development of Philippine national character in a postcolonial/neocolonial setting and, more specifically, how modernism becomes apparent in music. Numerous scholars have asserted the tie between the emergence of modernity and nationalist consciousness, though modernism and the means of representing modernity have been different for each nation (Gellner 1983; Smith 1998). While modernism has been used on a smaller scale to define specific movements, such as those in architecture, painting, and music, modernism is also an umbrella term that encompasses ways of thinking and processes of change in larger conceptual categories, including technology, economy, infrastructure, and the arts. In this book, the term "modernism" refers broadly to the ideological impulses that urge society and culture toward an ideal of modernity, whatever contextual specifics that may entail. Yet, while the apparent teleology of modernism is the achievement of modernity, modernity is itself an idea—one that is linked closely to Westernization, the desire to belong to a global community of nations, and the legitimation of self-rule. Further, modernity is an ideal that can be realized only incompletely and with inherent "contradictory and contingent processes" (Dube and Dube 2006: 2). Thus, modernity is not an era that can be measured in universal time, but a condition that has occurred in different places during different times and has as much to do with ideology as it does with evidence of modernization (Gilroy 1993; Appadurai 1996). If modernity is a "mood" rather than a "sociocultural form"—or if it is a mood that arises from and also causes the production of sociocultural forms in a kind of feedback loop (see Rengger 1995)—then modernism is the impetus that propels people and society toward modernity. Most insightful for the Philippine case in this text, Néstor García-Canclini outlines four projects that characterize the aspect of modernity, and each appears in some form in the chapters that follow as a corollary of modernism: emancipation, expansion, renovation, and democratization (1995: 12). Further, his summary is particularly applicable to formerly colonial nations where troubling associations between progress and the West have persisted, the precolonial past takes on great symbolic import when defining the present, and identity constructions must take into account a cultural legacy of syncretism, whether in an effort to accept or negate it.

Consequently, the second theme is the condition of hybridity that pervades nationalistic expression as much as it does other aspects of individual, community, and national identity. For Jameson, modernism is an "uneven moment of social development" in which one experiences "the coexistence of realities from radically different moments of history—handicrafts alongside the great cartels, peasant fields with the Krupp factories or the Ford plant in the distance" (1991: 307). Thus follows García-Canclini's observation that the development of a modern, postcolonial nation is also always postmodern, since it exhibits an endemic hybridity that is often read as syncretism or pastiche (1995: 6). In this scenario, traditions transcend anachronism, existing with the modern in what Chatterjee calls "heterogeneous time" (1999: 132). Theorized this way, hybridity may indeed be viewed as the natural disposition of all modern nations, making the case of the Philippines more wholeheartedly universal than exceptional. Yet, the easy applicability of hybridity as a theoretical framework in different national case studies does not mean there is nothing to be learned through a closer examination of a specific locale. As an example, pervasive hybridity is not only a matter of temporal disjuncture and juxtaposition, as outlined by the previous theorists, but also one of transnationalism understood in the senses of border crossings and internationalist perspectives. The regional and historical specifics of these crossings reveal themselves in local understandings of the nation. Benedict Anderson offers the illuminating observation that internal "imaginings" of the Philippines "have been profoundly shaped by the [United States]" (1998: 47). The United States does figure prominently throughout this book, not merely as a foil for nationalist aims, but also as an inescapable part of Filipino culture. The Philippines was, after all, a U.S. colony during early American ascendancy as a world power, and the "special relationship" forged through hegemony and ambivalent dependency was colored by a global perception of the expanding U.S. empire. While other Southeast Asian countries formed nationalist movements against representatives of the Old World, the Philippines underwent a modernizing project under the tutelage of the New World. These experiences, translated into the representation of self, resulted in external and internal projections of a hybridity unique to the Philippines that required cogent articulation. The case studies in this book are emblematic examples of national self-articulation through musical performance.

The third theme deals with who is making these articulations and encompasses the tensions between official statements and the multifarious expressions of artists that are variously in compliance with and in contestation against the aims of the state. At the proverbial top are various Philippine governments and arts institutions that act as dominant but nonmonolithic structures. Throughout the bottom and middle, individuals and groups negotiate their subjective positions and illustrate how nationalist strategies ranging from indigenous recuperation to modernism have direct correspondences in a variety of musical expressions. As the functional needs of the Philippine state have evolved, so too have the official articulations of nationalism and the uses of music in support of the nation-state. The network of meanings attributed to music—tapped into variously by the state, private institutions, influential ensembles, and individual actors—depends upon discourse about musical sound and musical genre. At times, this discourse imbues musical aesthetic markers with a kind of metaphoric naturalness, but even these interpretations are subject to debate. The populace may understand modern anthems that follow the model of European marches as symbolic of the right of self-governance or the validation of revolutionary militancy against the state. Snippets of folk music or explorations of indigenous scales may be understood as a shared sense of history or a strategy of nativism. Whatever form they take, most of these symbols of nation are dependent upon a collective understanding of a national history, even if impelled by an insurgent desire to rewrite the narrative of a nation-state's inevitability found in the status quo. The following chapters take up the question of national narratives and representations, and as the book's three themes intersect and overlap, myriad readings of music and its role in shaping and articulating ideologies of nation become apparent.

Music and the Nation

Music carries multifaceted meanings whose illumination is made possible through examinations of intent and reception. Undoubtedly, the many possibilities of meaning are what make music so significant as a human expression and so rich a topic to explore. There is no single music in any given nation that provides the key to the puzzle. In fact, in many places throughout the world there is no single word for music but rather a variety of terms referring to instruments, types of dance and theater, or particular types of music. To better understand the difficulties in even approaching the question, "music" and "nation" should be considered as discursive formations and the relationship between them viewed as a network of meanings contingent upon context. In claiming such, I do not conclude that music is music only if we talk about it. I do mean that the process by which music comes to be defined first as music and second as a specific kind of music is perceptual, subjective, and based on experience and existing knowledge. This discourse contains many points of view and shifts over time. The process can be slow, such that change is shrouded in evolutionary mystery; or it can happen drastically, pressured by actors who have something at stake in reconstituting the characteristics and functions of music. Music that has transformed from folk to professional is a prime example. It is through discourse and experience that music can be defined as characteristic of a people or a nation—sometimes as an essential characteristic.

Importantly, even judgments about the aesthetics of music and how music creates meaning are subjective and socially constructed over time. Though having a grammar, music is not a language in the linguistic sense and is capable of conveying a multiplicity of meanings. Yet it seems clear from historical examples that, while meaning is unstable, music has the power to convey an epistemology of national identity and nationalism through aesthetics. In other words, people not only come to know something about their nation through music—for instance, through the lyrics of patriotic songs that are paired with rousing marching music—they also learn how they should experience nationalism as they make, listen to, and remember music. As such, historical musicologists and ethnomusicologists have provided insight into why the study of music is uniquely elucidating about nationhood.[4] More than other art forms, music can be a powerful social practice in the private and public realms. Music can be didactic or revolutionary, among many other things, and its power has been recognized throughout history, whether considering the danger assigned to music or the use of music in support of regimes. Music is a shaper as much as a reflector of society, leaving scholars to analyze how these effects are possible. Music signifies through text, context, and aural markers, and though it may seem straightforward to establish conventionalized interpretations of sound and song, the inescapable conditions of plurality and contradiction in meaning make simplistic conclusions and metanarratives untenable. Instead, interpretation grounded in context, the hallmark of most ethnomusicological studies, produces tantalizingly complex but comprehendible narratives. The question of how music might sound out nation, then, is a gateway to the history and sociology of a given people.[5]

The connection between music and nation is an abstraction that is not only imagined but is also performed, and the affective nature of music intensifies the power of this perceptual and discursive marriage. That music and nation could ever be linked denotes a process rather than a fact. One might wonder whether there even is such a thing as national music, since the very idea of a national essence is unsustainable when examined too closely. To simplify matters, in his reference work on Filipino music, Raymundo Bañas defines a national song simply as "one that belongs to the nation" (1975: 79).[6] This statement, at the very least, illustrates the authority of perception. Importantly, music of and for the nation is not merely a question of genre perception and has everything to do with the construction of ideas.

"Nation," like "music," is one such construct that is rooted in ideas as well as in tangible artifacts and physical realities. As Benedict Anderson (1991) made clear, nation is the shared imagining of a community of people made possible through secularization, technology, and other radical circumstances that allow for the wide dissemination of mutual ideas about identity and place. The Philippine nation is a conceived entity, and various historical forces have come into play in order for the conception of nation to be communally held. In many cases, the nation is hardly a given, and separatist movements, religious and ethnic differences, and internal instability continue to plague governing bodies. This is certainly true in the Philippines, where movements for autonomous governance, regional loyalty, and competing languages have existed throughout colonialism and independent nationhood. In addition, practical issues of land sovereignty have pitted neighboring nations against one another, such that cartographic borders are subject to shifting.

It is also important to separate the nation, as it were, from the state, or the governing structure of that nation. The notion of the nation-state arises when the two are understood as being in tandem, thereby legitimizing state rulers.[7] To consider the Philippine nation and the Philippine nation-state as separate but similar concepts is heuristically useful, because it allows for a variety of insights into cultural politics. Music, in this scenario, may be associated with either the nation or the state, or it may comprehend both. The nation-state asserts its power best when people interpret authority as a manifestation of their own will, and their understanding of ethnoculture becomes a means for defining the national self (Pickett 1996: 68). Ethnoculture and nationalism, however, are open to interpretation. As an example, music promoted by the state likely serves the state by using the image of the nation. In contrast, it is because of the distinction between nation and state that some patriotic music may be suppressed, because love of the nation (or country) can be used as a subversive message against the aims of the state. Nationalism must therefore be understood as subsuming a plurality of ideologies and, though it is often tied to the legitimation of the nation-state, this is not always the case.[8]

For the purposes of the present book, I define nationalism as the authorizing ideologies of nation. It is a field of ideas from diverse sources that can be examined through subcategories—including political nationalism, the sentiment of patriotism (love of country), cultural nationalism, and, specifically, musical nationalism.[9] Yet, more than just a psychological predisposition (Giddens 1985), nationalism authors nation, ceaselessly propelling the projection of ideas and production of culture in a multidirectional circuit. There are many other ways to theorize nationalism, including such contemporary iterations as balkanization and a resurgence of tribalism in the global context, but those uses of the term, at least, are constricted and do not apply well to the earlier Philippine context (Appadurai 1996). I consider nationalism in its romantic (e.g. Herderian) sense, but only to the extent that blood and land can be popularly believed as tying Filipinos together. After all, as stated above, the Philippines is not distinguished by a single language, ethnicity, or religion. The country is an archipelago with lowlands and mountains and with numerous ethnic and regional divisions. Nationalism, therefore, works at shoring up understandings of mutual belonging and exclusion among a diverse population.

A past president of the University of the Philippines, José Abueva, defined nationalism in the context of the Philippines in a more conventional and rhetorical way, declaring that "Filipino nationalism is love of our country.... It is also love of country and God.... It is cherishing what is Filipino, what makes us a nation distinct from other nation.... It extends to our love of freedom, liberty, and democracy as Filipino values and ideals." Moreover, to Abueva, Filipino nationalism is shared, can be secular, is based in part on indigenous values, is an ideology rather than merely a sentiment, is political, social, and is an answer to a history of colonialism (1999: xix). In other words, even in the case of a single nation, nationalism may take on a variety of forms and can be expressed in many ways—patriotism included.

Romeo Cruz outlines a particularly interesting point of view revealing a very early (and also limited) transnational understanding of Filipino identity that highlights the complex development of nationalism within a colonial context. He theorizes Philippine nationalism as a sense of belonging to the larger community of Catholics and Hispanics, accompanied by the perception that Filipinos were "integral" and "co-equal" with all peoples in the Spanish empire (1989: 57). This description of Filipino nationalism—or perhaps prenationalism—in which the Empire is a global unit that is constituted as much by sameness as it is by difference, sheds light on the complexities of identity formation in a colonized site. One's sense of self is not merely colored by the intrusion of others and the conversions that result, but also by the tendency to look outward and to frame oneself relative to external standards. After all, as Lucila Hosillos points out, nationalism and internationalism have been closely linked with one another throughout history (1970: 311). Hosillos's internationalism is the recognition of one nation's place within a community of nations and the pursuit of relations between nations, and it can extend into a generic definition of transnationalism as a phenomenon of the global system of nations in which people cultivate ties to more than one nation and participate in networks that transcend national boundaries. While the large-scale migratory patterns typical of Filipinos points toward theorizations of postnationality in which "nation" holds less meaning than it ever has before, the imagination of nation is actually magnified and simplified—in other words, essentialized—through the phenomenon of distanced citizenship that arises from a vast population of overseas workers and other emigrants. The nation takes on the powerful symbolism of home, such that diasporic Filipinos, wherever they may be, continue to identify the nation as the space of Filipino people and culture. Space may be reproducible on a micro level by community activities, but the nation remains source and core. This attachment to the idea of a place can be understood as a habitual handcuffing between race and place that, whether theorized or not, is felt on a deeply personal level (Kahn 1998 22). The discourse between those who are home and those who are away from home enforces traditional attachments to and perceptions about nation, even as more and more Filipinos spend the majority of their time abroad.[10] Hence, I continue to consider the concept of nation and expressions of nationalism as potent interventions into Philippine identity, even while coming to terms with the internationalism, transnationalism, and globalization inherent in the reality of everyday life. While the nuts and bolts of Philippine identity and culture cannot be itemized like a recipe, nationalism is still understandable as a "variety of human belonging," and a very strong sense of belonging at that (Shafer 1982: 6).

Amidst all this talk of hybridity, migration, and flux, it is significant to note that cultural nationalism is underpinned by the conviction that a nation does indeed have a shared culture (see Hutchinson 1987).[11] Following from my prior arguments, and demonstrated in the different case studies of this book, cultural nationalism is an umbrella term for ideologies that do not necessarily agree on the distinctive characteristics of the nation, but that do have in common an underlying nationalist utilitarianism. Whether propagated by the state or by a single artist, expressions of cultural nationalism seek to stabilize the vagaries of everything that "culture" is said to stand for into tangible facets of national identity. One strategy of cultural nationalism is nationalization, a process that defines, produces, and, most important, controls products of culture.

Nationalization in regard to the arts describes two processes. The first applies to music or performers adopted by the state and elevated to national status, in most cases because the perceived ideals of the musical product or declarations of the artists support those of the state. Music may originate from a sector of civil society, from a single region of the country, or from outside sources, and its nationalization represents a modernist interaction between citizens and the state (Chatterjee 1998: 60–61). In some cases, the state will appropriate or adopt music, likely to support an agenda of cultural nationalism, and process it through nationalization. This is the kind of nationalization that appears most commonly in the chapters that follow. The second use of the term refers to the widespread diffusion and popularity of music and artists on a national (and perhaps international) scale accomplished through successful commoditization (see Frishkopf 2008). Other kinds of music that become nationalized may parallel state nationalist ideology or even oppositional ideology; the important aspect is that the process of nationalization is one of mass media and commoditization without deliberate state intervention. Of course, there are many ways in which the two overlap and impinge on one another. The genres and artists in this book either express ideologies of the nation, have undergone nationalization, or both. In addition, one should distinguish between nationalized music and music as propaganda. The process of nationalization merges John Hutchinson's theorization of political nationalism as a cosmopolitan and rationalist impulse with cultural nationalism as national character and offers a more nuanced evaluation of nationalized expressions than simple propaganda (1987). While propaganda may employ the languages of cosmopolitanism and rationality, nationalized music involves levels of production and consumption that may or may not be in the control of the state. In fact, it is the diffuse nature of cosmopolitanism—both in its common usage and in Turino's theorization of the cosmopolitan's translocal *habitus* (2000)—that mitigates against nationalization as a purely local and insular process under the purview of any single institution of a given society.

Finally, tying together this discussion of nation, the corollaries of nationalism and transnationalism, and the process of nationalization is a thematic concern with performance in the public realm. I am interested in how the idea of nation circulates publicly through performance and how nationalism culminates in spectacle. The process of nationalization occurs in both public and private, but it is critical that nationalized performances occur in public. Public performance provides a text of the nation that is made legible to citizens, even though it may contain internal contradictions and elicit ambivalent reactions. Further, the public sphere extends to a global level where musical actors, as it were, perform their nation (see Ebron 2002). The case studies in this book involve all of these ideas in one way or another, and they represent a diverse range of musical and performance expressions. They bring to light persistent shared ideologies regarding local and global identities and illustrate the significance of music in shaping notions of the individual and national self in very public ways.

Time, Place, and the Narrative Voice

The articulation of nation through music is a story told diachronically and with regard to multiple points of view. To provide structure, this book is primarily chronological, though at times the narrative moves backward and forward through time to provide necessary contexts. This is my retelling of the past, using written histories, archived materials, and the memories of consultants as my guides. Stuart Hall observed that "the past is not waiting for us back there to recoup our identities against. It is always retold, rediscovered, reinvented. It has to be narrativized. We go to our own pasts through history, through memory, through desire, not as literal fact" (1997: 58). The book follows a strategy of capturing certain generalities of the time periods under scrutiny and relating them to the details of individuals, groups, and even singular events. Each chapter hinges on particular moments of time that, like performance utterances, are transitory and telling. Yet, while there is logic in situating each performance vignette with historical particularity, all the performers in this book span multiple time periods, causing narrative overflow, overlap, and gapping. Historian Vicente Rafael has remarked that the ironic disjuncture of episodic versus epic histories "forestalls and interrupts the establishment of a single-overarching narrative about the nation" (2000: 4). By focusing on episodes and ordering them in understandable ways, I forgo the metanarrative in favor of historical pointillism.

In addition to time periods, I am also specific about my choice of the place under consideration. A great portion of the material in this book centers on the capital city of the Philippines, Manila, even though musical materials and people often originate from other parts of the country. The city and its surroundings, also called Metropolitan or Metro Manila (as well as the National Capital Region), has historically been the seat of national government and the financial polestar. As a center of communications, politics, and industry, Filipinos and outsiders perceive Manila as the national center, even if events there sometimes appear to have little impact on local life (Dolan 1993: 94). Further, the manner in which Manila has been treated extensively in Filipino movies, books, newspapers, and other media suggests a "Manila bias" in popular imagination and calls attention to what appears to be an exaggerated center-periphery model of urban and rural in the Philippines.

Still, Metro Manila depends upon the rest of the country, and this multi-directional relationship, along with the growth of other urban locales, blurs the dichotomy between the center and periphery. There are many other factors to consider as well, including the distribution of political power. In the countryside, landowning families are masters of their own fiefdoms, often fielding private armies and taking care of affairs through a well-established system of patronage. These same families comprise the oligarchy that today supplies the Philippines with its high-ranking politicians in Manila and throughout the nation. Historically, these families have also controlled the production of raw materials from the countryside that are exported to other nations. Manufactured goods arrive into the ports of major cities that then filter back out into the countryside. In contemporary life, labor is the primary commodity. Workers migrate to urban centers, but they maintain a sense of regional loyalty and keep ties with their families back in the countryside. Notably, the arrival of workers to Metro Manila and the lack of jobs available for them create the conditions for what Andrés calls "pseudo-urbanization," a process in which rural migrants cannot be absorbed adequately by the city. Instead, they form a subgroup of the population living in squatter communities where regional practices continue in a new context (2002: 80). At the same time that the city absorbs the people and cultural practices of the countryside, it remains a cosmopolitan arena where international goods are elevated as cultural capital, and transnational images and ideas permeate the communal psyche. Indeed, the city is a modern and hybrid space where regional sensibilities and national ideals continuously intermingle.

Most important to this study, Metro Manila is the home of the political and intellectual elites who have been concerned with the building of nationhood. The city area also contains the largest, most powerful, and most well funded arts institutions in the country, including the Cultural Center of the Philippines, the National Commission on Culture and the Arts, and a variety of important universities. My consideration of Metro Manila does not negate the cultural importance of other urban centers and rural regions. Simply, Manila is crucial to the Philippines in all aspects of national development and therefore must be considered with all of its idiosyncrasies in discussions about national identity. Those who deny urban culture in a quest to uncover "authentic" Filipino identity are faced with the paradox of overemphasizing the rural while negating the setting that gave rise to the majority of these discussions. Manila, then, is a self-conscious and egocentric urban center, but also a place of invention, struggle, diversity, and cultural production on a national scale. This book is merely a starting point, and others hopefully will follow with more attention to sites outside of the capital area.

A Glance at the Philippine Context

Space permits only the most cursory gloss of history before the twentieth century. The Philippines is an archipelago of several thousand islands located in Southeast Asia. By 2008 the population had reached over 90 million people with multiple languages and dialects in common usage, including Cebuano, Ilocano, and Tagalog. Filipino (the contemporary re-visioning of

Tagalog and other regional languages) and English are the main languages of business, government, and mass media.[12] The period before the arrival of the Spaniards is not well documented.[13] Most contemporary scholars believe that there was a core population of racially similar people throughout the Philippines and Southeast Asia who engaged in trade and intermarriage among themselves and with others in the region (Cortes et al. 2000: 14–18). Muslim missionaries traveled to the area along these trade routes, supporting Islamic communities and sharing their religion with neighboring populations (Majul 1988: 50). Beginning in Sulu, Islam diffused through the southern region of the Philippines, most probably circulated by travelers from Malaysia who, in turn, may have been descended from Arabs (ibid. 97).

The Spaniards first alighted on the island of Cebu in 1521 under the command of the Portuguese mariner-soldier Ferdinand Magellan, who, after making blood compacts with local chieftains, lost his life to another local chief named Lapu Lapu. The Spanish Basque Miguel López de Legazpi arrived from Mexico (then called New Spain) in 1565, conquered Cebu, and established the settlement of Manila in 1571 (Cortes et al. 2000: 29–31).[14] Roman Catholic religious orders established mission provinces in the islands over the next four decades, tasked with converting the natives. They made religious conversion palatable to the population through strategies such as the translation of the mass into local dialects and the training of native boys as liturgical musicians.[15]

In 1610, a Tagalog named Tomas Pinpin published *Librong Pagaaralan nang manga Tagalog nang uicang Castila* (The book with which Tagalogs can learn Castilian). The title of the book assumes an inherent truth to the very *category* "Tagalog," a separation between the Tagalogs and the Spanish, and a burgeoning imagined community among the mixed lowland populations (Rafael 1993: 56). In fact, the communities existing in the Philippines during the seventeenth century were quite varied. Besides the Muslims in the south and the natives who kept to the mountains to avoid Spanish rule, there were Iberian Spaniards (*peninsulares*), Spaniards born in the Philippines (the first "Filipinos"), natives of the islands (initially called *indios* or *indios filipinos* by the Spanish), and Chinese (both first and later generations). In Manila itself, traders and journeymen from all over the world came, went, and sometimes settled. These different groups intermarried, and it was the mix of Spanish and Chinese that formed the original *mestizo* class (Agoncillo 1967: 4).

The intervention of Europeans in Southeast Asia laid the groundwork for future nations in two ways: first by separating the region according to colonial design, and second by introducing the very idea of a nation-state that was both internally cohesive and distinct from other nations. The first clear manifestations of nationalism in the islands occurred through localized insurgencies—harbingers of later nationalisms—that reveal a sense of community among natives based in local beliefs (often spiritual in nature) and a unified opposition to oppression by perceived outsiders (Constantino 1975). Some insurgencies arose as natives balked at their harsh treatment by Spanish authorities and landowners, while others protested the power structure of the Catholic Church that limited the role of natives. Rural religious movements against the Spanish and political movements directed at the Spanish state merged along with the developing sense of the native as "Filipino," a perception cultivated during the nineteenth century and one crucial to modern Philippine nationalism (ibid.).

It is not surprising that natives became exposed to ideas from outside the country, not merely because foreigners came to the islands, but also because natives sought education abroad. Those from the upper economic classes who could afford the highest levels of university training sent their sons to Europe. These highly educated Filipinos, known as the *ilustrados*, became a class unto themselves based on education and sometimes economic standing, and they brought European ideologies of nationalism to the Philippines (Cullinane 1989).[16] One of the most prominent members of the *ilustrado* class, José Rizal, became a pivotal figure in Philippine nationalism through his writings on reform. By the end of the nineteenth century, Rizal's works reveal the emergence of a national imaginary, at least among the intellectual elite of the Philippines (Anderson 1991: 27). The Spanish put Rizal on trial and ordered his execution on December 30, 1896.[17] Following Rizal's martyrdom, and in the footsteps of insurgencies that had transpired in previous years, working-class hero Andrés Bonifacio formed the revolutionary organization Katipunan in 1896, along with Teodoro Plata and Ladislao Diwa (de Viana 2006: 25). The revolutionaries polarized Filipinos against their Spanish overlords, and in the last decade of the nineteenth century, waged war against the Spaniards. The notion of the *indio* inhabitants of the islands as "Filipinos"—a name that in its beginnings referred to Spaniards born in the Philippines—had been developing over the years, and the war served as a declaration of the *indios'* right to self-rule (Ileto 2005: 218).[18]

Scholars of Philippine history have examined these early roots of Filipino nationalism from a variety of standpoints, ranging from the transmission of a European nationalist consciousness to anticolonial Filipino elites to grassroots movements that developed during the Spanish regime (see Agoncillo 1974 and Constantino 1982). Filipino nationalism has also been associated with conceptions of the church hierarchy and the Catholic religion, whether viewed as a manifestation of the resentment toward the power of the Spanish clergy or as mass movements based on a theology of liberation (see Schumacher 1981). In *Pasyon and Revolution* (1997), Ileto proposes that peasants who supported the revolution and those who participated in the religious movements against the Spanish had aims and ideologies about the nation that were locally specific and not in line with the burgeoning Filipino nationalists. The interests of peasants did not necessarily include fighting for or with the Filipino elites. Related to the role of the church in daily life, Niels Mulder has asserted that the patriotism of the rebels in the revolution against Spain was nothing short of "nationalism as religion," complete with a sense of mystique and brotherhood (1997: 107). It was, then, the culmination of numerous rebellions with many underlying impetuses that together constitute a long revolution against Spanish rule. Yet, on the verge of self-rule, even after the declaration of the first republic by self-declared president Emilio Aguinaldo, another colonial era was set to commence.

The Spanish-American War brought the U.S. military to the Philippines, and the colony became U.S. territory through the Treaty of Paris signed on December 10, 1898. With the decision made to annex the Philippines, the United States refused to recognize Aguinaldo's republic. The Philippine army resumed fighting, but this time against the Americans. The Philippine-American War (or insurrection, as the Americans blithely called it) began in 1899.[19] After two years of fighting, Aguinaldo fell into American hands and swore his allegiance to the United States (see Miller 1982). The Americans set up military bases, gained majority control of businesses, set up unequal parameters of trade, and imported American media and mass culture in the course of its civilizing mission. For better or for worse, one could argue that the comparatively short stay of the Americans had as great or greater an influence on the Philippines as the long tenure of the Spanish colonial government.

This broad sketch of time illustrates the complexity inherent in the development of the Philippine nation that directly impacts the diversity of nationalist expressions. Chapter 1 takes up the narrative once more with a closer examination of music during the first half of the twentieth century and the role of composers in expressing nationalist ideologies of liberation and postcolonial modernity. Chapter 2 covers the 1950s and 1960s through a case study of the Bayanihan Philippine Dance Company and its connection to an official cultural nationalism of renovation. A prominent aspect of this performance of modernism was a nostalgia for a pre-U.S. colonial past and a co-optation of cultural hybridity from throughout the nation. Chapter 3 illustrates the institutionalization of culture, modernization, and the display of modernism under the Marcos dictatorship through the creation of the Cultural Center of the Philippines in the late 1960s and into the 1970s. Chapter 4 deals with the rise of the Philippine Madrigal Singers as ambassadors of a modern nation expanding into an international community and delves into the cultural politics that members of a nationalized ensemble experienced during the New Society of the Marcos regime. Chapter 5 reenvisions expressions of nationalism as separate from the nation-state but connected to a long history of revolutionary song through a study of music during the 1986 People Power Revolution. In this chapter, an assorted array of songs herald democratization as a hallmark of global modernity that is at odds with the aims of the state. The conclusion of the book integrates material from the previous chapters, as the diverse nationalist history of the Philippines is celebrated and retold in music during the 1998 Centennial of Philippine independence from Spain.

A Note on the Interludes

The interludes that precede each chapter are reflexive in tone and are meant to serve as self-positioning statements during an age of scholarship in which the omniscience of the authorial voice is looked upon with suspicion, particularly in fields such as anthropology and ethnomusicology. As a technique, the ethnographic present and overt implications of "I was there" writing, may seem self-justifying. This is, fortunately, not the goal of contemporary reflexive writing, in which the inclusion of the self is—while not a guilty confession of fallibility—a disruption of the illusory authority of third person text. If one believes that the scholar-writer of musical ethnographies is another kind of artist, one who communicates knowledge and experience as mediation rather than exegesis, then one must know something of that writer in order to make better sense of the text.[20] At the same time, using a format of interludes between chapters corrals passages of overt reflexive writing for the benefit of readers averse to coming upon them without forewarning.

L UCRECIA KASILAG HAS A KIND face whose eyes, especially when she smiles, reveal a healthy reserve of mischief. She has a forthright manner and a quiet command of presence, despite her diminutive stature. A couple of years prior, she donated a set of Philippine string instruments to the Iskwelahang Pilipino Rondalla of Boston, delighted that the art form was being carried on overseas. On this visit, she invites my family to her eightieth birthday celebration, featuring performances of some of her important works. The written invitation requests "Filipiniana" attire, so that night I opt for a simple embroidered Filipino kimona top over a long skirt. As with most kimona designs that you can buy in department stores in the Filipiniana section, it is loose fitting and somewhat translucent, for it is meant to be worn over a camisole and to keep the user cool in the tropical heat. Upon arrival, I find I have taken the invitation too literally. The chandelier-lit lobby of the Cultural Center of the Philippines is already humming with Manila's cultural elite, dressed to the nines in fashionable evening gowns that would be right at home in New York City or Tokyo. I, the U.S. American, appear very much the provincial, eliciting sidelong glances from beneath the mascara.[1] The employees are the only other women wearing the Filipiniana attire of kimona and skirt.

The concert features a bonanza of nationalized performing groups, including the Philippine Philharmonic Orchestra (PPO) with Francisco Feliciano conducting, Ballet Philippines, Bayanihan Philippine National Folk Dance Company, and the Philippine Music Ensemble.[2] Bayanihan, near and dear to Dr. Kasilag's heart, performs the first number, a suite called "Legend of Sarimanok" (1963), accompanied by the PPO and the Philippine Music Ensemble playing ethnic instruments. Following the dance and music suite, the PPO interprets Kasilag's "Divertissement for Piano and Orchestra" (1960) with Zenas Reyes Lozada as the piano soloist.

After intermission, the PPO returns with another suite entitled "Philippine Scenes" (1974). Finally, the last number of the evening features the world premiere of Kasilag's "Violin Concerto No. 2 in G" (1994–1998) with Grigori Zhislin as a visiting soloist on the violin.

Throughout, I witness a whirlwind history of Kasilag's contributions to Philippine nationalism in the arts. When it is all done, I search the lobby for recordings, but I cannot locate any. In fact, over the next few years, though I check in record stores throughout Manila, I find it exceedingly difficult to find any recordings of Lucrecia Kasilag's compositions. Art music, in general, does not sell well in the Philippines, just as it does not in the United States. But there is the added problem in the Philippines that Filipino art composers must compete with Western art music's greatest hits, and that the music of prominent and influential composers like Kasilag, José Maceda, and Ramón Santos are considered difficult to understand. I am finally able to obtain an LP record of Filipino nationalistic art music with one recording of a Kasilag piece from the librarian at the Cultural Center of the Philippines. The records have never been in demand, she tells me, and she is merely glad to find someone who is interested. The boxed record is in lovely condition, likely having never been opened. It is a commemorative album of the tenth anniversary of the Cultural Center of the Philippines, featuring rare recordings of compositions by members of the League of Filipino Composers. The 1979 album is called *Pagdiriwang*, meaning "celebration."

CHAPTER ONE | Composing for an Incipient Nation

This very Westernization of Filipino tastes is responsible for the modern excellence
and sophistication of Filipino music performers. All other peoples in Asia and the
Pacific have only five notes in their ears. We Filipinos, thanks to the assiduous
friars who made choirboys and musicians out of the Filipinos, carry seven notes, the
do-re-mi of the European octave and have the distinct advantage of familiarity
with the inventory, repertoire, and musical codes of Western music.

Carmen Guerrero Nakpil (1997)

CONFRONTED WITH RECAPPING A HISTORY of the development of the
sovereign Philippine nation-state and nationalist composers from the
late nineteenth century until the mid-1950s, I have chosen only a few narratives over the legion possible. Much like the musical vignettes of Kasilag's
birthday concert, the composers and musical works in this chapter tell a
larger story about the early development of the Philippine nation-state and
the approaches of nationalist composers. The first half of the twentieth
century is a particularly interesting time period to discuss in terms of nationalist art music composition, because it represents a long transitional era from
Spanish and U.S. colonialism to commonwealth status to independence.
During these eventful years, the works and ideologies of nationalist composers took on heightened importance in authoring the nation as it struggled

into coalescence, and composers wrote into history their understandings of what the modern Philippine nation could be and the role of music in national culture. Many had affiliations with the University of the Philippines—founded in 1908 and the only government-supported university in the nation until 1955 (Martin 1980: 353)—and all were supported by the state through commissions and other kinds of patronage. Interestingly, the relationships between state actors and composers during this period do not appear to have been coercive in nature and were likely built upon shared interests in concretizing a nationalist (and therefore national) culture, though certainly the state had further goals in consolidating political power. Rather than being subsumed by the machinery of a ministry of culture, the legacy of composers in this chapter reads much like that of the "great moderns" of arts in many nations (Jameson 1991: 306). Their ideologies and compositions have been treated in historical texts and in public memory as evidence of individual genius that endure as gifts to the Philippine nation. As Hilarion Rubio, a prominent composer, trumpeted, "The reverence for our heroes should be extended to native conductors and native music" (1941: 61). The famous historian Teodoro Agoncillo concurred, deeming the composers "heroic" in his epic textbook history of the Philippine nation (1967: 669).[3]

For these composers, nationalism was strongly linked with emancipation and the recognition of self-rule—a common theme relating nationalism to modernity—since colonialism under Spain and then the United States reigned as the dominant political paradigm of their times. At the end of the nineteenth century, this vantage point fit squarely into the goals of the newly burgeoning Philippine state, comprised of revolutionaries who belonged primarily to the elite class and who were ambivalent in their relationship with the U.S. colonial government. For Commonwealth (1934–1946) and post–World War II nationalist composers, the use of folk music melodies, native instruments, and native art forms like the *sarswela* was a declaration against colonial culture that complemented the goals of a young state needing to define the national purview.[4] Like the nationalist composers of Europe, these composers looked to folk sources to help define a Filipino identity in music and, even further, experimented with metaphorically decolonizing musical expression by finding a native voice, while still maintaining the Western musical aesthetics that symbolized modernity.

The impact of colonialism on hybridizing the arts of the Philippines, including and especially nationalistic music, cannot be overstated. This is a cultural dilemma faced by early iterations of the postcolonial Philippine state in arenas that stretch beyond music. Many expressions of Filipino cultural nationalism, from music to art to literature, incorporate ideas and aesthetics that at one time were considered foreign but became localized through repeated use and adaptation.[5] Additionally, the inevitable change of music as it becomes a part of native expression relates to the natural internalization of aesthetics as much as it does to the spell of hegemony. Tonality is at once an outside influence, an assimilated musical aesthetic, and a "universal" musical paradigm, such that what is foreign is difficult to definitively separate from what is native. There are fundamental reasons for this difficulty. First, when music types mix, aesthetic traits of both may transform in the newer expression and will likely continue to change over time. Second, when there are distinguishable traits of older musics in a hybrid expression, one must remember the problem of aesthetic overlap, in which similar traits between two disparate musics cause them to be amenable to one another and therefore difficult to parse out once they have been combined. Third, the perception of mixing and even of foreignness does not necessarily carry over into every passing generation. Once a new music arrives and is introduced into the native repertoire, its expression can become a natural part of the soundscape of the next generation. Artists have also learned about a variety of musics from travels and studies abroad, for Filipinos are a cosmopolitan people, whether considering seafarers before and during the Spanish colonial period, the students in Europe and the United States from the nineteenth century on, or the explosion of overseas workers from even the poorest economic classes in the twentieth century. The borders for acculturation are exceedingly porous, so even while different manifestations of Filipino nationalism have tended to seek an identity differentiated from a colonized one, nationalistic expressions have not been strictly indigenous from an aesthetic standpoint.

Even more significant, Western tonality represents an early form of musical modernism in many Asian countries, symbolic of superiority, cultivation, and even technological advancement (Santos 2002: 38). Thus, musical modernism in the Philippines begins with the adoption of tonality and includes the development of a class of musicians who labeled themselves composers in the European sense of the word (ibid. 39). Modernism in this sense only later directly relates to the musical modernist movements of Europe. Instead, Filipino nationalist composers of the late nineteenth century were the modernists of their time, adopting for their own use tonality, romanticism, and European musical forms. Critics could argue that they were subject to a larger colonial hegemonic project, but cultural modernism is a complex issue, since mastering the arts of the colonizer and taking ownership over them for symbolic reasons is an exercise of agency. The dialectic of colonial mentality and creative will is evident in music itself, and, regardless of composers' intents, we can simultaneously perceive evidence of colonialism, hybridity, and nationalistic modernism.

Accordingly, musical nationalism in the Philippines has appeared in a variety of forms and styles, ranging from references to precolonial music to the sounds of the musical avant-garde movement. It is unclear exactly what precolonial music sounded like, though in addition to indigenous forms, we might suspect some South Asian influences and perhaps even borrowings from China as a result of trade patterns (Bañas 1975: 14). In the southern islands, Islamic missionaries arrived in the fourteenth century, bringing with them Arabic influences, including those that had become localized in the areas that would become Malaysia and Indonesia. More than three hundred years of Spanish colonization thrust Western scales upon the Filipino, as well as a variety of musical instruments, and numerous music and dance genres—most of which underwent a syncretic or hybridizing process of adaptation. The Filipinos also adopted the European classical repertoire along with its accompanying hegemonic value system. Almost fifty years of U.S. colonization furthered the Filipino internalization of the West, this time equated with popular music, the commercialization of music in general that occurred during the first half of the twentieth century, and American folk tunes. Because of several centuries of musical inculcation in the colonized areas of the Philippines and the tendency of imperialized peoples to look outward as much as inward, cultural nationalists of the postcolonial era produced hybrid styles of music that epitomize Filipino modernity while still containing the imprints of a complicated history. To put their work in context, as well as set the stage for the rest of the book, it is important to review the foundation set by the earliest nationalist composers of the Philippines leading up to the end of World War II.

The Musical Nationalist Experience

Filipinos began composing music that used Western idioms during Spanish colonialism. While it would be tempting to mark liturgical music as the beginnings of nationalism in Filipino composers, the successful foray of the native into European art music was a natural outgrowth of exposure, creativity, and the desire to participate in church functions.[6] As an example, Marcelo Adonay (1848–1928) is best remembered for his church music, and his role as a pioneering Filipino composer during the late nineteenth century lends him some cachet as a national hero of sorts. Elena Rivera Mirano, however, warns against this, writing that the romanticist impulse to include him as a national hero is more associated with his time period than with his intentions or the nature of his work (2009: 6). He did compose a number of secular pieces, including a hymn for the reformist hero Jose Rizal called "Rizal Glorified" (Kasilag 2009), but the question of whether intention or genre matters in regard to modernist constructions of a national patrimony remains.

Still, by the nineteenth century when currents of early nationalism had become stronger, even religious music shows some evidence of, or at least can be tied to, nationalist thinking. The most well known analysis comes from historian Reynaldo Ileto's work on the recitation of the Passion of the Christ in *Pasyon and Revolution* (1997) and its relationship with ideologies of liberation theology.[7] Thinking inclusively, then, both religious and secular music from the past can come to represent the nation or can be selected as part of a nation's exalted patrimony. Cultural nationalists have used this strategy of recuperating the past effectively when constructing their country's histories. In the realm of music, composers or particular musical works can be designated as nationalist retrospectively as part of present-day strategies, whether or not the composer had any such intent. In the Philippines, most composers considered to be nationalist have themselves expressed such overt concerns.

All of the composers in this chapter have been labeled as nationalists in Filipino sources, and they exemplify the important expressions of cultural nationalism of their day. These composers have become artifacts in national historiography, just as their musical pieces have evolved into an integral part of nationalist culture and its active articulation.[8] The extant literature on Filipino nationalistic music focuses on a small sample of songs that appear just prior to the revolution against Spain, and the earliest nationalist composers that we have records of emerge simultaneously with the struggle for sovereignty. Not merely by-products of a movement, these composers were also purveyors of nationalistic ideology. During the last decade of the nineteenth century, when Filipino nationalists were primarily concerned with overthrowing Spanish control of the structures of power in the church and the government, Filipino musical compositions reflected political concerns. Two anthems came to light in support of the two rival Filipino rebel leaders, Andrés Bonifacio and Emilio Aguinaldo, who became embroiled in an internal struggle for control over the revolution. Through political maneuverings, Aguinaldo's men declared Bonifacio guilty of treason and ordered his execution and that of his brother in 1897. The elite, through the person of Aguinaldo, managed to wrest control during the revolution against Spain, and therefore were able to articulate their own ideas on nationalism while ostensibly serving as mouthpieces of the people (see Zaide 1999). History's regard for these two leaders has changed over time, with Aguinaldo's reputation suffering from, among other follies, his responsibility for the death of Bonifacio. The controversy over the roles of both in the revolution, who better represented the Filipino people at that time, and who served as the better leader remains. Most significant for this work is the importance both political leaders placed on the modern symbols of nation, not merely internally, but for the international community of nations as well. Thus, anthems and flags are early evidence of "official nationalism" in the Philippines, a potent top-down strategy for an "emerging nationally-imagined community" (Anderson 1991: 101).[9] Interestingly, national anthems change over time and contain evidence of shifting historical contexts.[10] Moreover, unlike flags, anthems are regularly performed by the people at whom they are directed, and therefore, music is deeply rooted as a communal expression of nationalism.

Bonifacio requested the first of the two anthems in 1896 from Julio Nakpil (1876–1960), who wrote the music and lyrics and called his composition "Marangal na Dalit ng Katagalugan (Honorable Hymn of Katagalugan)," also known as the "Himno Nacional." Nakpil was not only a musician and composer, but he was also a soldier who fought alongside Bonifacio and served as a procurer of arms and ammunitions during the revolution against Spain (Constantino 1964: 15).[11] When Aguinaldo ordered Bonifacio executed on charges of treason, the hymn lost its place. In 1898 Aguinaldo commissioned Julián Felipe (1861–1941), a composer from Aguinaldo's home province of Cavite, to pen a march to play during his declaration of independence from Spain. The result was the "Marcha Nacional Filipina (Filipino National March)" (ibid.). The piece followed the template of the Spanish Royal March, and its rousing refrain displays influences from the French "Marseillaise" (Nettl 1967: 168). As has been famously proposed, history is written by the victors; and so it was that with the death of Bonifacio and the singular ascendance of Aguinaldo, Julián Felipe's composition began its destined path to become the national anthem of the Philippines.[12] The "Marcha Nacional Filipina" made its musical debut on June 12, 1898, along with Aguinaldo's reading of the Act of Proclamation of Philippine Independence. Copies of the music were made for dissemination around the Philippines, and two of these were sent to Admiral George Dewey to bring back to the United States (Ocampo 1998: 267). (See figure 1.1.) Aguinaldo's own claim to the presidency of the First Republic was short-lived, as the liberated Filipinos almost immediately plunged into another war, this time against the Americans.

In 1898 the United States, under President William McKinley, annexed the Philippines after decisive victories in the Spanish-American War and with the added incentive of a $20 million payment to Spain for the islands. The Filipinos

FIGURE I.I. The national anthem of the Philippines (transcription by author)

took up arms once more, and in 1899, so that Filipinos could actually sing the anthem, the first text for the "Marcha Nacional Filipina" was added. The lyrics, from a poem called "Filipinas" by José Palma that was published in the newspaper *La Independencia*, extol the land, calling the Philippines a daughter of the Eastern sun. The mother country is a place of heroes and of love (capitalized and indicative of patriotic love), where invaders should never tread (an anticolonial message), and for whom the children of the land may die with glory if necessary. The final section offers an uplifting vision of the nation as a land of happiness, sun, and love (this time lowercase and plural, allowing for multiple interpretations). The place of rest for all sons of the country—in life and presumably in death too—is the sweet lap of the motherland. Interestingly, death is the fate not just of fallen heroes, but also of sons who in some way offend the motherland. This version of the anthem had appropriately heroic and poignant lyrics that resonated with the current war and into American colonization.

> Tierra adorada
> Hija del Sol de Oriente,
> Su fuego ardiente
> En tí latiendo está.
> Patria de Amores,
> Del heroismo cuna,
> Los invasores
> No te hollaran jamás
>
> Tierra de dichas, de sol y amores,
> En tu regazo dulce es vivir,
> Es una gloria para tus hijos,
> Cuando te ofenden, por tí morir.

Following the protracted and brutal Philippine-American War of 1899 to 1902, U.S. colonial rule metamorphosed the society from one colonial state to another.[13] The rule of the Americans through the first part of the twentieth century brought about another kind of national consciousness that was secularized and linked with modernization. It was, after all, the Americans who instituted a system reflective of their own government for the Filipinos (Karnow 1989). Instead of brandishing weaponry for the cause of self-rule, the Filipino elite began agitating in a manner quite distinct from that of the revolutionary Katipunan. They formed overt political parties that drew fluid lines around ideologies involving the relationship of their emerging nation and the United States. The first political party, called the *Federalistas* (Federal Party), was made up of conservative Filipino politicians who sought colonial annexation as a path toward U.S. statehood (Kramer 2006: 173). A newer party begun in 1907 reflected less conservative ideologies; the *Nacionalista's* platform called for independence from the United States and immediate self-government (ibid. 299). In reality, this political nationalism bombastically hid the very real ambivalence of many Filipino politicians who recognized the advantages of a connection with the powerful United States.

During the colonial period, the United States dramatically refashioned the social and political landscape of the Philippines, weakening the vise grip of the Roman Catholic Church and establishing American-style institutions in the country's infrastructure. They also introduced new music that permeated the sonic landscape, especially in urban areas, that initially spread through public education and through music schools and conservatories. The musical soundscape included folk songs from other nations, Western art music, and popular music aired on the radio and in movie soundtracks (Kasilag 1977: 2583).

In many ways, American popular music and folk songs supplanted traditional Filipino music and competed with European forms that had prospered during Spanish colonization. Yet, throughout the U.S. colonial era, Filipino composers responded to imperialism and the spread of American music with compositions of their own. The composers and writers of *zarzuelas* (also *sarswelas*), a light music theater form that arrived in the Philippines from Spain in the late nineteenth century, hid seditious messages in their productions through symbolically archetypal characters, costuming, and props that contained references to the Filipino flag (see chapter 5). These signs of hope for the appreciative audiences were especially significant between 1907 and 1919 when the Filipino flag, along with the national anthem by Julián Felipe, were banned by the American government in the Philippines through the infamous Flag Law.[14] When the law was repealed by the newly established Philippine legislature, patriotic and nationalist feelings ran high (Quirino 1956). The key of the national anthem changed from C to G, putting it within a more manageable vocal range, and the time signature switched from the 2/4 meter of a march to a more genre-defying 4/4 (Ocampo 2005).

It is a telling sign of the times that in 1934, on the eve of the declaration of the Philippine Commonwealth, Camilo Osias made an English translation of Julián Felipe's anthem.[15] Thus, when made official in 1938, the national anthem of the Commonwealth had English lyrics. The U.S. officials in the Philippines allowed this version to be sung, regulating that it must always be followed by a rendition of the "Star-Spangled Banner" (Nettl 1967: 170). Much of the message from the Spanish text is retained, including a poetic reference to the country's location in the east with an implication of the youthfulness of an emerging nation. A warning against invaders is coupled with a reference to sons of the land as heroes. This land, despite U.S. secularization, is sacred, and the Filipinos are possessed of souls. Later in the text, the Philippines is no longer the lap of a mother, but rather the embrace of a lover, an intriguing shift in national character to one of virile masculinity, with the feeling of liberty described as nothing short of a glorious throb. The Filipino flag, freed from the Flag Law, has a place in the lyrics as a symbol of nation, as does the history of colonial tyranny and the communal suffering of the Filipino people.

> Land of the morning,
> Child of the sun returning,
> With fervor burning,
> Thee do our souls adore.
> Land dear and holy,
> Cradle of noble heroes,
> Ne'er shall invaders
> Trample thy sacred shore.
>
> Ever within thy skies and through thy clouds
> And o'er thy hills and sea,
> Do we behold the radiance, feel and throb,
> Of glorious liberty.
> Thy banner, dear to all our hearts,
> Its sun and stars alight,
> O never shall its shining field
> Be dimmed by tyrant's might!

Beautiful land of love, O land of light,
In thine embrace'tis rapture to lie,
But it is glory ever, when thou art wronged,
For us, thy sons to suffer and die.

Roland Sintos Coloma comments that Osias's utilization of English was a native expression of nationalism that "refashioned the codes and language of the dominant power" (2005: 19). This perceptive statement might well apply to all prior nationalist musical compositions in Western idioms, both musical and linguistic. Yet, at least when analyzing music of the late nineteenth century to the early twentieth in the Philippines, this extrapolation would exaggerate the politicization of art. Filipino nationalist composers of that time period would not have considered the romantic musical style prevalent in their music to be foreign in the same way that classical pieces from abroad were. They were writing in the musical style that was aesthetically appropriate for them and that appeared to have at least some of its precursors in native music (even if these precursors were themselves mixtures of local and foreign influences).

Multiple transformations over time can obscure musical origins. Julio Nakpil's national anthem for Bonifacio, for instance, was written as a *dalit*, defined by Bañas as "an ancient type of native song. It was at first a prayer to the Virgin but it later became a prayer song for the soul of the dead. Occasionally it was also a love ditty" (1975: 85). He categorizes the *dalit* as a Filipino folk song, but its religious function reveals the transformation of the *dalit* from native song to Spanish religious hymn before the time of Nakpil. In this case, the cloudiness of musical origins is less important than an examination of processes of indigenization and localization that shapes perception from past to present.[16] In sum, early nationalist composers' use of the Western scale and rules of harmony were not subversive, and, if anything, defined their work as Western and modern in style. The native voice had been so effectively conscripted into the aesthetics of tonality and harmony that composers did not have to "refashion" musical codes so much as cater to their own sense of aesthetics. Francisco Santiago fits well into this paradigm of the early nationalist composers.

Francisco Santiago (1889–1947) has been referred to as the "Father of Philippine Nationalism in Music," precisely because he felt "propelled" by a feeling of Filipino nationalism when he composed (Manuel 1997: 20–21). In fact, he was actually one of three prominent composers who formed what Lucrecia Kasilag called "the Philippine musical triumvirate in nationalism," along with Nicanór Abelardo and Antonio Molina (1977: 2584). As with many Filipino composers who followed him, Santiago received advanced education in the West, attending the Chicago Musical College for his master's and doctoral degrees (ibid. 2584). The practice of going overseas for education had its predecessors as far back as the late Spanish colonial period, when members of the Filipino elite studied art and other subjects in various European locales. Their experience and exposure to European nationalism fed into their own understanding of the colonial situation in the Philippines, and this cosmopolitanism is part and parcel of the development of Filipino nationalism among the elite. As evidenced from Santiago's written and musical output, his sense of nationalism was less driven by the liberation politics of his late-nineteenth-century predecessors than by the impetus to cultivate Filipinism in the arts. "Filipinism" results from "Filipinization," the process of making culture more Filipino in order to counter the effects of colonialism and/or further a stronger sense of localized identity. This relates well to nationalism, which, though it has taken many forms, has often been associated with the desire for a national identity separate from a colonial one. Significantly, Santiago saw the work of nationalists as specialized, and institutionalization, an effective tie with the state, as the proper channel for dissemination. Thus, he took a modernist stance during the U.S. colonial period when he wrote, "I would suggest to the public that all the songs for the public schools should be those which are really Filipino, but the work of composing appropriate music to our songs can only be delegated to experts" (1928: 21). This positioning of composing as within the purview of experts was part of a modernist approach whose secular nature and treatment of the arts as an academic pursuit corresponded with societal changes under U.S. colonization.[17]

Perhaps the most nationalist and patriotic of all Santiago's compositions is the well-known "Pilipinas Kong Mahal (My Beloved Philippines)." Interestingly, the English version of the song is as widespread as the Filipino one, though it is not a direct translation. The Filipino version praises the Philippines as the "one and only country" and anthropomorphic "love" of the singer, who willingly serves and protects this love as a "duty." The English version also weds the singer to the country, pledging heart and hand to the Philippines, but it lacks the sense of duty of the Filipino text, and instead it extols the landscape as inspiring of devotion. Though the song is often used during flag ceremonies, the music is much more hymn than march In fact, the melody is particularly lyrical and inviting to solo singers, including both minor second intervals amenable to crooning and a leap of a major sixth at the beginning of the B section that instills a sense of uplift.

One approach that Santiago followed was to write in the Filipino *kundiman* style, producing some of the earliest in the genre to be considered art music (though his *kundiman* might better be described as popular art music). Another manner of achieving this goal was to use well-known folk melodies in his compositions. The composer, musician, and academic Antonio Molina claims that Santiago was the first Filipino composer to engage in this practice, an opinion shared by the anthropologist and folklorist E. Arsenio Manuel (1997: 18). Folk music materials were elevated as expressions of the inner self of the Filipino, and despite the syncretic nature of many tunes, they did not carry the taint of foreignness (Pájaro 1957: 35). The strategy of utilizing vernacular folk music on a national scale and tying a conception of antiquity to modernity parallels Anderson's focus on printing in vernacular languages as an "embryo of the nationally imagined community" (1991: 44). The national repertoire of folk music, expertly arranged for performance and pedagogy, likewise gave fixity to the imagined national self (ibid. 44). At times composers used only melodic fragments, and at others entire melodies served as the foundation of a symphonic piece. Some experimented with different ways of harmonizing the melodies and with transforming rhythmic structures (Santos 1991: 161).

More than just raw material, composers felt that folk music tapped into a kind of essential Filipino identity, even if the sound of the music displayed foreign influence (see Osit 1984). This sense of a national identity has the power to obscure regional and even ethnic differences in the Philippines and caters to nationalism's aspiration for unity. Folk music from lowland colonized areas is particularly flexible in reception, because, within this subset of the country's music, musical distinctions are more difficult to make. Hence, folk songs can become part of the national repertoire by rising above regional renown and becoming well known throughout the country. The folk song "Pobreng Alindahaw," which originates from the Visayas region, is a good example, because the melody is commonly known despite having lyrics in Visayan rather than Tagalog (or Filipino). The purposeful and widespread diffusion of folk songs as performed artifacts of patrimony is a nationalist strategy[18] and can be transmitted through folkloric presentations, elementary school music curriculums, and other modes of performance and education. The message embedded in the spread of music and its acceptance as "Filipino" throughout various provinces in the country is one of connectedness. This is made possible due to a shared understanding of musical sounds that are marked as "Filipino traditional" rather than simply "traditional" or even "regionally traditional." Because the musical markers are easy to hear and lack a unique correspondence with any one region of the Philippines, these aesthetic cues have been extremely efficacious for composers writing music that can embody the nation.

Like Béla Bartók of Hungary, Santiago spent many years collecting and recording folk songs. In 1930 he formalized his collecting after being invited to join a research project of Dr. Jorge Bocobo, the former president of the University of the Philippines (see chapter 2). Notably, the researchers on the team along with Santiago—Francisca Reyes Tolentino (dance), Antonio Molina (music), and Antonino Buenaventura (music)—have all been enshrined in the cultural history of the Philippines as important contributors to nation-building (Kasilag 1977: 2586). Besides collecting for reasons of preservation, Reyes Tolentino (later Reyes Aquino) notated dance steps in pictures and prose, and the musicians transcribed melodies in order to create a standard that could be taught in schools. The point clearly was to introduce Filipinos to a folkloric heritage in public schools. Santiago, in particular, has become notable for his practice of harmonizing folk music from various parts of the islands (Cavan 1924).

This practice led to legal problems for Santiago, the first occurring in 1928 when he attempted to copyright his harmonized version of the folksong "*Ay Kalisud*" and, in the face of some controversy, had to drop that request before it went to court. The second happened in 1939 when another composer, José Estella (well known for his *sarswela* music), complained that Santiago's "*Ano Kaya ang Kapalaran*" plagiarized his own "*Campanadas de Gloria.*" Importantly, the well-publicized case concluded with the court declaring that both composers had based their compositions on folk music, and neither could declare original ownership of those motifs (Manuel 1997: 43–44). The affair illustrates the extent to which folk music served as raw material for nationalist composers in the Philippines as well as the fluidity of those melodies through the folk, popular, and art music realms. Though the court case caused a scandal in its heyday, Santiago's ascension to nationalist divinity was only briefly curtailed. His achievements as a musical nationalist have been canonized in Philippine history, and many of his compositions and arrangements of folk music remain staples in the repertoires of singers, instrumentalists, and folkloric ensembles. Santiago fell victim to a paralyzing heart attack during World War II and died in 1947.

At the end of the commonwealth period under the United States, which lasted from 1935 to 1946, the Japanese occupied the Philippines. Filipino composers responded to Japanese propaganda against the Western colonial legacy with music that still had a distinctively Western sound (using Western scales and based on harmonic principles), but this was easily tolerated. After all, the Japanese themselves had undergone Westernization in some of their own music, and it was not tonality as much as popular songs directly from the United States that symbolized the colonial past.[19] During World War II, the Japanese propped up the Second Republic government in the Philippines and attempted to establish a more Asian-focused society there. The Japanese welcomed music with native roots and promoted Filipino composers and musicians, overseeing the first all-Filipino orchestras in the country. The resultant musical cycle proved beneficial for numerous Filipino artists, since more work for composers meant more pieces for orchestras and more opportunities for conductors (Santiago-Felipe 1977: 2502). In this atmosphere, musical nationalism became even more closely associated with the extinguishing of Western hegemony, despite the continued predominance of Western musical aesthetics that had become naturalized among Filipinos. The strategies were, on the surface, simple. Composers could "nativize" their music by using a local language instead of English. They could also make use of folk song material and patriotic themes that suggested Filipino nationalism but did not defy Japanese imperial designs.

During this time period, the experiences of Felipe de Leon illustrate a more complicated and subversive approach in expressing nationalism. Educated at the University of the Philippines Conservatory of Music under the composers Colonel Antonino Buenaventura, Antonio Molina, Rodolfo Cornejo, and Hilarión Rubio (all future members of the League of Filipino Composers), de Leon was already accomplished in the musical arts before the Japanese occupation (1942–1945). During World War II, the Japanese banned the national anthem by Julián Felipe and ordered de Leon to write another one in 1942. According to Helen Samson, biographer of several Filipino composers, Japanese officers presented de Leon with a prize-winning poem by Catalino Dionisio and compelled him to write the musical accompaniment. "De Leon stressed that he never expected the song to be anything more than just an ordinary march. He never thought it would almost be a national anthem . . . especially during the time when the Philippine National Anthem was prohibited" (Samson 1976: 115–116). Faced with working for the Japanese, de Leon attempted to secretly thwart the propaganda by manipulating fragments of the original national anthem in his "Awit sa Paglikha ng Bagong Pilipinas (Hymn of the Birth of the New Philippines)."

> The vocal part, starting with the phrase "Tindig, aking inang bayan," was premised on the commencing phrase of the national anthem. The same principle applied to the phrase "Hawakan ang watawat. . . ." Its instrumental passage, harmoniously bridging the song's first part and the chorus, echoed the third part of the anthem up to the seventh

measure. De Leon augmented...the banned anthem's melody, and he effectively used the reverse technique, to deflect possible suspicion by the Japanese Imperial Army. The third part of our anthem, used in the introduction of the march, was also evident. (Osit 1984: 77)

After the war ended, de Leon explained how he had inserted hidden musical messages into his compositions, and the People's Court absolved him of collaboration charges (Samson 1976: 116). His wartime experiences reveal how artists attempted to circumvent pressure with creative tactics, even as they acceded to demands for the manufacture of public culture to feed into a propaganda campaign. The story also displays the symbolic flexibility music has to express many sentiments and why it is so difficult to come to terms with how music means.

On the other side of the coin, the Japanese military campaign in the Philippines was notoriously brutal, inspiring a musical repertoire among Filipino guerrilla fighters that followed in the tradition of revolutionary songs from the war against Spain. The *Hukbo ng Bayan Laban sa Hapon* (People's Army Against the Japanese), commonly known as the Huks, sang as they traversed the countryside and engaged with Japanese soldiers (T. Maceda: 132–133). These nationalist expressions of the people would, like those who called themselves Huks, become increasingly anti-Philippine state after the war. Schools of thought regarding Filipino nationalism would split radically as the political stances between communists and activists became more at odds with the government. Still, during the time of World War II, Huk composers toting guns in the jungles and art music composers with pen to score in Manila shared similar ideals about the nation. Nationalism not only expressed and evoked a love of Pilipinas—the motherland that had long been a captive of the Spanish, Americans, and now the Japanese—but it also voiced a longing for liberation and self-rule.

A Nation Born Again

When the United States recognized the independence of the Philippines on July 4, 1946, the country established its Third Republic. It was a time of rebuilding from the devastation of World War II, and the newly independent Philippine government was charged with massive reconstruction on a budget that was already in arrears. Yet, the rubble of the capital city Manila was only the surface wreckage; societal infrastructures from the educational system to law enforcement required rebuilding as well. Filipinos in power found themselves tasked with nation-building, a process that went beyond putting into place the mechanics of the new republic and also encompassed the shaping of nationalistic ideologies, both for internal and external consumption. These ideologies emanated from various camps high and low on the social totem pole, but it should be noted that nationalism specifically in the service of nation-building remained primarily the purview of the Filipino elites. Since nation-building included the cementing of hierarchies of power after the dismantling of colonial structures, the elite needed to play a primary role in the process to safeguard their political, economic, and social positions. Likewise, many members of the intellectual and artistic elite, who were not always or even usually from the upper class, became active in nation-building. They were either invited or conscripted by the state to participate, or they simply continued their work and were recognized for it. Hence, with various players involved in the burgeoning arena of postcolonial national identity, the abundance of contesting views on what could or should constitute the Philippine nation comes as little surprise.

The government of the new nation-state was populated primarily by the Filipino elites, and their articulations of nationalism proved to be separate, though sometimes inclusive of, the liberation ideologies that fueled its earliest expressions. The politicians of the state turned their attention to nation-building, which for cultural nationalists in particular included coming to terms with postcolonial Filipino identity. Much of what comprised the everyday life of Filipinos originated as a result of colonial experiences, from religion to language. Two of the most widely read writers of all time in the Philippines, N.V.M Gonzalez and F. Sionil José, began to mature into prominence during the first decade of the postwar period, and they produced articles, short stories, and novels in English. The question of national language (as opposed to the local languages spoken throughout the archipelago) has been ongoing since the commonwealth period and has been an important factor in Philippine identity at the national level. With the Spanish language never really a contender, nationalists felt that Pilipino should supplant, or at least stand alongside, English.[20] Spanish had not been taught in the Philippines during colonial times in the Philippines the way it had been in Latin America, and the preferred languages of religious conversion were local ones.[21] By the time World War II had ended, there were relatively few Spanish speakers, many of whom were part of the *mestizo* upper class. English, however, was widely spoken among the elite, and it was the medium of public education and governance during American rule. As Gonzalez and Sionil José proved, writing in English was not necessarily antinationalist or colonialist, because what has mattered in retrospect has been the subject matter of their works. Still, the debate about what language should be the primary one of public education for present and future generations remains important in the country, because the command of English is a marketable commodity even inside the country (for instance, in the call center industry). After 1946, English continued to be used in government and business, and it was the first language of the growing mass media industries. Alongside English, Filipino (formerly Pilipino, a development of Tagalog with the addition of words from other regional languages) grew in national importance and was spread through mass media.

Technology changed the information landscape and became an important way of disseminating popular culture and its associated images of modern Filipino identity. Elizabeth Enriquez calls 1946 until 1957 the "Golden Years of Philippine Radio," due to the widening availability and affordability of radio equipment and the expansion of programming. As radio became more prominent, Filipinos took over the airwaves from Americans and introduced local languages in order to better communicate with their regional audiences. Most radio content comprised American popular music as well as more local fare, including amateur singing contests, quiz shows, children's programs, talk shows, and on-air poets who engaged in oratorical jousts with one another (E. Enriquez 2003: 22–26). Of course, this change in musical tastes caused some chagrin. The nationalist composer Felipe de Leon wrote, "It is rather lamentable that the creative genius of our composers suffered a great deal with the advent of the new environment which offered nothing but ear-splitting and somewhat distorted music of the jazz type, not to mention the boogie, *guaracha*, *mambo*, a-go-go, and others of their kind" (1976: 161).[22] Filipino audiences continued to have a taste for Western pop, and local artists often remade hits from overseas that replicated the originals with uncanny accuracy. While the copycat singers found fame and success, reaching the airwaves and making their own recordings, other Filipino singers attempted to cultivate an audience for Filipino popular music sung in Tagalog. Radio and the recording industry, now under the control of Filipinos, afforded new postwar opportunities.

In the meantime, television also began to make headway into Filipino society. While radio had a more freewheeling style, television programming was primarily made up of shows from the United States. Few Filipinos were capable of producing programming in the early years, and shows like *Candid Camera, I Love Lucy,* and *Life with Father* were popular in the 1950s Philippines (del Mundo 2003: 7). Whether through radio, television, or the continuing popularity of movies, Filipino national identity continued to be caught up with American popular culture, and this posed a problem for cultural nationalists.

Perhaps predictably, the first independent republic in Asia maintained its close ties with the United States, and the time period could be characterized as a neocolonial period in terms of both economic and political matters. Because of unfair trade policies that favored American interests, the Philippine economy remained closely linked to U.S. markets as well as the valuation of the U.S. dollar (Jenkins 1954). In the 1950s, the country experienced an influx of monies from international sources, including the United States and Japan, for projects ranging from health care to the military, all of it a boon to the burgeoning economy. At the same time, money also translated to international meddling in Philippine affairs. Not surprisingly, the United States asserted influence within the office of the Philippine president, despite the stream of nationalistic rhetoric glorifying independence that was fed to the public.

President Manuel Quezon, who served from 1935 until his exile in 1941 during the Japanese occupation, set a fiery tone for Filipino politicians when he famously declared, "I'd rather have a government run like hell by Filipinos to one run like heaven by the Americans" (Mulder 1997: 109). Conversely, the three Filipino presidents who followed after independence evinced a much more pro-American sentiment. President Manuel Roxas (served 1946–1948) ascended as the first postwar president amidst accusations of collaboration with Japanese forces during the war. The issue of collaboration loomed over many politicians of the time, but Roxas had the shielding and support of the American general Douglas MacArthur. Roxas declared an amnesty for collaborators during his presidency, ostensibly as a gesture toward moving forward, but many Filipinos equated this with an absolution of the elite in order that they retain power (Dolan 1993: 43). He also adopted a foreign policy favorable to American interests that was continued by his vice president, Elpidio Quirino (served 1948–1953), when he died in office (Zaide 1999: 357–358).

The next president, Ramón Magsaysay (served 1953–1957), adopted "Mambo Magsaysay," a catchy tune written by another prominent politician named Raul Manglapus, as his campaign song in the early 1950s. The song aired on radio stations, signaling the populist tone of Magsaysay's presidency. English was still widely spoken in the Philippines in the 1950s, especially in more urbanized areas, and Magsaysay's campaign slogan was "Magsaysay is my guy" (del Mundo 2003: 6). Perceived to be a kind of "man of the people," Magsaysay promulgated stories of his lower class past in order to differentiate himself from the elite, who were perceived to be irreversibly corrupt. He toured Philippine villages to talk with rural people, and he visited soldiers in the field. His past as a guerilla fighter against the Japanese during World War II gave him credibility as the commander in chief of the armed forces and endeared him even more to the masses as a military hero.

During and after his campaign he courted newsmen and actually increased the importance of the media in politics as he promoted himself.[23] Amando Doronila, the respected Filipino journalist and historian, sees Magsaysay's presidency as a turning point, directing politics from localism to centralism, providing a single figure of power and capturing the imagination of the masses, and increasing the role of the middle class in bureaucracy and business (1992: 95–97). The romantic ideology surrounding Magsaysay and permeating those years was one of reform, honest government, and attention to the regular people; he matched well the archetype of the benign king.

While the poets Ildefonso Santos and Julián Cruz Balmaceda had written Tagalog lyrics for the national anthem in 1948—calling it "O Sintang Lupa"—it was not until Magsaysay's tenure that Julián Felipe's march for Emilio Aguinaldo became the national anthem of postwar, independent Philippines. "Lupang Hinirang (Chosen Land)" became official in 1956 and underwent only slight changes in the following decades to alter the text from Tagalog to Pilipino (now Filipino) that reflect the development of the national language of the nation.

> Bayang magiliw
> Perlas ng Silanganan
> Alab ng puso
> Sa dibdib mo'y buhay
>
> Lupang hinirang
> Duyan ka ng magiting
> Sa manlulupig
> 'Di ka pasisiil
>
> Sa dagat at bundok
> Sa simoy at sa langit mong bughaw
> May dilag ang tula at awit
> Sa paglayang minamahal
>
> Ang kislap ng watawat mo'y
> Tagumpay na nagniningning
> Ang bituin at araw niya
> Kailan pa ma'y 'di magdidilim
>
> Lupa ng araw, ng luwalhati't pagsinta
> Buhay ay langit sa piling mo

Aming ligaya, na 'pag may mang-aapi
Ang mamatay nang dahil sa 'yo

English translation:
Beloved country
Pearl of the Orient
The fervor of the heart
Is alive in your chest

Chosen land
You are the cradle of the brave
To conquerors
You will not surrender

Through the seas and mountains
Through the air and your blue sky
There is majesty in your poems and songs
For beloved freedom

The brightness of your flag
Shines victoriously
Its stars and sun
Will never dim

Land of the sun, glory, and our love
Life is heaven in your arms
It is our pleasure, when there are oppressors
To die for you[24]

After being banned for periods during American colonization and Japanese occupation, the final reinstatement of the anthem in a native language was appropriately nationalist for the times. Still, Magsaysay's legacy is commonly remembered as pro-American, particularly since some believe he came to power under the tutelage of the CIA.[25] Less than a decade after World War II, many Filipinos continued to perceive Philippine and American interests as the same or as overlapping, making Magsaysay the model of a new kind of pro-Western nationalism (Lumbera 1996: 10). This tight post–World War II (and Cold War) alignment with the United States differentiated the Philippines from other postcolonial countries, particularly those in Southeast Asia from whom the general population of the Philippines felt distant. The historian Nicholas Tarling denotes that despite being the first Asian colony to gain independence, "Filipino statements praising the United States at an Asian Relations Conference held in New Delhi in March 1947, only months after the Philippines became independent, shocked other delegates, as did a statement at the Manila Treaty conference in 1954 that Filipinos did not regard themselves as Asians" (1999: 265). Magsaysay supported U.S. enterprises and rode high on an anticommunist platform, firmly subduing the communist Huk insurrectionists (with American aid) for the time being. Even so, one might wonder whether the peasants in the countryside who took up communism as well as arms against the Philippine government after World War II were the true heirs to the revolutionary spirit that marked the nationalism of the past fifty years.[26]

With such competing and changing notions of nationalism in the ideological arena of nation-building during the decade after World War II—and faced with the rapid dissemination of American popular culture aided by technological advances—cultural nationalists in the Philippines had a difficult task ahead of them. Was the postcolonial nationalist approach in the arts to be defined by a purging of colonial vestiges? How, then, was one to stave off the advance of popular culture that was clearly not rooted in indigenous forms? Or did approaches that block out the history of colonialism also deny something essential about the identity of the contemporary Filipino? Nationalist composers of the 1950s in the Philippines were undaunted, and they took up the debate amongst themselves and in public forums, including the popular mediums of newspapers and magazines.

The Composer's Responsibility

In October 1955, less than ten years after the end of American colonization of the Philippine Islands, eleven composers inaugurated the League of Filipino Composers as a member of the Regional Music Commission of Southeast Asia.[27] While the League's founding generated no fanfare among the populace at large, the rhetoric surrounding the formation of the group articulated an important nationalist consciousness that held great sway among Filipino cultural and political elites of the time.[28] The League did not require its members to be nationalists; yet, the ideological tenor of the times was such that art music composers felt a personal responsibility to achieve success in the service of nation-building. Eliseo Pájaro, described by Ramón Santos as a modernist and neoclassicist who experimented with twentieth-century techniques, served as the first chairman of the League of Filipino Composers (1991: 161). In the following lengthy quote, Dr. Pájaro articulates eloquently a position of musical elites regarding the role, and even obligation, of composers in advancing the Filipino race (which, here, he tellingly equates with nation).

> The contribution of a nation or race to civilization and culture is measured by the achievements of its scientists, scholars, thinkers, and artists.... And so our country's contribution to music as an art will have to be made through our serious composers, and the importance of that contribution will depend entirely on the quality and durability of their works. Bearing this in mind what have we Pilipinos done to promote the growth of music as an art in our country? Or, to be more specific, what have we done to encourage the Pilipino composer in his efforts to promote the growth of music as an art in our country? What can we do to help the Pilipino composer develop to full maturity and possibly attain the greatness of a Stravinsky, a Hindemith, or a Schoenberg? What can we do to inspire our composers to produce great works that are expressive of our aspirations and feelings as a people, and which would be reflective of our national customs and traditions, aesthetic sense, our own way of life? (1966: 9)

Following from Pájaro's rhetorical opine, the early goals of the League centered on encouraging artistic musical creation as well as fostering national pride.[29] That this pride could be accomplished only by contributing to the musical arts within a global context is significant. Filipino composers could achieve success in their own country, but, Pájaro reminds us, these same composers become representatives of their nation when evaluated from the outside. The reference to Stravinsky, Hindemith, and Schoenberg, is in this case an invocation of nationalism that equates the talents of Filipino composers with Europeans.[30] Moreover, Pájaro implies that the great works of European composers have contributed to all of human civilization, illustrating that a Filipino composer with nationalist concerns would not have a narrowed purview, as long as the compositions themselves exhibited excellence. Indeed, through the "greatness" of works one can achieve "universal success" that, when measured by external validation, requires global dissemination and lasting impact outside of an originary national context. Later in his life, Pájaro wrote, "A lot of the serious music that have [*sic*] come to us belongs to the whole world, hence, is universal" (1976: 3). One could argue that the very notion of universal music masks cultural hegemony, for in practice, universality in art music has been applied only to the Western classical musical tradition. Yet, it is with national pride that Pájaro espoused the possibility of Filipino composers achieving equal musical immortality, a hope made possible by the amelioration of an inferiority complex imposed by colonialism. Felipe de Leon, an original member of the League illustrated this when he said, "American singers and instrumental players come to the Philippines to give us their music, and we Filipinos go to America to give the Americans also their own music. It is a pity. It should not be just one commodity on the two-way traffic. That is not fair exchange and it does not advance our own music. Why don't we reverse the direction of the cultural flow by popularizing our own music in, say, Europe or America" (Osit 1984: 98). This quote reveals a ground-level understanding of how multidirectional cultural flows intervene in perceptions of national identity. Further, through the discourse of composers, an incipient connection between the responsibility of artists and the politics of postcolonial nationalism becomes apparent. Locating music and nationalism in this fashion adds a new component to conventional arguments that postcolonial nationalism should be primarily concerned with anticolonialism or state-sponsored nation-building, for the arts can—and for some, must—reach places that politicking cannot. In various ways, individual artists contribute to the nationalist debates while negotiating a complex field of politics, and their concerns activate music as nationalist undertaking. Thus, the issue of state patronage against artistic autonomy should also have appeared in the writings of nationalist composers, but it is largely absent.

On a practical level, the composers benefited from the League's annual Philippines Music Festival, which featured commissioned works by the members. In tandem with the Music Promotion Foundation (headed by the operatic diva Jovita Fuentes), the League featured a number of interesting works in the 1950s. These included the "Toccata for Percussion and Winds (for orthodox Western instruments and Muslim percussions)" by Lucrecia Kasilag, the "Philippine Symphony No. 1" by Eliseo Pájaro, and the "Suite Pastorale" by Lucio San Pedro (Kasilag 1977: 2587). The rest of the eleven original members of the League of Filipino Composers—Colonel Antonino Buenaventura, Rodolfo Cornejo, Bernadino Custodio, Felipe de Leon, Antonio Molina, Hilarión Rubio, Lucino Sacramento, and Ramón Tapales—also contributed important works to the first festivals.[31]

While all of these composers should be considered nationalists, at least in regard to some of their works, the following section focuses on Lucio San Pedro and Lucrecia Kasilag as two important models of modernism in

Philippine nationalist music. San Pedro is among the most widely recognized composers of the League, primarily because his output has been extremely accessible to Filipino audiences. His music has been remade into popular songs, and many Filipino musical ensembles rely on his arrangements of folk music. Conversely, while Kasilag's compositions generally find a home only in concert halls, her approach reveals an enthusiasm for local instruments and performance practices that is important in understanding musical nationalism in the Philippines. Both were modernists in their own way, despite the utilization of contrasting strategies. While Kasilag's trajectory fits more easily into conventional narratives of musical modernism of the twentieth century, San Pedro's romanticism conforms to Jameson's dialectical vision of modernism, in which a strain of "antimodern" is aesthetically represented by "pastoral visions" that are symbolic in their spiritualism and general opposition to the machinery and rationality of modernity (1991: 304).

Lucio San Pedro and the Cradle of Folk

Lucio San Pedro's childhood surroundings were similar to those of many Filipino composers of the first part of the twentieth century.[32] As a child, Lucio San Pedro (1913–2002) pumped air for the church organ played by his grandfather while his grandmother sang in the choir. San Pedro began composing works while still a teenager and eventually inherited the job of church organist as well as the directorship of the choir. Along the way, he learned how to play the violin, the Filipino *banduria* and *octavina* (fourteen-string chordophones with European origins), the banjo, and several band and orchestra instruments.[33] He graduated from the University of the Philippines Conservatory of Music in 1938 with a teacher's diploma in composition and conducting, after studying with such nationalist composers as Francisco Santiago and Antonio Molina. Though he had taken some military training, it was San Pedro's music career that thrived during World War II.

He served as conductor of the Musical Philippines Philharmonic Orchestra, won three first prizes in composition contests held by the Japanese occupation government, and landed a faculty position in the composition department of Centro Escolar University (Samson 1976: 193–196). In 1946, the tone poem "Hope and Ambition," which he had written to celebrate the inauguration of the Third Philippine Republic, won a special prize in a national composition contest. Winning enabled him to study abroad, and in

1947 he left for the Juilliard School of Music. Though he had worked alongside Filipino nationalist composers at the University of the Philippines, it was under the mentorship of Professor Bernard Wagenaar that San Pedro finally realized the significance of creatively using folk music in original works. In one of his assignments, Wagenaar suggested to San Pedro that he develop only a part of a folk melody to "emphasize racial origin" but to avoid literal quotations that included entire folk songs (Hila 1998: 310). San Pedro approached this advice with conviction, and his attention to the essence of folk songs rather than the use of known melodies has been an integral aspect of his entire body of works. The historian Antonio Hila glowingly encapsulates San Pedro's legacy and writes him into nationalist history.

> In the Maestro's works, the creative, not the literal utilization of the folk idiom, which is clothed in a polished style, evoked a subtle effect that articulates a sense of identity, a consciousness that is unmistakably Filipino.... It is largely from this consideration that the Maestro has earned the plaudit "Creative Nationalist." And it is through this philosophy that his works came to be appreciated and ardently loved by countless Filipinos. Obviously, the Maestro keenly perceives the importance of the folk idiom in projecting relevance and identity in his works.... For indeed, folk songs are the spontaneous, unconscious expression of feelings, interests and aspirations of the people. And because the Maestro draws inspiration from them, his compositions are perceived as typical expressions of life itself. (1998: 307)[34]

How can the idiomatic essences of folk music rather than folk music itself evoke the same understandings in audiences who do not have specific melodies with which to associate memories? If composed "traditional" music is to be implicated in the aesthetics of nationalism, then we should first ask, what are the aesthetics of the traditional? This is a troublesome question to answer empirically, especially in the face of inescapable hybridity. Musical aesthetics, in the case of Filipino folk music, actually have great range. Regional pieces of various lowland Christian groups are quite different from the musics of non-Christian peoples in different parts of the country.[35] Lowland Christian folk music tends to use the diatonic scale, simple time signatures, simple harmonies, and are often verse-refrain or strophic in form. Yet, there are many different genres of folk music whose origins are foreign to the archipelago and whose musical styles are quite varied. These folk music types range from marches and *mazurkas* to *polkas* and *paso dobles*, with each displaying distinguishable musical characteristics that define the styles.

Moreover, each style has been to a greater or lesser degree adapted in its Filipino iteration. Hence, folk music is inextricably related to colonial dissemination, often bears the stamp of foreign sound structures, and yet has been remarkably well assimilated as a Filipino expression. Moreover, Western tonality has become inherent in the folk music aesthetic, especially following the harmonization of these tunes by composers such as Francisco Santiago during the early half of the twentieth century.

One by-product of this broad sense of the traditional is that some pieces that Filipinos consider to be folk songs actually have known composers who happened to be writing in a traditional style. By virtue of their content as well as the composers' intentions, these creations join the folk songs as part of a national tradition. That the melodies and themes of folk songs remain embedded in the minds of composers from childhood on indicates a kind of implicit awareness of the "Filipino-ness" of the music—that is, the meanings packed within the song itself that could have developed only through idiosyncratic history, setting, and cultural personality. Thus, folk music includes songs in the oral tradition with mixed regional and even international origins, songs composed in a traditional style that may or may not be attributed to a certain composer, and songs that contain folk song themes or consist of several folk songs put together. What all have in common is a perceived style that connotes the traditional. Important to musical nationalism, however, are those composed pieces that do not directly invoke the sound aesthetics of folk music but still encourage a deeply felt tie to the traditional. Pursuing this strategy requires sensitivity not only to musical technique, but also to the discourse of the traditional that affects reception. In the Filipino case, as in many others, tradition is closely associated with a timeless sense of the past and the romanticized countryside.

The feeling of romanticism in San Pedro's music that seems to evoke qualities of Filipino folk music is aptly displayed in his 1956 "Suite Pastorale," a five-movement piece premiered by the Manila Symphony Orchestra and Chorus that sweeps through scenes of his hometown, Angono, Rizal. The fourth movement of the suite, a lullaby entitled "Sa Ugoy ng Duyan (The Sway of the Baby Hammock)," has become quite well known in the Philippines. More haunting than sweet, the song has a modal quality that lends itself to exoticism or, more aptly, a distancing from the present-day self in imagination or in time. The past—an implied shared past—is both metaphoric for the nation and real for many as a memory from childhood. The song is based on a tune that San Pedro's mother hummed when putting him

FIGURE 1.2. Undulation motif of San Pedro's "Sa Ugoy ng Duyan" (transcription by author)

to sleep, and the tones that undulate smoothly beneath the melody clearly paint the memory of gentle rocking. This rocking serves as a constant motif throughout much of the piece (see figure 1.2).

San Pedro had actually written the piece for a song contest more than ten years earlier, but it did not have any text until he happened upon the lyricist Levi Celerio during his return to the Philippines from Julliard (Hila 1998: 311). Celerio stayed true to San Pedro's maternally inspired music. The lyrics are personally nostalgic, containing allusions to specific memories rather than the abstractions a lullaby might contain. More than that, they achieve a plaintive nostalgia that link to the lyrics of Maria Clara's song in Jose Rizal's nationalist novel, *Noli Me Tangere* (Touch Me Not). In Rizal's version, the mother(land) is remembered and longed for at a time when the Philippines was still under Spanish colonial rule. In "Sa Ugoy ng Duyan," the heart of the nation may be found in the ambiguous past, as lost to the singer as pastoral life is lost to the modern city dweller. San Pedro's music evolved from a lullaby and references the genre, but it is a song for adults.

> Sana'y di nagmaliw ang dati kong araw
> Nang munti pang bata sa piling ni Nanay
> Nais ko'y maulit ang awit ni, Inang mahal,
> Awit ng pagibig habang ako'y na sa duyan.
>
> Sa aking pagtulog na labis ang himbing
> Ang bantay ko'y tala ang tanod ko'y bit'win
> Sa piling ni Nanay, langit ang buhay
> Puso kong may dusa'y sabik sa ugoy ng duyan.
>
> Ibig kong matulog sa dating duyan ko Inang
> Oh! Ina.

English translation:
I wish my days of old would not fade
When I was a small child in Mother's arms
I wish to hear again the song of my beloved Mother
A song of love while I was in a baby's hammock.

In my slumber so deep
My guardian a bright star and my guide a star
In Mother's arms, heaven is alive
My sad heart yearns for the sway of the hammock

I yearn to sleep in my old hammock, Mother
Oh! Mother.

Because the suite as a whole deliberately harkens to San Pedro's notion of the countryside, the pastoral aspect carries throughout "Sa Ugoy ng Duyan," such that the rocking of the baby's hammock (a kind of hanging cradle of cloth widely used in the past and even in the present-day countryside) encapsulates too the swaying of tall grass, bamboo, and palm trees. The first fifteen measures of the piece are consumed by the movement of two tones over a pedal tone and the alternation of the tonic and fifth. By repeatedly ending the accompanying phrases on the sustained fourth chord, the music does not allow for a place of rest, just as the cradle itself would seem in perpetual motion until sleep. In measure sixteen, the piano accompaniment pauses on the minor second chord, only to resolve back to the tonic in the next measure in the middle of the word "love." The mood of the piece alters somewhat at this point, with the accompaniment shifting into a forward and upwardly directed motion. The movement toward the register of the melody in the tenor line suggests a minute focus on the singer, just as the world would melt away in the transition from wakefulness into sleep, and the sound of the lullaby would be one's only sensation. There is playfulness in the syncopation of the left-hand accompaniment at rehearsal letter B, while simultaneously the right hand plays a high-pitched melody that derives from the original theme. Here the mood switches from *semplice dolce* to *expressivo*, and the iterations of this melodic derivation are the most childlike moments of the composition. It is also worth commenting on San Pedro's use of grace note ornamentations to allow for melisma on several occasions (but with exception) when the word "awit," or "song," is sung, for the composition as a whole is a musical impression containing word painting as much as it is a lullaby about a time of lullabies.

At risk of elaborating on the melancholic lyrics with metaphors they may never have been intended to evoke, because San Pedro's references to the folk (read in this case as pastoral) are commonly touted as nationalistic, his music can be read on another level. "Mother," as is not uncommon in metaphor, may stand in for one's own land, extending from the locality of home to the expansiveness of a nation. Having a sense of motherland as a figurative and literal home is not specific to any particular people, and, likewise, the lullaby is a genre that exists all over the world, though aesthetics differ from place to place.[36] This duality corresponds with the universalism and localism implied by Western musical aesthetics in much of Filipino nationalistic music and encapsulates what has made San Pedro's compositions so appealing to so many.

Lucrecia Kasilag and Asian Modernism

Lucrecia Kasilag was born in 1918 in the Ilocos region, homeland of the future president and dictator Ferdinand Marcos. Because of her father's job as a government engineer, Kasilag's family moved south, and she grew up in Manila. Surrounded by music in her own family—her mother taught music to all of her children—Kasilag learned the violin, piano, guitar, and *banduria*. She went on to study music and liberal arts at the Philippine Women's University (PWU)—the first women's university in Asia administrated by Asians—and though she toyed with the notion of becoming a concert pianist at this stage, she ended up pursuing a degree in English. Afterward, Kasilag continued her study of music at St. Scholastica's College, and following graduation, she joined a Filipino group on a cultural tour of China and Japan. While performing concerts of Western art music there, she had her first exposure to East Asian music genres that would pique her interest and serve as inspiration for future works.

In 1946, the same year the Philippines achieved independence, Kasilag commenced teaching at the prestigious Conservatory of Music at the University of the Philippines. After one year, she left to join the faculty at her alma mater, PWU, and there she took the helm as dean of the newly opened College of Music and Fine Arts. She remained at PWU (while also holding other positions) for more than fifty years. While music education remained close to her heart, Kasilag's skills, drive, and engaging personality led her to become one of the most important brokers of Filipino culture within the Philippines as well as internationally. In later years, she would serve simultaneously as the musical director of the Philippines' most famous folkloric group, Bayanihan, as well as the artistic director of the Cultural Center of the Philippines. These two positions have overshadowed her work as a composer. Still, it is notable that she remains one of very few women composers included in histories of Filipino art music, and her works reveal interesting and innovative ideas about the expression of national identity through music. Two musical strategies in particular proved compelling in establishing her nationalistic ideologies: experimentation with modernist music and the use of Asian (including Filipino) instruments in orchestral works.

As a composer, Kasilag's antecedent influences were quite varied, including Johann Sebastian Bach, Robert Schumann, Claude Debussy, Béla Bartók, and Antonio Molina, and her writing in the 1940s and early 1950s emphasized folk song arrangements and the nineteenth-century Romantic style prevalent in Filipino art music (de la Torre 1985: 108–112). Kasilag's first exposure to European modernist music—music that was progressive, antiromanticist (in contradistinction with San Pedro), and distanced from tonality—occurred away from home. As with many of the composers and musicians in this book, Kasilag pursued advanced musical training overseas. On a Fulbright scholarship, she completed a master's degree in music from the Eastman School of Music at the University of Rochester in 1950 with a major in theory and a minor in composition. In the United States, she experienced atonal and electronic music for the first time while under the mentorship of Allen Irvine McHose and Wayne Barlow (ibid. 23–31). She became excited about the possibilities for modern Filipino compositions. How might an art music composer of the Philippines express a postcolonial Filipino sensibility? What were the aesthetics of societal hybridity? What could a composer contribute in sound and ideology to nation-building? These questions seemed to have an answer in modernist music, not merely because the work of composers like Schoenberg reflected well upon their home countries, but also because a liberation from the hegemony of Western tonality had symbolic import for a newly independent country.

During Spanish colonization, developments in Western art music taking place in Europe had parallel adaptations in the Philippines. By the time Americans arrived with their own repertoire of children's songs and popular music, Filipinos of the colonized areas had long internalized the naturalness of Western tonality and harmony. More than just emulative of the West, tonality had become foundational in art and popular music of the Philippines and had no separate identity. Folk music that had once been sung with notes that fell in between notes of the diatonic scale shifted gradually to the scale or disappeared from use. Newer folk music came into being with melodies generated from the diatonic scale. Beginning in the nineteenth century,

Filipino art music composers wrote in the Western music idiom (with a particular taste for the Romantic style, since it was prevalent in Europe during this time period), and their mastery of form and harmony was considered an achievement in the same way that fluency in the Spanish language, long withheld from the native, represented the advancement of the Filipino elite. The hegemony of tonality, then, could be read as analogous to the imposition and eventual localization of colonial values, not the least of which assumed the superiority of the West. Filipino music prior to colonization and music from areas that evaded Spanish control—including that found in the mountains and the Muslim south—used a variety of scales and different techniques for formulating melodies. From the repetitive hocketing of gongs and bamboo instruments to intricate microtonal melodies over drone, music perceived to be indigenous took on new significance in a postcolonial age. It was if sonic difference could answer, in part, the question of what Filipino could have been were it not for colonial influence.

José Maceda was an early pioneer in exploring indigenous music of the Philippines, European modernism in music, and deconstructions of Western music conventions in composition (Santos 2002: 49). Trained in Europe and in the United States in piano, composition, and ethnomusicology, he essentially founded the field of ethnomusicology in the Philippines (Santos 2005: 129). "In the 1950s," he himself pointed out, "few musicians in the Philippines have ever heard of the Jew's harp, or of the different types of gongs.... What I saw and discovered was a music realistically fresh but it needed to be studied and understood" (Samson 1976: 138). Maceda referenced a nationalist trope of connecting indigeneity to modernity when he wrote that native music has "hidden symbols and signifiers meaningful even now to a modern Philippine world" (1998b: viii). He also laid the groundwork for the study of ethnic minority music as a social science and musicological endeavor. As a composer, his exposure to the European avant-garde blended with his intellectual approach to indigenous music sound and practice. He committed himself to the decolonization of Asian music through the pushing of compositional boundaries (Santos 2002: 42). Maceda's elevation of tribal musical culture and insistence on its significance as an essential aspect of Filipino identity has continued to be a powerful postcolonial strategy, and his use of tribal musical aesthetics and practices in his compositions was metaphorical for the incorporation of ethnic minorities into the national imagination.[37] Moreover, Maceda's departure from simple strategies of musical quotation and his intellectual approach to composition paved the way for a new generation of Filipino composers whose creative output can be viewed as personal and as nationalist in intent (for a more thorough assessment of Maceda's work, see

Santos 2005). Yet, as with Kasilag, Maceda's body of compositions is not well known among the general Filipino population. He was certainly a nationalist thinker and composer, but his works did not engage the public at large, and his writings were at times too esoteric for students outside of music. This does not diminish his role in history nor his impact on musicology in the Philippines, but it does illustrate how nationalism does not always coincide with populism. At the same time, his work in the field of Philippine ethnomusicology and his dogged intellectualization of music remain a profound legacy of nationalist modernism.

In general, European and American musical modernism of the early twentieth century, like most other movements in the arts, did not have a unified approach. Some modernist works represented a rejection of the past and a break from "tradition," while other works acknowledged a relationship with the past—for instance, Schoenberg's view that his work in the 1920s was an extension of German musical tradition rather than a complete departure (Greenberg 1971: 171). In music, modernism signaled a general movement away from tonality and the dissolution of vertical relationships dictated only by harmonic progression. That Kasilag should have been attracted to modernism as a nationalist strategy for Filipino composers while studying in the West is not as ironic as it appears, for modernism was flexible in its approaches and therefore not tied so strictly to a single place as it was to its time. Moreover, modernism's openness to temporal continuity in aesthetic expression allowed a Filipino composer to anchor works in historical import and relevance, even while engaging in the radical. At the same time, modernist composers like Hindemith and Schoenberg are also considered to be neoclassicists in their insistence on order, balance, and rational principles rather than the emotionalism that propelled the music of nineteenth-century Romanticism.[38] As Ferenc Bonís put it succinctly, "[Neoclassicists] revive the means of musical expression of the period before 1800 or 1750, in certain cases with the declared intention of showing the 'Day-before Yesterday', as an aspect of 'Today', for the public of the Present" (1983: 73). This definition has clear overlap with concepts of modernism. In the context of the 1950s Philippines, the musical strategy of ambiguous tonality and neoclassicist principles of balance and anti-Romanticism had the nationalist implications of metaphorically dissolving colonial aesthetic values while not denying the unchangeable facts of history.

As the ethnomusicologist Gerard Béhague theorized in regard to art music composers of Latin America, modernist music that combined the romantically distilled essences of the native with European musical models defied conceptions of colonial mentality in art (2006: 37). Kasilag revealed her motivations in her own writings.

In the light of contemporary aesthetics, the apparent divergence between Western and Eastern music should appear less, since they have a common heritage. Western music developed from older forms identified with the East, where musical traditions have enjoyed a long and ancient history.... Modern composers like Debussy, Bartók, Stravinsky, and Messiaen became fascinated with the musics of the East and reflected these in their works.... With its rich, cultural, mosaic background of Eastern-Western complexion, indeed the Philippines, which is so well-situated in the Pacific and so dually civilized, presents an ideally centrical place for an ambivalent training in East-West cultures. Our local audience could get used to concerts featuring the of occidental and Oriental repertory as performed on varied instruments peculiar to the international musical systems of both worlds. (1967: 71–73)

Accordingly, the second strategy that Kasilag essayed in several of her works involved the use of Asian instruments in formal compositions. Her inclination toward what she referred to as "so-called East-West flavor" developed in part out of creativity and in part from a feeling of Asian-oriented nationalism (de la Torre 1985: 61). Kasilag revealed her interest in indigenous Filipino music in the late 1940s, during which time she asked students to collect instruments on their journeys and deposit them at the University of the Philippines library. She continued this practice when she became dean at PWU and enlarged her collection of instruments, especially those from Asia, while on international trips of her own (ibid. 44–45). She incorporated non-tuned rhythmic instruments, such as gourds, sticks, and gongs, into the Western orchestra, and the unfamiliar timbres clearly signified the combination of East and West. In addition, at times she scored for Asian instruments only, including those from different regions in the Philippines. Kasilag was not the only composer in the Philippines or in Asia expressing an Asian identity through art music. During World War II, Japanese propaganda implicated the arts in purging Western influences and embracing local ones. Moreover, Japan's idea of the Greater East Asia Co-Prosperity Sphere had pan-Asian overtones.

This same conviction that Filipinos had neglected their Asian roots complemented Kasilag's adoption of modernist ideas from the West. But, it is worth noting, modernism did not in and of itself provide a solution to a colonial mentality in music, especially since, as a movement originating in Western elite thought, it could be construed as inappropriate for a postcolonial nation. Especially concerning, the musical modernism of Kasilag and others produced sonic "modern art"—even "high art"—that mirror García-Canclini's observation of an elite "aesthetic disposition" (1995: 16). The modernity expressed in Kasilag's music highlights elite sensibilities in nationalism that favor "symbolic distinction" over utilitarianism (ibid. 17). While modernism has taken many forms in different arts and different places, Jameson insists they are all linked to the idea of modernity in their high valuation on innovation, transformation of the old into the new, and technology (1991: 304). In music these strategies may alienate listeners, because the transcendence of the familiar weakens the power of musical symbolism as contextually meaningful. The arguments for and against the adoption of modernist and Western techniques to further nationalist aims could persist endlessly, especially in light of the discussion of folk music's transformation during colonialism.

Still, there are other aspects of musical practice beyond sound. Kasilag embraced the inherent spirit of innovation in the modernist movement and took advantage of the weakening of traditional tonality with the inclusion of dissonant instruments and pitches. She had the opportunity to experience many different types of music in her role as a cultural ambassador and as music director of the Bayanihan Philippine Dance Company, and this international exposure became a part of her understanding of musical modernism. Her travels in Asia inspired her to combine traditions, and her choice to explore and use Asian instruments related to the already Westernized nature of the Philippine music tradition. She summarized her approach by saying, "On the one hand is the material; on the other is the technique. I simply take it one step further and put in a bit of innovative creativity" (ibid. 61).

The blending of Eastern and Western instruments renders literal the performance of hybridity—both in blood and culture—that underlies much of postcolonial Filipino identity. While playing Western music of any kind in the Philippines by a Filipino is partially an outgrowth of the colonial experience, it is a performance in which the native identity is not completely subsumed by the colonizer. From a nationalist standpoint, the adoption of Western music might better be unpacked theoretically as a potentially empowering mimetic act as much as an expression of hegemony. Even more symbolically potent, however, hybridity in composition and performance practice is the deliberate carving out of space for the native. It creates a partnership of equal grounding that, significantly, has been manipulated creatively by the native. Hybridity validates the claim of the native on Western music, not as an immutable universal product, but rather as birthright. Hybridity, as a nationalist and creative strategy, might even be construed as a hallmark of Filipino modernism.

Kasilag would continue to play an important role as both a nationalist in the field of music and as an active leader in nationalizing music. Among her many accomplishments, she received a Presidential Award of Merit as Woman Composer and penned a number of significant works, including "Toccata for Percussions and Winds" (1958) (which combined instruments from Mindanao with a Western orchestra), "Fantasy on a Muslim Theme" (1962), "The Legend of the Sarimanok" (1963), "Filasiana Choral Dance Kaleidoscope of Asia" (1965), and "Misang Pilipino" (1966) (a mass incorporating tribal chants) (see Samson 1976). Her work as a composer, as music director of the Bayanihan folkloric group, artistic director and president of the Cultural Center of the Philippines, and delegate to the International Music Council of UNESCO, the International Society for Music Education, and other international forums earned her a National Artist Award for lifetime achievement in music in 1989 (see Santiago-Felipe 1998).

This chapter has been concerned with expressions of nationalism in Filipino music from the nineteenth century until the mid-1950s. While nationalism as an ideology existed in various forms among different segments of the population, early nationalist composers were in step with political nationalists and primarily concerned with the theme of liberation. After World War II, members of the League of Filipino Composers accepted responsibility for nation-building through the arts, and because they collectively composed the bulk of native art music during their lifetimes, they influenced the shape of nationalism in Filipino art music for future generations. A common compositional technique since the late nineteenth century has been to use Filipino folk music from various areas of the country, some of which were already known from the composers' childhoods and others that were collected on research trips. While some composers quoted fragments or entire melodies and reworked them in ways that would please their concert audiences, others attempted to distill the essence of folk music to create a new repertoire of native pieces. Modernism became apparent in music both as a linking of the past to the present and, dialectically, as a rejection of the past. It provided a whole new approach to sound that could vibrantly suggest a superfluity of meanings about postcolonial Filipino identity. Yet, modernism and neoclassicism, rather than cleaving Filipino composers from the past, suggested that the present and future could accommodate the past while still expurgating its colonial connotations.

THE MEN DANCING IN CIRCLES each wear the hand-loomed loincloth called *bahag* and little else. Bound together by the rhythmic stamping of their feet, they alternately goad one another with shield and spear and then retreat without fear. There are four or five men kneeling in a line to one side with small flat gongs on their laps, and they begin playing together, hands slapping and brushing the metal faces of their instruments to produce interlocking ostinato patterns. The women arrive shortly thereafter, balancing graduated stacks of clay pots on their heads. Watching and listening to them, the experience is akin to venturing upon a pristine and exotic locale where modernity has yet to intrude and where the basic needs of survival are tenuous but largely uncomplicated. Bodies move comfortably in the present and past tense; they represent a living people who tie us all to what seems a darker yet purer age. Conveniently, these colorful moments are realized as a spectacle that one merely has to pay to see, for it is a performance by Bayanihan, the Philippine National Folk Dance Company. It is 2006, and I am in a large campus auditorium in Virginia with a sold-out audience primarily made up of other Filipino Americans.

Filipino Americans, like other diasporic Filipino populations, are fond of engaging in and watching folk dance and music spectacles rooted in traditions from the homeland. It is a way of connecting to the Philippines and participating in a culture that by now is perceived as national rather than regional. While the original dances are attributed to one place or one ethnic group, folkloric dance belongs to a national corpus that has been defined by Bayanihan and groups like it. One Filipino cultural producer in New York described the need for cultural shows in the community in the following way:

When you are on foreign soil, the influence of the dominant culture is tremendous. You could spin around and get completely lost and begin to question yourself. And this is why Filipinos long for affirmation. When you are projecting Filipino culture, you are projecting to the entire world, beginning with Filipino Americans.... That's how you bring people and talents to the world instead of just relying on television images of havoc in the Philippines. (Pajaron 2000)

In fact, my parents are first-generation immigrants who met at a party following a performance of Philippine folk dances during an international program at Boston University. My mother had always loved folk dancing, from the required lessons in elementary school to the clubs in high school and college. Yet, in the United States both the setting and experience of folk dancing was quite different. Certainly, she enjoyed the social aspect of practicing with her *barkada* (group of friends) with its obligatory home-cooked food, laughing banter in their native language of Tagalog, and mutual understanding of circumstance. Even more, the fascination held by non-Filipino U.S. audiences intrigued her. They remarked on the colorful costumes (such as the "butterfly-sleeve" *balintawak* dress) and the grace of the dancers, reveling in the quaintness of a culture that seemed to them utterly alien. Americans liked the dances and were especially tickled by the "Tinikling," good-naturedly volunteering to try the dance at the end of each performance.[1]

Perhaps like other Filipino Americans, I learned a slow version of the "Tinikling" before graduating to the faster one immortalized on a Bayanihan recording. Later, I learned how to play the Bayanihan version of the "Tinikling" during my first lesson on *rondalla* instruments. So, when a group of friends and I went to take music and dance lessons in the Philippines with Bayanihan, we asked them to teach us different dances. We learned several dances from the Bayanihan repertoire, all of which came from regions in the Philippines that neither we nor our teachers had ever been. It was ironic but telling, then, that we headed back to the United States several weeks later feeling as if our time in the dance studio had somehow brought us closer to our cultural heritage. What was authenticity, after all, if it could not be measured by the impact of our own experiences in childhood and from the memories of our parents? *To watch, to dance, and to play music.* All perform connections over distance and time that let us imagine something true about ourselves.

CHAPTER TWO | Recuperating a National Past

The Bayanihan Philippine National Folk Dance Company

The spirit of our ancestors is ever present, and dance is the way of communing with them.

Bayanihan film (1962)

B AYANIHAN IS THE MOST PROMINENT folkloric music and dance group of the Philippines and was one of the first performing groups to experience nationalization, a process whereby the Philippine state adopted the group as a resident company of a national institution and promoted them as cultural ambassadors at home and abroad. This chapter investigates the early development of Bayanihan from the 1950s through the 1960s in order to analyze how the nationalist ideologies of its founders are apparent in folkloric music and dance performance. The music and dance provide a reading of Philippine history and diversity that gives particular attention to the role of the past in shaping a modern national identity. The quest to build a modern state is, according to Clifford Geertz, common in young nations (1963: 108), though the validation of membership in global modernity can be a tricky proposition. The staged performance of national culture is one viable route, for it celebrates the distinctiveness of a given nation in a fashion appropriate for the international spotlight. Further, folklorization is a common strategy in many places, marking those who utilize this technique of self-representation as part of an international community of performing nations.

In addition, this chapter explores how narratives of the nation in staged productions condense both place and time in order to foster a sense of national unity. The performance of place, in which the remote and exotic are performed alongside the more familiar, reveals how national self-identity can be forged through an incorporation of internal Others. These Others, relegated to premodernity through cultural evolutionary discourse, are present-day evidence of the nation's past. Narratives of historical time disclose a concern with indigeneity, colonialism, postcolonialism, and modernity as seen through filters of nostalgia. Finally, the chapter takes into account how ideologies of gender, race (and more particularly, racial hybridity), and class weave through folkloric productions and present idealized models for the national citizenry through the staging of archetypes.

How do ideas of the nation come across so effectively in performance? Fundamentally, the folkloric repertoire of tribal, lowland Christian, and Muslim dances packaged together metaphorically depicts the Philippines as a diverse yet unified nation. That simple and powerful message can be gleaned intuitively, but a host of other meanings circulate through the aesthetics of performance. To read performances in expected ways, audiences must have opportunities to experience them and guidance to influence interpretation. During presentations, guidance may come through narration, for instance, spoken introductions or program notes. Children learn to understand how folkloric performances comprise an important part of the national cultural heritage during physical education classes in school where Filipino folk dances are commonly taught. These same dances, stylized to an even greater degree and performed by semiprofessionals, take on added meaning, but they are not separate from the dances with which the population has become familiar. Outside of performance spaces, discourse about the folkloric may circulate through mass media, imparting messages with leading rhetoric like "national," "pride," and "world renowned." While not limiting the fields of meaning, all of these factors contribute to what ethnomusicologist Katherine Hagedorn describes as "audience competence," the development of knowledge regarding rules of performance (2001: 58). When audiences have been cultivated and have expectations about what will be performed, the staged narratives become emblematic of a unified nation with a power that differs from written histories. More than writing a narrative of the national self, performance is a vivid and visceral experience that is both repetitive and unique in each enactment. A phenomenological approach to performance is inherently more open-ended and tied to subjective interpretation than generating meaning from language, but its cues are no less operative. Movement and sound can be read in many ways, but this field of meaning becomes narrower the more "performance literate" the audience is, and that literacy can be gained by exposure, outreach, and education. Philippine folkloric dancing is, after all, not limited to Bayanihan, though Bayanihan is the most prominent group in the country.[2] Many youth can and do learn the fundamental steps of folkloric dances through schools and clubs, even if the choreography and production standards are considerably less sophisticated than those of more professional ensembles. Over time, the folkloric becomes conventionalized, and its performance at any level may be considered an enactment of national tradition.

Promoting a sense of a consolidated nation foundational to state rhetoric on nationalism has never been a straightforward task in the Philippines. As in other places of the world, the territorial Philippines materialized as a result of colonialism, emerging from foreign imperial ventures rather than from the nineteenth-century romantic nationalist dream of blood and destiny. Illustrative of this, the 1935 Constitution of the Philippines designated the nation as comprising all territory ceded to the United States through treaties with Spain and Great Britain, and any other areas over which the Philippine government had been exercising jurisdiction. In addition, unlike other nations of East Asia and Southeast Asia, the Philippines as a whole lacked a large-scale monarchy or court tradition on which to base a postcolonial nation-state. The diversity of religion, ethnicities, languages and dialects, along with large class differences, contravene a durable feeling of Filipino nationalism and oppose the legitimacy of the nation-state.

The Philippine government has always depended upon the cooperation of landed families in the various regions of the country to influence voting and support the illusion of the centralized power of the state. And, as occurs elsewhere, groups within the Philippines deny belonging to the nation. Ethnic groups in the Philippines identify with religion, language, history, and place (among other things), and include tribal groups as well as a healthy number of Filipino Chinese in the urban areas. Though the large majority of Filipinos practice Roman Catholicism, Protestantism and localized Christian groups also have strong followings, tribal groups engage in a variety of religions, and Islam predominates in the far south of the country. The Islamic regions of the southern Philippines do not share the interests or identity that the central government represents and promotes and therefore do not feel aligned with the various ethnic groups that do look to Manila (Osborne 1997: 187). While the desire for autonomy in the Muslim area represents an extreme case of antinationalism, even relatively minor regional differences are magnified as a result of linguistic diversity. This regional loyalty helps to explain why, despite the contentious historical record of Ferdinand Marcos as president, his reputation remains strong among many supporters in his home region of Ilocos Norte.

Constitutionally, the government has been charged with maintaining and promoting this cultural integrity. The Preamble of the 1935 Constitution of the Philippines charges the government with culture management, vaguely mandating it to "conserve and develop the patrimony of the nation." The state's role in culture becomes much more clearly defined by the time of the 1973 Constitution. Article XV, Section 9 states, "Filipino culture shall be preserved and developed for national identity. Arts and letters shall be under the patronage of the State." This chapter engages with the time period in between these two constitutions and reveals the state's first forays into nationalizing the arts.

The success of the state's efforts would by no means imply a unitary national culture of the Philippines, but rather indicates the acceptance that the composite of diversity comprises the whole of the nation's culture. What, then, is this "culture" that it should be under the purview of the state? Because definition of the term is assumed and not clearly stated in the 1973 Constitution, in this context it may refer narrowly to Philippine material arts and the pursuing of artistic endeavors. This likely includes folk arts and supposedly "high" arts, but does not distinguish indigenous from foreign. These categories are significant in the larger debate about how to express identity in a postcolonial age. That "high" art should be included, despite its inevitable hybridity—or, in some cases, altogether Western origin—relates to many of the issues in chapter 1. The emphasis on "arts and letters" and the state's interest in culture "for national identity" supports arguments that folkloric performance, far from being spurious, was considered effective for expressing and promoting nationalism to a wide audience. This strategic co-optation of the arts is magnified when one considers that the 1973 Constitution was ratified during the martial law era under Marcos (considered in chapter 3). Hence, a concern with folkloric dance and music cannot be separated from an interest in ideologies of the nation, for there are instances where the two are provocatively intertwined.

Bayanihan is the most prominent dance and music ensemble of the Philippines. Reynaldo Alejandro comments that the decades of the 1950s and 1960s in the Philippines constitute "the years of rediscovering the past" that included not only the rise of Bayanihan, but also a general interest in "colonial furniture, *santos* (saints), Oriental ceramics, and ethnic dances" (1978: 91). The Bayanihan case study is extremely relevant to a discussion on nation, because, as Anthony Shay states matter-of-factly, "A national dance company embodies a nation. This mission forms the basic reason for the formation of these companies, and each in its own way, states this in its program notes and other publicity publications. They also attempt to find strategies to visually depict all of 'The People' of the nation-state" (1999b: 31). While Bayanihan did not define Filipino cultural identity, the company is similar to the nationalist composers of chapter 1 in its significant contributions to the nationalization of Philippine arts. It took until 1998 for Republic Act No. 8626 to designate Bayanihan as the national dance company of the Philippines, but the group served a similar role in an unofficial capacity since its inception.[3] The dance company established the standards for representing the nation in staged, folkloric performance and thereby gave the nation a personalized "face" domestically and through international touring. From an aesthetic vantage point, it is easy to become entranced with the whirling colors, the wash of musical sound, and the grace and *puissance* of the dancers. Even amidst accusations of inauthenticity (discussed further below), Bayanihan has continued to attract large audiences with its unshakeable insistence on the essential beauty of Filipino arts.

Who constitutes these Bayanihan audiences? The answer has varied throughout the history of the group. In 1950 private sources launched the Philippine Travel & Tourism Association to bring international visitors into the country, and six years later the Philippine congress took over the initiative and renamed the association the Board of Travel and Tourist Industry, the precursor to the contemporary Department of Tourism. The efforts to bring in foreign tourists were both economically salutary and nationalist in spirit, and their success in attracting visitors provided a market for Bayanihan. According to Patricia Lim Yusah, a Bayanihan dancer from 1969 to 1973, most of the domestic performances catered to foreign audiences of visiting Americans (2006). This is not surprising, because Americans had become fascinated with native expressions since the beginning of the colonial period, with particular attention paid to tribal peoples. "The American penchant for highlanders' performances of Igorot dances and songs were well-known. In contrast, there appears to have been little, if any, American interest in lowland cultural displays" (Finin 2005: 279). Over time, as the company developed in size and reputation, Bayanihan created several subgroups to accommodate demand. Part of the company maintained a regular show for tourists at the Manila Hotel and other local engagements, some members made it into the international touring group, and some were part of outreach to different areas of the Philippines. Any given member might participate in one or all of these performance types at different times, depending upon their skill and level of experience. Yusah characterized local performances as "business deals" in which the ensemble was hired for a fee to participate in a *fiesta* or perform at an event that might or might not be free for the public. Unsurprisingly, during free events sponsored by an organization, audiences could be quite large. Was it national pride or curiosity that drew the crowds? Yusah noted with amusement, "Generally, the Filipino loves a show. The longer-drawn the better (*sarswela* influence), so whether it is the same old 'Pandanggo sa Ilaw (dance of lights)' dance or the 'Tinikling,' we stay and appreciate it like it's the first time we've seen it" (2006).[4] Conversely, Yusah observed, "The rich would only appreciate our folk entertainment for the purpose of entertaining their 'foreign' visitors, because they would rather go to the CCP (Cultural Center of the Philippines) to watch *Miss Saigon* or the Vienna Boys Choir—you don't go telling your bejeweled girlfriends that you just watched a folk dance show. Horrors no!" (2000). Foreign visitors included diplomats and heads of state, and Bayanihan has been called upon many times by the Philippine government for command performances. Finally, developing away from its initial focus on tourists and elite audiences, Bayanihan has made an effort to participate in outreach programs, popularizing the folkloric as an expression of cultural pride among the wider population of Filipinos and training dance teachers. Considered over the whole of its existence, the audiences for Bayanihan have been a mixed group, ranging from tourists to schoolchildren to socialites to international dignitaries and more. This wide exposure helps to explain Bayanihan's ascendance as the national dance company of the Philippines.

As a national dance company, the responsibility of Bayanihan in international touring is to showcase the music and dance of the country in a way that not only differentiates the Philippines from other nations but also affirms its place in the community of nations. This implies that the proficiency of the musicians and dancers is at a high level and that the production standards—from lighting to sound to costuming—conform to an international level of professionalism. Therefore, appealing to tourist audiences at home and foreign audiences abroad must be considered an essential determinant of performance aesthetics in Bayanihan productions. The tendency to look outward in order to define what is within conforms to a general transnational and cosmopolitan impulse in nationalistic exercises, but the movement of ideas about how to stage culture was not unidirectional from West to East and has involved a fluid exchange of ideas from world tours, international expositions, and visiting artists. Helena Benitez wrote, "The most uplifting among its achievements is the fact that Bayanihan has inspired other countries to exploit their own folk material for international theater presentation. Among these is Mexico whose international folkloric ballet company [was] formed after Bayanihan's first performance there" (1987: 6). Likewise,

Bayanihan benefited from visiting dance groups and choreographers. The Philippines does not have its own classical dance tradition, and elements of ballet and modern dance that arrived during the U.S. colonial period have influenced the development and stylizations of folkloric groups like Bayanihan (see Alejandro 1978). This kind of international exchange has been invigorating in the development of the Philippine folkloric tradition. In the case of Bayanihan, the raw materials of dance and music combine with professional standards of production and choreography to produce a highly localized expression presented in an internationally accepted manner.

From Folk to Folkloric

Bayanihan helped to shape the Filipinos' own perception of their national culture. Its towering influence in inspiring other folkloric ensembles in the Philippines and among diasporic Filipinos sets the stage, as it were, for folkloric music and dance to be considered Filipino culture in and of itself and not merely a stylized copy of "real culture." Yet, if we are to consider the folkloric as cultural tradition, it is important to make a differentiation between *folk* and *folkloric* music and dance. In its most old-fashioned use, *folk* is "of the people" and may describe materials, practices, values, and ways of life. What the word has actually been used to encompass is as horizontally broad as *culture*, ranging from that which is perceived as traditional to contemporary revivals of these same traditions. Taken altogether, practices and material culture of the folk (noun for people), or all that is considered to be folk (adjective to describe things of the people), is sometimes referred to as *folklore*. Like folk, folklore has connotations of the rural, the traditional, and even the essential. While some may define folk music as having no known author, this definition is inadequate in the context of theorizing nationalism. In Germany, Johann Gottfried Herder (1744–1803) provided a framework for understanding the folk as the source of identity; the folk, or the people of a nation, embodied the essential spirit of the nation, and folk song was an essential expression. Cultural nationalism equates the coalescence of a national body based on territory with a natural grouping of people based on shared culture (including and especially language). The nation, while not defined only by its folk, was populated by the folk, who in turn provided the colorful substance of national identity. The common usage of folk in relation to the nation has changed since Herder's time, due in no small part to the inherent diversity of national populations. Scholars now speak of folk expression within one nation in plural rather than singular terms, where different ethnic groups may practice different folk culture in juxtaposition.

Folk culture may also have large overlap with popular culture, or even be part of popular culture, as is sometimes the case with folk music revivals. In some definitions that differentiate between folk and popular, folk has class overtones, while popular is entwined with commodification. For elite, middle class, and urban populations of the Philippines, for instance, folk music and dance would be understood as the culture of the lower rural classes, paralleled by stereotypes evoked by words like *bakya* and *promdi*. *Bakya* refers literally to a wooden slipper or clog worn through the 1950s, but now has a connotation of something or someone that is "low class." *Promdi* is a contraction in Taglish (English and Tagalog) of "from the," as in "from the provinces," but the term is less concerned with the real demarcation of provinces than with the perceived differences between rural and urban dwellers. *Promdi* is usually used pejoratively to indicate that someone is unsophisticated and likely of the lowest class. There are also combinations of the two terms. Popular folk music, which includes folk music that has been refashioned using contemporary instruments as well as newly composed music, is often recorded as well as performed live, and implies a closer relationship with the marketplace of sound media than traditional folk music.

As with class, folk also allows for a plural understanding of time. While folk may exist in the present tense, the term itself often references the past. In the postcolonial Philippines, the term *folk* is tied to an essentialist vision of national culture, but the significance of folk is in its differentiation from "the modern," "the urban," and even "the foreign." One of the interesting offshoots of this temporal flexibility is that the negative connotations of folk described above tend to dissolve as the past takes on a more romantic tinge. Because folk is no longer taken to represent a "real" working rural class, it can encompass the past of all national citizens. As such, social dances of the elite class can be absorbed by the folk moniker, because they are performances of antiquity. Additionally, folk is resurrected from its class associations to provide entertainment for all classes when transformed into the folkloric.

Folkloric usually refers to performance practices and the associated material culture deriving from the folk but recontextualized for audiences. Folkloric is not equivalent to the commodification of cultural practices, but there are certainly many cases in which both would apply. Folkloric performers may be tradition bearers or complete outsiders. Importantly, the aesthetics of folk and folkloric are not always the same. All that said, it is most useful to dispense with binary definitions that pit one against the other, either in a unidirectional or bifurcated model in which folk is the source and folkloric is the benefactor, for both are not mutually exclusive. Anthony Shay's (1999b) proposition that the folk and folkloric exist as "parallel traditions" that impinge upon one another over time fits neatly with an anecdote from former music director of Bayanihan, Leonilo "Boy" Angos. He recalled that the dancers at the time learned their steps from a research film, but since there was no sound, he had to create accompanying music. At a later time, while visiting the tribe who originated the dance, Angos felt concern over what the people would think of his music. More than mere approval, the locals learned his version and adopted it as part of their own repertoire (1996).

Angos's story begs the question of how to define authenticity in relation to the folkloric, and who has the authority to define what authenticity comprises. On its surface, authenticity in the folkloric is nothing more than a myth of origin, since decontextualization for the purposes of staging makes authenticity in its strictest interpretation impossible. Lucrecia Reyes-Urtula defines authenticity in Bayanihan dance as "retaining the original flavor and feeling of the indigenous dance and not offending the sensibilities of the ethnic group from which the dance originated" (Albano-Imperial 1998: 342). Because of her role as an educated expert in dance at the national level, Reyes-Urtula had the authority to support this definition; however, her point of view on authenticity is no longer widely accepted in regards to the representation of ethnic minorities.

As a result of changes made in movements, costuming, and music (discussed further below), staged folkloric dance has taken on the burden of being considered inauthentic. After all, even the field of ethnomusicology was, early on, suffused with a "salvage" mentality, where native musics had to be recorded and protected before they disappeared in the wake of Western and popular musics. Important to this philosophical and disciplinary approach was the notion of cultural purity and authenticity. If this idea of authenticity is taken in tandem with ideologies of decolonization, internal and local understandings of truth and genuineness in culture become potently meaningful. For a purist, any folkloric undertaking for stage is already decontextualized and inauthentic; however, the tolerance for what constitutes authenticity has expanded to suit a modern and cosmopolitan age. For nationalists, tourists, and vendors alike, authenticity has far too much utilitarian value to remain itself a pure concept. In practice, authenticity can be measured rhetorically in degrees as more or less, and folkloric dance from the parlor to the professional stage are often judged using criteria that distinguishes the very traditional from the very hybrid and contemporary while allowing for much in between. The powers of a state must then ask, what does a population want and/or need to see in order to "buy into" official nationalism as an authentic articulation of culture?

What and who determine perceptions of authenticity? The folkloric group has an obligation to present itself in the light it wishes to be seen, and it can take advantage of an audience's understanding of the subject material (or lack thereof) by highlighting aspects of performances that people have come to expect as markers of authenticity. Since Bayanihan installed its own authority during its development, audience cultivation was akin to establishing standards of authenticity, backed by the narratives of fieldwork among different peoples. For most audience members, the traditions on stage were not originally their own, though the standardization of folklorization resulted in a very effective nationalization of many dances. A folkloric group, then, can purvey authenticity, in publicity, costuming, choreography, movement, and music. Conversely, limitations that dancers and musicians place upon themselves in the name of authenticity would at first seem not to have the same import among folkloric groups that belong to a community in which folk traditions still exist. These performers should have much more flexibility in staged productions, since the performers are themselves an iteration of the so-called culture bearer. Yet, as the folkloric has become nationalized, standardizations have affected local traditions with equal force. Local and national-level competitions reify traditions in the name of preservation, such that innovation is sometimes a barrier to success measured in prizes and possible funding opportunities. In another twist, these same audiences may be highly critical of reproductions done outside their own community, since in these cases, authenticity is all about representation and misrepresentation rather than self-representation.

Folkloric performance has the power to reestablish the very terms of authenticity. The way that Bayanihan presents (or re-presents) dance and music is authentically Bayanihan, whatever its relation to the "original," and student groups copying taped performances may strive to be true to the Bayanihan models. The folkloric group creates a new ground zero, and Bayanihan may be considered an authentic expression of the national folkloric, touting an official vision of the nation's performance culture. This is a noteworthy standardization of folk dance and music, because it reveals that the folkloric is itself a cultural tradition separate from its source. When this phenomenon occurs with companies like Bayanihan, the folkloric becomes representative of national culture, and the degree to which any given performance must remain faithful to its folk origins becomes a decision for music directors and choreographers. The liberties taken by Bayanihan in the past in terms of music and choreography have drawn criticism from a number of sources concerned with the problematic nature of authenticity and representation (these appear later in the chapter), but despite this, the impact of the group as cultural ambassador has been tremendous.

Dancing a Nation United

Bayanihan is a Tagalog word meaning "working together," while the *bayani-han* spirit is a sense of communal helpfulness usually associated with a rural setting. The root word *bayan* translates as "country," "nation," and may also connote people of the nation.[5] The most common example is that of a community gathering together to help in the moving of a bamboo house from one spot to another. But the term has come to encompass a great deal more through the legacy of the folkloric ensemble that took Bayanihan as its name. As the group's founder, Helena Benitez declared proudly, "Bayanihan in the Philippines today has become synonymous with folk dance and folk ways.... Throughout the Philippines, it appears, Bayanihan means a prestigious return to the native and a high premium on things Philippines—clearly a revival with international overtones" (1987: 6). The revival of "things Philippines" meant the collection and transformation of folk traditions to folkloric in order to promote a nationalist agenda through cultural standardization. As in many places around the world, the folklorization of music and dance in the Philippines depended initially upon research, since daily life in the capital city is remote from folk practices. That research begins the process of creating folkloric performance, and it is an inherent trope in stagings that serves to legitimate a kind of secondhand authenticity. Folkloric presentations rely on the narrative of originary research in the absence of native performers.

In 1934, Dr. Jorge Bocobo, a lawyer and dean of the College of Law at the University of the Philippines, became president of the university (Rivera 1978: 5). He positioned himself as a prominent nationalist who had been active in politics and in negotiating for Philippine independence during the American colonial period. Now, with resources, he directed his efforts toward authoring—and authorizing through his political power—a national cultural heritage. Bocobo's modernizing effort to standardize culture had precedents in his work with drafting a civil code for the Philippines. As a part of this effort, he proposed mining indigenous customs for "moral principles" and designating them as law (ibid. 8). In an analogous manner, the construction of a cultural heritage of music and dance could be guided and then dictated from above (if not legislated at this early juncture). Though folk song research had been done before this time, Bocobo's project to collect folk dances and music from all over the Philippines for eventual publishing had overtly nationalistic overtones. He enlisted a student instructor named Francisca Reyes Aquino (then Tolentino) to put together a performance of folk dances that would help to exemplify Filipino culture.[6] Alejandro documents that Aquino had few materials to work with, since American ethnologists had recorded only dances and music of the mountain people and not those, for instance, of lowlanders in various provinces of the country. She was inspired to undertake more research under the auspices of the University of the Philippines (UP) physical education program (1978: 37).[7] Bocobo also supported a team of specialists that included Aquino, the composer and musician Antonino Buenaventura (later titled Colonel), and the photographer Ramón P. Tolentino to undertake further folk dance and music research. Aquino eventually published a six-volume series of Philippine folk dances intended for educators, complete with a short background on each dance, standardized choreography, pictures of "costumes," and music transcribed for piano. She, in effect, created a canon of national dance and music for the nation-state. Her work led to the UP Folksong-Dance Troupe and the Philippine Folk Dance Society, and, afterward, the Filipiniana Folk Arts dance and music group of the Philippines Women's University (PWU) relied on much of this research to put together their own presentations.

In 1953, Lucrecia Kasilag, Aurora Diño, and José Maceda went on the first of several research trips to record music from remote areas of the islands that earlier folk song collecting had not covered. The first mission took them to Oriental Mindoro to study the Mangyan people. During this and subsequent trips, the researchers realized that the dance and music practices of many tribes were in danger of disappearing, and the goal of the research tilted toward the preservation of a Filipino cultural heritage in all of its diversity (Santos 2004: 7–10). During the same time period, dance researchers like Lucrecia Reyes Urtula traveled the archipelago to film dances and make sketches of the clothing and accessories that typified different peoples and would serve as the foundation for folkloric costuming.

PWU, under the direction of Conrado and Francisca Benitez, served as the primary institutional resource for these trips. Conrado Benitez, former journalist and dean at UP, was a nationalist and a great supporter of modernization of the Philippines. He had a divided stance on Philippine nationalism, however, favoring English as a national language for its modernizing possibilities and vernacular languages in schools and newspapers for their nationalist symbolism (Gaerlan 1998: 142–143). The Benitez couple believed strongly that the young ladies of their university, the Philwomenian, should be "learned in the country's history and trained to take part in nation-building" (de Guzman 1987: 79). This legacy persevered through their daughter Helena, and PWU would buzz as a hub of folklorization and nationalism for decades to come (Santos 2004: 6). She realized that archiving dances and music achieved only one aspect of preservation. For Helena Benitez, transmitting this performative culture to Filipinos, as well as internationally, would further a sense of nationalism and a love of country (Benitez 1987: 7). The pre-1950s performances of folk dance and music that resulted from the research trips took place at PWU in the form of recitals by the Physical Education (P.E.) Club with male members recruited from the outside, and it took several years for the performances to expand more elaborately for public consumption.

In 1955, Lucrecia Kasilag, who was then dean of PWU, led a delegation to Dacca, Bangladesh (formerly East Pakistan) for an international festival of dance and music. A fascinating anecdote from that trip illuminates the search for cultural identity that Filipinos were engaged in during that time period. Doctor Kasilag had been accompanying the dancers on piano and requested a piano from the organizers for their performance. The organizers were sorry to say that no piano was available, for it was not anticipated that one would be required in an Asian festival. Kasilag made due with a guitar, but the experience made her and all of the other members realize how Western-sounding the music she had been playing was. When they returned home, the "identity crisis" that arose from being among other Asians gave them the determination to "probe deeper into authentic Filipino cultural heritage" (de Guzman 1987: 81).

The next formative event occurred the following year. In 1956 the international Rotary Club in the Philippines was geared up to celebrate its anniversary, with Conrado Benitez of PWU serving as the head Rotarian at the time. Among the invited guests were then Philippine president Ramón Magsaysay and the president of Rotary International, A. Z. Barker. Helena Benitez suggested a folkloric presentation to highlight the traditions of the country and the nationalistic optimism of the times, and the planning committee decided upon the theme "Magbayanihan Tayo (Us Working Together)." The performance featured a choreographed re-creation of farmers engaged in the rice cycle, including planting, harvesting, threshing, winnowing, and pounding. This was followed by dances of celebration from different villages (I. Santos 2004: 14–15). It was as if Filipinos in the urban setting were locating national identity in representations of rurality and distinguishing the essentials of Philippine selfhood from the homogenization of urban life in a global age. Perhaps, too, the sense of connection with the countryside even alleviated, for at least a few colorful moments, the alienation from the land that accompanied modernity, with its emphasis on urbanization and industrialization. At any rate, the success of the debut ensured the development of a more professional ensemble to portray Filipino folk music and dance.

Later in 1956, student performers from PWU traveled to Japan—the first group recognized officially by the Philippine state to make the trip in the wake of World War II. It was a memorable excursion, representing a small attempt at reconciliation between two nations that only a decade earlier had been at brutal odds. It also triggered the formal beginning of Bayanihan. As a result of the hospitality and appreciation shown by their Japanese hosts, the group's leaders and members realized that an official ensemble could tour other countries to promote Philippine arts (ibid. 15). Accordingly, in 1957 the Bayanihan Folk Arts Center came to fruition at PWU, guided by the music director, Lucrecia Kasilag, and the dance director, Lucrecia Reyes-Urtula. As Kasilag appeared at length in chapter 1, I will now turn to Reyes-Urtula's background.

Lucrecia Reyes-Urtula's spent her childhood drifting with her family throughout the varicolored regions of the Philippines, exposing her to an assortment of distinctive ethnic groups. Enthralled by the dances and music she beheld at festivals and public rituals, she mimicked the movements of the participants at home and eventually enrolled in formal dance classes to hone her craft. After graduating from PWU with majors in physical education and education, she entered into a dance apprenticeship with the dance scholar Francisca Reyes Aquino. Following this, Urtula fed her abiding interest in the folk arts by joining the Filipiniana Folk Music and Dance Committee at PWU and embarking on research trips around the Philippines. After pursuing graduate study in dance drama at San Francisco University, the University of California–Los Angeles, and the Hanayagi School of Dancing in Japan, she received her Ph.D. in Theater Management in Dance from the Polytechnic University of the Philippines (Albano-Imperial 1998). Throughout, Urtula stamped her mark on Bayanihan with her personal vision of how to stylize folk dance for stage productions. Her own words on stylization follow:

> The dance undergoes compression, enhancement, highlighting. By compression, a performance lasting several hours in its original is shortened to a normal two hours apportioned over a number of regional dance suites. In highlighting, all the resources of color and movement are employed to attain a visual emotional climax so that each dance suite projects its distinctive character, and each stands out as unique. Enhancing involves a certain measure of exaggeration, directed towards the present-day audience which, unlike its ethnic predecessors in the original setting, is set apart from the performers physically and otherwise. For instance, the small, mincing steps of an original dance have to be made bigger to suit the scale of the theater. (ibid. 342)

Fortunately for the group, her strategies to transform folk dance and folkloric performance to staged spectacle paid off from the start.

Bayanihan's coming of age occurred in 1958 at the Universal Exposition held in Brussels, Belgium. The Philippine government headed by President Magsaysay had accepted an invitation to participate but had no budget for dispatching representatives to Europe. Still, officials optimistically asked a committee of specialists in the arts to convene. The committee fielded, but ultimately rejected, suggestions to send works of art or a Filipino singer to Brussels. As with the Rotary Club event, again Helena Benitez advocated the dancers and musicians from Bayanihan, the performing group that had emerged from her university's P.E. club. The newly formed Bayanihan Folk Arts Association, Inc., and not the Philippine government, would be responsible for coming up with the necessary funding. This led to a peculiar selection process in which the first performers chosen for the trip were those who could afford to pay their own way, while contributions would fund the rest (de Guzman 1987: 85). The Bayanihan Philippine Dance Company was on the way to its baptism of international acclaim.

When the young performers reached Brussels, they ambled over to the Philippine pavilion only to discover that the exhibits from the Philippines had not yet arrived. The college students culled together the handicrafts that they happened to have brought with them, put them on display, and roosted at the pavilion in their costumes in order to advertise their upcoming performance. Because they were unused to the cold, the dancers were allowed to drink a single shot of whiskey and smoke cigarettes if needed (C. Benitez 1987: 10).

Bayanihan's pageant in Brussels has become legendary in the annals of Philippine performance lore, for they reportedly were judged as the best of the thirteen national companies at the exposition (de la Torre 1985: 33). Ed Sullivan, the American television host, was so impressed with Bayanihan that he contracted with them to come to the United States in order to dance on his famous variety program. This engagement followed with a booking by the impresario Sol Hurok at the Winter Garden Theater on Broadway as part of another international festival. In 1961, Columbia Artists Management scheduled Bayanihan to appear in over fifty cities in the United States. They traveled to Mexico for Christmas and returned to Europe to appear in Britain, Belgium, Italy, France, and Israel. Still under Columbia, Bayanihan revamped their program entirely and went on another world tour in 1964. The international touring would continue with glowing praise, as the Bayanihan Philippine Dance Company settled into its role as the most prolific and renowned cultural ambassadors from the Philippines for the next several decades.

To put the group's international stature in context, Anthony Shay sees the 1950s as a period in which state-sponsored folk dance ensembles were blossoming throughout the world, following the model of the former Soviet Union's Moiseyev Dance Company (1999a: 29). While the Moiseyev Dance Company may have provided a model for how a national company could present itself and tour internationally, each dance ensemble that arose in the 1950s did so with very local aims and needs. Bayanihan may have been part of a global trend, but it also articulated and addressed specifically Filipino concerns, many of which were separate from the state. Though it began without state funding, Bayanihan did garner the full support of the Philippine government and represented the nation during its many international tours. Not only were they cultural ambassadors, but the touring groups served pragmatic purposes for the state as well, most especially in the realm of tourism. The deputy music director Lito Vale Cruz, in a 2001 Bayanihan handout, explained: "Each time Bayanihan travels, we carry with us the idea of bringing people to visit the Philippines." The long relationship with the state eventually led to the declaration of Bayanihan as "the Philippines National Folk Dance Company in 1998, a year that was strongly doused with patriotism, for it was the centennial of the Philippine declaration of independence from Spain (see conclusion). Even back in its early days, however, the company seemed to embody the optimism and verve of a nation that had begun to prosper after the devastation of World War II and was establishing itself as one of the strongest economies of modern Asia.

A Modern Nation Breeds Nostalgia for an Imagined Past

The Philippine nation-state had strong footing from the late 1950s through the mid-1960s with a growing economy, a literate population, and a strong industrial sector. In an assessment of economic growth in Southeast Asia written in 1963, the Philippines showed the most growth in per capita real income of all the countries in the region (Paauw 1963: 69). Most of the postwar exports from the Philippines were agricultural and mineral, and the principal market had been the United States. As the 1950s and 1960s progressed, the importance of the Japanese market grew while that of the United States diminished, and the Philippine government reached out more to Asian neighbors than it had during the immediate postwar years.[8] Unsurprisingly, the primary benefactors of rapid economic growth remained the oligarchy who had long prospered under the traditional land-ownership system. Measures that limited foreign competition put forth by Filipino politicians appeared to be nationalist in intent, but these too served the interests of the elites in power (who in turn had no qualms about making profitable partnerships with foreign investors). In summary, the rehabilitation and growth occurring after World War II provided a healthy economy during the critical years of nation-building for a newly independent nation, but the extant power structures favoring the elite persisted even as political and social institutions underwent transformation. In fact, according to Wurfel, the barriers between classes actually became more difficult to overcome after the war (1988: 69–70). The widening of class divisions in the 1950s to the 1960s helps to explain some of the inherent tensions in expressions of Filipino nationalism, because the economic and political elite (often the same) had vastly different agendas from the predominant population of poor farmers and urban workers. This continuing shift toward an ideology of the idealized nation and away from the concerns of the masses was punctuated by the end of the Magsaysay era.

Following the sudden death of President Ramón Magsaysay in a plane crash in 1957, his vice president, Carlos García, took the oath of office. García's agenda encouraged local arts and business, and he adopted the nationalist-sounding "Filipino First" policy that protected the positions of the Filipino elite and went against the International Monetary Fund (ibid. 15). He also negotiated with the United States to release land that had once been held for U.S. military bases in order to further his goal of "respectable independence" (Dolan 1993: 48). Following García, Diosdado Macapagal held the presidency from 1961 to 1965, sailing to victory on the campaign song "Happy Days Are Here Again." Despite his choice of the American popular music hit, Macapagal promoted the Filipino language, and, in a move suffused with nationalistic symbolism, changed the official date of Independence Day from July 4 to June 12 (Zaide 1999: 363). This transfer had import to Filipinos, because June 12 marks the declaration of independence from Spain, while July 4 is the date that the United States ended the commonwealth status of the Philippines and allowed for the inauguration of the Third Republic. The purposeful coincidence of July 4 as Independence Day for both served as a reminder of the unequal ties between the countries, and Macapagal favored a declaration of independence from a time of revolution (as elusive as that victory actually was) over the granting of independence by a world power that still held influence over the Philippines. During his tenure, Macapagal attempted to expand foreign investment, as he viewed García's "Filipino First" drive as protectionism rather than economic nationalism (Doronila 1997: 9).

Yet, Macapagal had a very keen sense of Filipino nationalism that grew out of a very different perspective on the country than his predecessors, for he had been born into a peasant family. In retrospect, he did not produce significant changes in the face of stiff opposition from the elite, but his "New Era" ideals of social and land reform, a crackdown on corruption in government, and the strengthening of ties with other Southeast Asian countries gave life to the hope of toppling the status quo. During Macapagal's time, the countries of Southeast Asia wavered between various regional alliances before the formation of ASEAN, and he was involved with the Association of Southeast Asia (Malaya, the Philippines, and Thailand) and the short-lived Maphilindo (Malaysia-Philippines-Indonesia). In contrast, Macapagal was also the standing president when the Philippines asserted national boundaries by claiming Sabah, a confrontation engaging Malaysia and Indonesia that was eventually resolved peacefully. At any rate, Macapagal's attention to interests besides and sometimes against those of the United States is notable, since he is likely to have received American money during his campaign for the presidency (Wurfel 1988: 16).

The building of relationships between the Philippines and its neighbors is important during this period, for in previous years much of the country's focus had been on its entanglement with the United States. Filipino politicians had grown steadily more aware during the 1950s into the 1960s that their relationship with the United States subjected them to criticism from Asian neighbors, and they sought to improve their image (ibid. 179). In fact, Lela Garner Noble believes that as relative novices in foreign relations, Filipino presidents before Marcos "conceptualized the national interest in Asia almost entirely in terms of the national image; the primary considerations affecting opinions and actions were those of status. . . . To achieve their objectives, even if only image was involved, Filipinos were dependent on the perceptions as well as the responses of others" (1973: 561–562). Noble's invocation of the "image" as paramount in substantiating the national self on a global scale is theoretically attractive. It is unmistakably relevant in considerations of how nationally recognized folkloric groups like Bayanihan can become a physical manifestation of the nation, because it is representative of the national image. When Bayanihan triumphed at the Brussels Exposition, the Philippine state gained capital as a viable nation in the community of nations, though it did not serve any pragmatic goals. The significance internally of Bayanihan's achievement was magnified precisely because "image" (or, perhaps appropriate in an Asian setting, "face") was such an important consideration in national-level relationships.

While Bayanihan showcased Filipino music and dance traditions with magnetic flair, everyday life in the cities hurtled forward with very little relation to what was being enacted on stage. Television had reached new levels of accessibility, with a diversity of stations running popular American shows like *Mission: Impossible, The Untouchables, Ben Casey*, and *Wild Wild West*. At the same time, local programming began to flourish, and Filipino personalities, especially singers like Pilita Corrales, became television stars (del Mundo 2003: 11). The radio and movie industries continued to thrive alongside television, not only bringing in a steady stream of foreign (usually U.S.) sounds and images, but also instigating domestic production for the mass media outlets. More magnified than the liberalization in media that scandalized conservatives in U.S. society during the 1960s, the onslaught of Western values in radio, television, literature, and movies, and the weakening of the church rankled social critics in the Philippines. One author wrote that the introduction of Western movies and literature had "disastrous effects upon the lives of Filipinos since they do not always portray what is good," and that "they have contributed to immorality and delinquency particularly among the young people" (Quiambao 1976: 89). Another was more sanguine, insisting that "the 'boogaloo' and 'shing-a-ling,' progenies of the 'rock-n-roll' and the older 'boogie' will, of course, soon fade away as just another flash in the cultural pan, their passing hardly causing a dent on the local scene" (Villa 1967: 164).

The cities of the Philippines were a part of the modern age, and, as in other industrialized sites, Filipinos were forced to confront the attendant changes. In other words, this time period represents a moment of rapid transformation from old to new, rendering precarious the practice of tradition and providing fertile ground for Hobsbawm's "invention of tradition."[9] As Metro Manila continued to expand, city dwellers became more remote from life in the countryside where some had grown up and about which others could only imagine. Similar to other countries such as Japan, the countryside came to symbolize the idea of "Filipino traditional," which contrasted with the conditions of modernity and urbanization exemplified in popular media, particularly that imported from the West. As the composer Felipe de Leon bemoaned, "Aside from the sudden alienation of our people from the noble traditions of our glorious past, we can observe today a huge spiritual vacuum created by the abundance of things that minister only to the gross and baser side of their sensibilities, thereby slowly killing their basic aspirations for a higher humanity" (1966: 255). Traditions of the past could be equated with safety and with self, while change, modernism, and the importation of things Western represented a threat to the self. Even ballet engendered suspicion in the 1950s, undergoing a ban in Manila's convent schools where it became designated as "immoral" (Alejandro 1978: 57). This strong conservative wave in urban society provided conditions under which a sense of nostalgia could easily thrive.

The word *nostalgia*, originally coined by the Swiss physician Johannes Hofer from the Greek *nostos* (to return home) and *algia* (a painful condition), described a medical condition of extreme homesickness, exhibited by physical symptoms such as weeping and loss of appetite (Davis 1979: 1). Over time the term lost favor in the field of medicine but gained a place in lay lexicon. Nostalgia came to be characterized by a romanticized longing for the past, a metaphorical extension of geographical "home." But, while the clinical ailment could be alleviated by the actual or strong possibility of return to "home," the temporally based experience of nostalgia is fundamentally predicated on the impossibility of return. As a consequence, the implacable feeling of absence contrasts a lost past with the present, each essentialized respectively as models of positive or negative human experience. Rather than merely an act of remembering, itself a subjective process, nostalgia as a mode of thought is inherently comparative, leading to the common understanding that currently experienced anxieties often precipitate nostalgic remembrance.

In contemporary scholarship, conceptions of nostalgia are unbound from individual experience to describe a collective phenomenology (see Davis 1979). In this sense, nostalgia does not depend on firsthand experience of the past by any or all members of a group, but rather a general elevation of particular past eras in a common history that represent values felt on a wide scale to be lost or in decline. This construction of the past to serve the needs of the present is fundamental to a theoretical understanding of the performance of nostalgia. The evocation of sentiment depends upon manipulation of the aesthetics of nostalgia, cultural constructs normalized as semiotic triggers that, because of their efficacy in promoting pleasurable feeling, are highly successful when commoditized. Put succinctly, "the good old days" need not be a part of personal experience in order to be desired, and how the past is represented (constructed without particular regard to verity) reveals exigencies of the present that confer value on the past. Moreover, the performance of the past helps bind a national community, despite the diversity of the populace, so that those in the community can imagine themselves as having a common history (see Anderson 1991).

How can this theorizing of nostalgia illuminate issues of folkloric representation, particularly in relation to ideas of the nation? Nostalgia lends itself readily as an interpretive strategy with regard to performance. While the everyday experience of nostalgia is highly dependent upon individual experience, performance typically depends on nostalgic significance through the repetition of markers on many levels—from the understanding of archetypes and common plot devices to the physical experience of costuming and music. The extravagant dresses, frilly shirts, and accoutrements like fans and hats of the Spanish colonial era are as evocative as the string band music. The colorful butterfly-sleeve dresses and rolled up pants of the rural suite, accented by the singing of folk songs, harken back to a bygone era of simplicity. Delicate hand movements emulating birds, accompanied by the gentle twang of bamboo instruments carry audiences to a time when people were closer to nature and to the earth. Lighting, from the contrived dimness of the ancient past to the brightness of fiesta, conspires with movement and sound in transporting the audience to different times and places. Those involved with the nostalgic experience, whether performers or audience, are often aware that they are participants in a particular brand of memory project, although they may not be conscious of the possible effects of that project. In examining acts of performance, the nostalgic lens provides a powerful analytical tool in decoding the staged representation of the Philippine nation, particularly in light of race and gender ideologies. Theorizing the performance of nostalgia as spectacle, we can examine the folkloric treatment of a past era as a space for working out competing ideologies of race, class, and gender.

Nostalgia in the folkloric spectacle is evoked by aesthetics that are learned through repeated performance, experienced consciously and unconsciously by performers and audience, and understood on some level as a commentary on a condition of the present. Nostalgia found a welcome nesting place within Filipino nationalism of the postcolonial age, because both phenomena have a concern with defining a relationship between past and present. On the one hand, nation-building includes promoting a useful narrative of history that supports the idea of nation and the legitimacy of the nation-state. On the other, nostalgia manifests itself as idealizations of the past that help to ease tensions of the present.

Before moving on, there is a distinction to make between the activity of preservation and the construction of memory understood as nostalgia. While preservation may actually encompass processes of nostalgia, in some manifestations it implies rigidity and faithfulness to idealized "tradition." The repertoire of Bayanihan is the accomplishment of a preservationist impetus, but the continuing relevance of contemporary performance is a repetitive act of nostalgia. This nostalgia works in conjunction with the nationalist need to affirm a shared past and, as Hobsbawm articulates, to "use history as a legitimator of action and cement group cohesion" (1983, 1992: 12). For a nationalized group such as Bayanihan to repetitively perform constructions of the past for both local and international audiences is something analogous to a communal civics lesson. Over time, the folkloric has become so well engrained in the consciousness of the concertgoing public that the fulfillment of expectations is like the experience of singing the national anthem together or watching an epic in which everyone knows what is going to happen next. In this way, the folkloric, a constructed tradition, becomes naturalized as a tradition in and of itself, and its practice ties together the present and past through nationalism and nostalgia.

In the next section, I will describe four suites from a typical Bayanihan production, the Mountain Suite, Spanish Colonial Suite, Muslim Suite, and Rural Suite. I leave out descriptions of the Regional Variations Suite, which is similar in representational issues to the Mountain Province Suite as well as the Rural Suite, as it contains a potpourri of unrelated dances from various provinces of the country. While the titling of the suites is problematic due to the variety of names used over the years, the basic groupings remain consistent, and I will provide some general and alternate titles to avoid confusion. The following sections are presented in the order they would normally fall during a typical show.

Dances of the Mountain Province

Full-length Bayanihan productions begin with a set of dances called one among a variety of names, including Dances of the Mountain Province, Northern Suite, Highland Suite, Tribal Suite, or even Highland Tribal Suite. The mountain province, or the eponymous *highland*, refers to the Cordillera mountain range in the northern part of the country, though there are other highland and tribal peoples in the central and southern parts of the Philippines as well. The designation *tribal* still exists in common parlance in the Philippines, a category invented by the Spaniards to designate the populations of people that lived in the mountains or moved there to elude Spanish authority. The Americans continued this categorization when they colonized the country at the turn of the twentieth century, as did the Filipino governments of 1946 and beyond. Insulated from the Spanish throughout the colonial era by virtue of their almost inaccessible geographical location, these tribes continued to develop with little European influence, though they engaged in trade with their lowland Christian neighbors. In contemporary Philippines, both *tribal* and *highland* may be attributed with negative connotations, but people of the Cordillera region have recouped the word *tribal* as a strategic self-designation.

The contents of the suite derive mostly from research conducted in the first half of the twentieth century and generally portray religious rituals, courtship dances, and other music and dance events from varied tribes such as the Kalinga, Ifugao, Kankanay, Isneg, Ibaloi, and Bontoc. Typical of the suite are graceful numbers that depict birds, such as the Kalinga "*Idaw*"; somber re-creations of ritual settings, such as the "*Bangibang* Funeral Dance" of the Ifugao and the Bontoc "War Dance"; stylized life activities, such as Kalinga women carrying wine jars and Bontoc men hunting wild boar; and festive dances of courtship and weddings, such as the Kalinga "*Salip*" (see figure 2.1). As Urtula iterated, most of these dances are condensed, standardized, and self-contained units that exhibit more variety in movement and sound than would have been experienced in their places of origin. Generally, folklorization harnesses musical repetition through shortening and the juxtaposition of distinct music and dance genres.

FIGURE 2.1. *Banga* dance from the Mountain Province Suite (photo from the Bayanihan collection; reprinted with permission)

The musical sound of this suite had been generally unfamiliar to most lowland Filipinos before Bayanihan (and before composers began to use native instruments in concert halls). Hence, Bayanihan's contribution to folkloric culture was also educational and entertaining for the general population. The music throbbed with exoticism, giving audiences entrée to the remote worlds of their internal Others. Tribal music in the Philippines differs throughout the mountain province, and indeed through the whole of the country, but there are certain regional similarities in instruments used. As a consequence, while the same types of instruments may be found all over the Cordillera mountain range, they may be known by many names, complicating to a certain extent the task of taxonomy. Bayanihan musicians have made use of many of the most common bamboo instruments as well as gongs, but their adherence to native musical principles has been mixed.

The flat gongs played by Bayanihan dancers as well as musicians are usually referred to as *gangsa*, though they may also be called *gangha* or *hansa* among different peoples. While musical repertoires vary from place to place, the gongs are always played by a group of men and are hit either with the palms of the hands (*topayya*) or with sticks (*palook*) in interlocking rhythms.[10] Often played in sets of six or more graduated gongs (with different pitches from one another), the men may either be dancing with the gongs in one hand or sitting with the gongs on their laps, attached to a belt loop. Buzzers are made up of pieces of bamboo split at one end and struck against the hand; a hole near the handle end allows users to vary the timbre between open and closed. The *bunkaka* (as they are named by the Kalinga) buzzers are used to scare off evil spirits and are often played in a group of six with a method similar to the gong music described above. Bamboo stamping tubes called *tongatong* are tuned to different pitches through length, and, like the gongs, they play in the interlocking style called hocketing. Bamboo instruments—such as jaw's harps, bamboo flutes, and idiophone zithers—are also nonpercussive. Flutes come in transverse, vertical, whistle, and raft, among other types, are played through the mouth or the nose, and are common enough to be known under a variety of names (for instance, *kaleleng* by the Bontoc and Kankanay, *tongali* by the Ifugao and Kalinga). Bayanihan often features a solo nose flute at the beginning or in the midst of the Mountain Suite to provide a sound atmosphere that lulls the audience into constructed mystique as effectively as a fog machine. Finally, singing, with or without accompaniment, is extremely common among all tribes of the Philippines, and Bayanihan performers will sometimes engage in a group song to transition between numbers or while dancing.[11] Music, then, is not only for the accompaniment of dance. Musical performance is often portrayed alongside the performance of dance in this suite, a successful integration that is less apparent in other suites, where the musicians produce the primary music on stage to the side or off stage within sight of the audience and dancers. In either placement, to me the musicians have always seemed separate from the dancers, a disjunction that does not translate well from the original sources where the performance of dance and music is a community activity. When the dancers take up gongs or sing songs, their representation of tribal music is marked as different from music of the Spanish, Rural, and Muslim suites.

The portrayal of tribal music and dance is intriguing in numerous ways, but there are two aspects in particular that are closely related to the representation of the Philippine nation as a whole. The first interrogates how the self is imagined against an internal Other, and the second relates colonial nostalgia to the national project. In regard to the first, the Cordillera people gradually became distinct from the lowlanders during the Spanish colonial period, though earlier evidence suggests that there had been many shared practices. Though trade continued between the native peoples, the Spanish were unable to maintain any sort of influence in the mountains, hindered by the rough terrain. In the meantime, the lowlanders within hearing of the church bells became more Hispanicized. The grouping of the unrelated highland tribes together occurred at the outset of U.S. occupation, when in 1901 they were put under the jurisdiction of the Bureau of Non-Christian Tribes. Even following independence, the Philippine state's relationship with ethnic minorities remained colored by a prejudice persistent in lowland Christian society. In 1943, General Carlos Romulo (who later served as president of the United Nations General Assembly) declared, "The fact remains that the Igorot is not Filipino and we are not related" (Romulo 1943). The perception that highland peoples are fundamentally different from the self is at the root of constructing an Other, and herein lies the prevalent racial tension found in the Mountain Suite. Despite the fact that ethnic minorities of the mountain province have had an abundance of contact with others, are often educated, and have experienced a large number of converts to Christianity, misconceptions about the contemporary life of tribal people persist. My parents were not alone in growing up with stern parental warnings that if they did not behave, the Igorots (an all-encompassing term for Cordillera mountain tribes that has had negative connotations) would come and take their heads—a reference to the former practice of groups like the Ilongots, the subjects of Michelle and Renato Rosaldo's writings. In fact, some speculate that the term *Igorot* derives from the Ilocano word *gerret*, for "cut off" or "slice" (Finin 2005: 11). The etymology of the word is subject to debate. Corpuz (1989) believes the source is from *gorrot*, *golod*, or *gorrod*, meaning "high ground." The prefix *i-* indicates "people of," so *igorot* would translate as "people of the mountains." As another example, Ramón Obusan, well-known choreographer and founder of a renowned dance ensemble bearing his name, fondly recalled his first viewing of Bayanihan, which began his lifelong engagement with the folkloric. Before Bayanihan, he had never heard the music of the mountain tribes nor considered their relationship with him as countrymen. In his desire to become a member of Bayanihan, he shed preconceived notions about other ethnic peoples in the Philippines specifically through the experience of folkloric performance (Obusan 2000). In the 1950s and 1960s, Bayanihan's folkloric presentations not only served as cultural remedy, but they also asserted that the highland people were an important part of the Philippine nation and a possible link to the past of all Filipinos. Paradoxically, the depiction of the Igorot as "noble savages" and staged allusions to a national past perpetuated the sense of separation between highland and lowland peoples and dismissed historical and present-day connections and interactions among them.

Conceiving of ethnic minorities as a trope for the past as well as a foil for present-day identity arises from how the suite is organized and descriptions found in Bayanihan material. Contemporary folkloric productions based on the Bayanihan model often refer to the music and dances of the Mountain Suite as *indigenous*, which invokes historical difference even more than it does ethnic difference. The ethnic minorities were representatives of the people who were in the area before the Spaniards came. As a consequence, it became easy for nationalists (just as it was for scholars who extrapolated from Darwin and proposed cultural evolution) to make the tautological but effective leap that tribal culture of their present day could stand in for precolonial culture. As seen in the last chapter, Filipinos had to find creative ways to make sense of colonialism in the context of nationalism. Some artists chose to accept the colonial heritage in music and shape sound into a locally relevant expression; others leaned heavily toward a search for the native. In the case of the Mountain Suite, representation of the native was a means for recovering a past to connect with the present.

In a more oblique but closely related analysis, this suite displays something of Rosaldo's sense of "imperialist nostalgia" in which "the agents of colonialism long for the very form of life they intentionally altered or destroyed" (1989, 1993: 69). In this case, the Filipino elite, the original proprietors of the folkloric, are inheritors of imperialist nostalgia analogous to their elevated positions on the social and political hierarchy in the postcolonial age. This point of view takes into account the more nuanced perspective on the uncomfortable dynamics between lowland Christian Filipinos and the ethnic minorities described above. Taken from this vantage point, tribal peoples are more than living symbols of a possible past; they are a connection to the past that has not been always welcome.

In contrast, Igorots began to see themselves as what Finin describes as "a distinctive 'kind' of Filipino" in the post–World War II years, during which time college education became more available to the youth (2005: 141). The subsequent development of sense of pan-Cordillera unity gave political strength to the once very disparate groups of the region. In the 1960s, the BIBAK organization (an acronym for the tribes Benguet, Ifugao, Bontoc, Apayao, and Kalinga) epitomized the movement toward regional community over tribal differences, leading to a movement for self-governance in the 1980s. Based on the colonial practices of categorizing and labeling as well as the local political movement toward cohesiveness, the Philippine government officially recognized Igorot not only as a designation for the larger community of tribes in the Cordillera region but as an ethnic minority of the nation (Finin 2005: 280). Bayanihan is sensitive to the separate groups in its programming but continues the historically based logic of categorization by maintaining a repertoire in this suite that excludes tribal and highland groups from all other regions of the nation, reserving another suite for the miscellaneous spillover.

At the end of the suite, there is invariably a blackout, and the soundscape vividly transitions the audience and performers from the Mountain Suite to the Spanish Suite. Leticia Perez de Guzman, long-time executive director of Bayanihan, describes the juxtaposition of the suites as a kind of performed historical narrative, though audiences generally need no notes to understand this internal logic.

> With the conquest by Spain in the sixteenth century [came] an overlay
> of Hispanic influence, from the fiery flamenco to the gracious charm of
> ballroom dances. For the next 300 years, the beat of primitive gongs
> and soft plaint of bamboo flutes were displaced by the rhythm of cas-
> tanets and guitars. The spectrum of Philippine dance broadened to
> include European modes of courtship and revelry as inspiration, where
> it used to be a primeval expression of tribal beliefs. (1987: 79)

In many stagings, and captured on audio recordings of Bayanihan, the Mountain Suite ends climatically with a ferocious scream by a male warrior that seems to punctuate the death of the "primitive" and lead to the dawning of the Spanish era.

Spanish Suite

The Spanish Suite (also called the Spanish Colonial Suite, Maria Clara Suite, El Salon Filipino, etc.) features local adaptations of European waltzes, mazurkas, polkas, and a panoply of Spanish *jotas* representative of the latter end of the colonial era that lasted from the first permanent settlement of 1565 until 1898. Bayanihan's original choreographer, Lucrecia Urtula, described the suite in the following manner (included here, because it encapsulates how the suite is described in many programs).

> Made up of Christian lowland dances of Hispanic influence, this suite has been sometimes titled *Galleon*, evoking the romance and adventure of the galleon trade, or *Aires de Verbena*, or—more affectionately for the Company—simply *Maria Clara*. . . . Dressed in satiny embroidered gowns with the typical large flowing sleeves and generous with their smiles, the female dancers make swaying, fluid, curvilinear movements with their arms and bodies to weave endless graceful patterns in the air. The gallant young men in their impeccable *barong tagalogs* serenade the young girls to the accompaniment of a guitar. A romantic air is conveyed in the dances of courtship where the young men woo and the damsels respond with a smile and a flutter of handkerchief or fan. . . . All in all, the dances of this suite exude an air of gracious sweetness and refined urbanity. (1987: 122)

The name Maria Clara comes from the archetypal Filipina maiden of the nineteenth century as idealized by the writer José Rizal in his novel *Noli Me Tangere* (1887). Maria Clara remains unsurpassed in Filipino literature as the epitome of the nineteenth-century Filipino woman. According to one writer of the 1950s, "Perhaps no other fiction character created by a Filipino novelist has captivated the abiding sympathy and affection of generations of readers. . . . She has become the idol of Filipino girls" (Alzona 1953: 13). Brought to life in José Rizal's novel describing the "social cancer" wrought by Spanish misdeeds in the Philippines, Maria Clara is beautiful, fair-skinned, intelligent, musically talented, and devoted to the man she believes to be her biological father, to Christ, and to the hero of the book. Secretly, she is the daughter of a Spanish friar and a Filipino woman who could not become pregnant with her Filipino husband, creating forevermore the embodiment of the racial merging of East and West.[12] Ironically, in the novel, Maria Clara is a tragic figure and one whose filial and romantic devotion ends tragically with her going mad in a nunnery. Not surprisingly, modern readings of *Noli* shed a less positive light on the heroine. Salvador Lopez, a writer, teacher, and statesman of the Philippines, criticizes the character as "far too weak to justify her being held up as a model for the women of our country. Her loyalty is the loyalty of the vanquished in spirit, her modesty the modesty of the timid.... We are left with the surmise that Rizal most probably intended the character of Maria Clara not as a glorification of the women of his time but rather as a satire upon their foibles and weaknesses" (1968: 83–84). Carmen Guerrero Nakpil, a well known Filipina writer, even describes Maria Clara as "the greatest misfortune that has befallen Filipino women in the last one hundred years" (1968: 85). She continues with the trenchant analysis that Maria Clara has influenced the understanding of Filipina femininity with an emphasis on fair skin, light hair, round eyes, and a perfect nose. "Rizal himself called her features 'semi-European,' and while this circumstance was clearly called for by the novel's plot, it was unfortunate for Filipino beauty. For in portraying his heroine in this guise, Rizal set up, unwittingly, one likes to think, a standard of feminine beauty that was untypical and unreal" (ibid. 89). Despite these and similar thoughtful criticisms, Maria Clara has retained her mystique over the years and remains well known to Filipinos. The novel still is required reading in schools, and its author, José Rizal, is revered as a national hero.

The Spanish Suite music and dances are closely associated with the Philippine aristocracy of the Spanish colonial age, such that folkloric costuming highlights issues of class and urban versus rural (see figure 2.2). The theatrics of performance tend to heighten the "Spanish-ness" of the Maria Clara suite repertoire, primarily through costuming, the use of props, choreography, and musical sound. Spanish dances in general were popular in the Philippines in the 1950s, and ballroom and social dancing appeared regularly on television (Alejandro 1978: 69).

Folklorization of Spanish-era courtship dances, then, connected with contemporary audiences through the musical accompaniment, and costumes lent a historical flair to the suite.[13] In addition to the *rondalla* ensemble, which I will describe below, little is more evocative of Spanish musical convention in the Philippines (and elsewhere) than the sound of castanets. Many dance pieces utilize castanets, especially to create dramatic effect in the choreography and sound, and the Spanish Suite as a whole often uses this convention for its striking opening sequence. It is notable that folkloric groups often use the Filipino adaptation of Spanish castanets—pairs of unattached rectangular bamboo pieces—even though they are more difficult to manage. While not all Spanish Suite pieces utilize the castanets, their recognizable clickety-clack sound, the ringing of *panderetas* (tambourines with jingles), and the shimmering timbre of the *rondalla* are musical markers of the Spanish era. In

FIGURE 2.2. Dancer from the Spanish Suite (photo from the Bayanihan collection; reprinted with permission)

addition to instrumentation, musical elements such as short references to the Phrygian mode and 6/8 rhythms also serve as distinctive aural cues.[14] All of these musical signs are meant to evoke specific qualities of a European past and its continuing cultural significance in the Philippines, but the folkloric representation wipes out any traces of the oppressive realities of the colonial period. Performed gentility becomes an homage to the past.

The folkloric representation of the Spanish colonial period and the accompanying implications for class and gender are implicated with institutionalized nostalgia. On stage, the characters of the suite tell a story—with bodies, movement, and music—cultivated to transport the audience to a time-space

understood as the colonial past. The story told is one in which racial hybridity is idealized, gender roles are strictly formulated, and class is a matter of manners rather than economy. Racial and gender-based metaphors are referenced overtly in actual performances of the folkloric Spanish Suite. Values represented by the sweet strains of music and graceful dances include feminine virtue, male gallantry, and physical control/restraint. I asked Zen Lopez, a former Bayanihan member who stands and moves with a dancer's poise, about the Spanish dances. She remarked, "We had to project refinement, grace, elegance of carriage and 'haughtiness' in the *jotas*. . . . In keeping with a concept common at that time, the dance movements for women were demure, coy and languid because they were modest and reserved. The men's movement more dynamic because they were brave and strong" (2006).[15] The kind of regulated courtship displayed in these dances is a large part of the nostalgic project.[16] This is significant, because in traditional courtship, stereotyped gender roles are emphasized. Feminine and masculine behavior are found in and promoted by choreographic movements, which in many cases focuses on the male/female dichotomy as much as their union. While Filipinos anecdotally have informed me that Filipina women are equal to men, as evidenced by the number of women in high political positions (including the presidency), standards for the behavior of women are relatively conservative. The Spanish are said to have "established a tradition of subordinating women, which is manifested in women's generally submissive attitudes and in a double standard of sexual conduct" (Dolan 1993: 98). A rather feminist declaration of nationalism juxtaposes the historical myth of precolonial gender egalitarianism with European patriarchy and imperialism.

Racial hybridity and class are also defined in the microcosm of the suite. It is fascinating that while the courtship of Spanish-flavored dance and music speaks to a union of cultures through male and female, the physical image presented by the actual dancers is closer to the offspring of such a union, the *mestizo*. According to former Bayanihan dancers Patricia Lim Yusah (member 1969-1973) and Marijo Castro Fadrigalan (member 1968–1972), it had been traditional within the casting practice of Bayanihan to prefer taller, light-skinned dancers for Spanish dances and to cast shorter, darker-skinned dancers for Rural Suite numbers. The cast members of Bayanihan often teased one another about their appearance, a preoccupation with race and skin color that is common in society at large in the Philippines (Yusah 2006). Incidentally, when I took lessons with Bayanihan during the summer of 1987, a similar casting of dancers occurred, although at the time I assumed the most important factor was height and not skin color. Hence, the reference to the suite as the Maria Clara Suite is as much about racial hybridity (Maria Clara is the

daughter of a Spaniard and a Filipina) as it is about the age it represents. Class too is effectively encapsulated by both the reference to Maria Clara and the dances of the suite, for all belong to a representation of Spanish and Filipino nobility of the nineteenth century. This is no space for the planting of rice or the unfurling of fishing nets. Rather, the dances are preoccupied with manners, grace, and courtship, and the repetition of these themes through the folkloric seems to validate the continuous replication of the upper class and its oligarchic control of the country.

How effective could a folkloric performance of the past be in evoking nostalgia and connecting with a Filipino audience? Yusah commented that many dancers in her generation had living family members who experienced the end of the nineteenth century under Spanish rule, giving the Maria Clara Suite particular resonance (2006). This time period would stand in sharp contrast to the American colonial era—also lived through by those same family members—which is typified by rapid changes in society, the secularization of the country, and the advent of Filipino modernity. Isabel Santos of Bayanihan describes the "graciousness and old-world charm of the Spanish suite" (2004:46), a description that clearly makes a differentiation from the New World values of the Americans and all of the anxieties attendant to "progress" and "change." Folkloric presentations of the Spanish colonial era are charged with this dichotomy between old and new, and they are public displays of culture in a contemporary narrative of postcolonial identity.

Do the performers, artistic directors, and audiences desire something as simple as a return to the "age of manners," when men were men and women were women (so to speak)? Of course, this would be a faulty conclusion. The efficacy of nostalgia as an aesthetic, and therefore as a theoretical lens for analysis, is in the ability to completely transcend reality. The performance provides a basis for imaginary temporal transport, but it encourages audiences to connect with a sense of self and a shared national identity rather than to indulge in escapism. The nationalized folkloric offered by Bayanihan and groups like it is a kind of "edutainment" with the extended benefits of promoting participation on a national scale.

Muslim Suite

Featured in the Muslim Suite are the ethnic groups from the southernmost region of the Philippines, including the Maranao, Maguindanao, Tausug, and the Badjao, who absorbed Islam from missionaries during the four-

teenth century. The ethnic groups are not interchangeable with the term *Muslim*, but the Muslim Suite consolidates them into one performance segment. Bayanihan program notes, when available, often make more specific attributions as to which people a particular dance should be associated. Aggregated despite their historical separateness from one another, they have become known as the Moros in the Philippines, a term that originated with the Spanish who related them to the Moors of their own country's history. While the original word referred to the inhabitants of Morocco, Moors, or *moros*, of Spain generally described North African peoples; however, it is the religious connotation of practicing Islam, and not a racial distinction, that defined Moro in the Philippines. Though the moniker originally carried negative connotations—and continues to do so to a certain extent in Spain—Moros of the 1960s reclaimed the name as a political gesture. Like the tribal groups presented in the Mountain Province Suite, the various peoples placed under the Muslim umbrella are an internal Other that is not racially distinct from the majority of the country's population but is perceived as being quite different. Politically, the Moros contribute to the sense of difference by resisting belonging to the Philippine nation in explicitly pronounced ways. While the Moros in total represent around 5 percent of the population, this relatively small number garners considerable attention in national politics, because most occupy a single area of the country, and because of the long history of separatist movements. Primary complaints include the contradictions between national laws and local laws and leadership, and government support for settlements of Christian Filipinos in Muslim areas. Even during U.S. colonization, when the Muslim areas were finally subsumed by military force, administrators by and large did not follow through on President McKinley's stated goal of Christianization (and, after all, the country as a whole was already around 80 percent Roman Catholic), and the Muslims remained a distinct population from the national mainstream (see Majul 1988). This historical separateness, as well as an Orientalism inherited from hundreds of years of colonization by Western powers, contributes to the exoticism inherent in the folklorization of Muslim music and dance.

Barbara Gaerlan, in her examination of how Filipino Americans have drawn from the Bayanihan Muslim dances, describes how the folkloric constructs an exotic and haughty Other (1999). The danger lies in a general ignorance about the people being represented, such that folkloric performance becomes a substitute for a heterogeneous people, despite highly narrow and stereotypical characterizations. She is not alone in her critique of Bayanihan in general and of the Muslim Suite in particular.

Usopay Cadar, an ethnomusicologist from the Maranao people, complained about dances and costuming fabricated for this suite (1970) and has worked to present a more balanced image of his own cultural traditions through teaching and performance. Even Ramón Obusan, who gave credit to Bayanihan for inspiring him in his younger years, disagreed with the group's stylizations for stage and opted for stage representations closer to what he encountered in fieldwork (2000). Bayanihan's reproductions support Orientalist stereotypes from within the Philippine nation, simultaneously incorporating the dangerous Other while declaring its essential difference. Ties to the past are integral to the folkloric Othering, for without the advent of the Spanish, it seems likely that in time much of the archipelago would have been converted to Islam. Moreover, it is believed that the Moros maintained much of their pre-Islamic practices, further implanting their reputation as "authentic" natives to the islands and illustrating how adaptation and the hybridity of culture contact continually undergo processes of naturalization. The religion and its practitioners, therefore, connect Filipinos with a pre-Hispanic past that had the possibility of shaping the present in an alternate universe. In line with this, the Muslims in this suite are re-created in the folkloric realm as a kind of substitute for the court culture that the rest of the Philippines lacks in contrast to its Asian neighbors. Indeed, the Bayanihan Muslim Suite seems itself intoxicated with the richness of a reimagined sultanate culture, bearing such loaded adjectives as "regal splendor" and "elegant hauteur" (Urtula 1987: 122). Alejandro characterizes Muslim dance as having an emphasis on the upper torso, bent knees, upturned toes, and the use of hands to express feeling. He continues, "Moslem dances move with a peculiar elasticity and almost serpentine suppleness; curves are emphasized in the apparently jointless, backturned hands, flexible arms, and rounded posture of the body" (1978: 167–169). Costuming, lighting, and sound enhance the exoticism of choreographed movements and stylized carriage, all simulating in tandem a world of mystery and barbarism matched equally with grace. Isabel Santos, costume designer for Bayanihan, describes the Muslim Suite as "an exotic world of sultry colors and sinuous movements," showcasing *malongs* (tubular pieces of cloth that can be worn by men and women in a variety of ways), embroidered jackets, outsize fans, fringed umbrellas, jewelry, and the famous wave-bladed *kris* weapon (2004: 48).

This exoticism ties directly into notions of the precolonial past, not to elicit nostalgia but to propel a nationalism that feeds from the pride of a people who were never colonized by the Spanish and who appear to share a closer heritage with other populations of Southeast Asia.[17] It also furthers a classicist agenda, in which people of the present day construct connections to a proud past in order to validate modernist nationalism.[18] The sense of external reaching is exemplified by the *Vinta*, a dance of balancing skill atop two bamboo poles hoisted on the shoulders of two men, that celebrates the small boat of the same name. The *vinta* symbolizes the seafaring ways of the southern people and extrapolates to the Filipinos as a whole, implying that they are natural ocean travelers. In post–World War II Philippines, this perception tied nicely to the large number of Filipino sailors who joined the United States Navy as well as to the many workers on freight and passenger ships traversing the world's waterways.[19] Other ties to the outside, and particularly to Asia, evident in this suite include dances with silver fingernail extensions, movements from Southeast Asian martial arts, the use of bamboo poles, ankle bells, and the drum and bossed gong instrumentation. The music, especially, distinguishes the Muslim Suite, with its nondiatonic scales (the gongs are tuned to accommodate pentatonic modes) and use of rhythmic modes. While there is a great variety of musical styles and instrumentation among the various Muslim groups, the Muslim Suite primarily features the *kulintang* ensemble.

The *kulintang* ensemble is very expertly covered in a number of sources, so I will merely summarize it here for the convenience of the reader.[20] The *kulintang* (or *kulintangan*) denotes the ensemble as a whole as well as a single instrument with eight bossed gongs laid horizontally in pitch order (lowest on the left to highest on the right) in a rectangular frame. While also played by non-Muslim tribal Filipinos in the south, the music and ensembles best known inside and outside of the Philippines are those of the Muslim Maguindanao, Maranao, and Tausug. The *kulintang* ensemble differs somewhat among ethnic groups. Among the Maguindanao, the ensemble includes the *kulintang*, *agung* (two large hanging knobbed gongs), a set of *gandingan* (four shallow, hanging, knobbed gongs), a *babandil* (small time-keeping gong), and a *dabakan* (goblet drum hit with thin bamboo sticks). This instrumentation reflects that found in Bayanihan, but the musical repertoire is actually quite different. Unlike the circumscribed melodic improvisation and interaction between musicians found in original settings, the folkloric ensemble relies not only on standardized tunes but also on ones that are either completely fabricated or extremely simplified to highlight repetitive rhythmic patterns.

Including the Muslim Suite in Bayanihan presentations makes absolute sense from the standpoint of showcasing the diversity of the country. And, even more than the other suites, its incorporation helps to divert attention from very real and very rancorous divisions within the nation. The performance dialectic in which Muslims of the south are portrayed as heroic warriors and an important part of the Filipino cultural fabric, while being simultaneously Othered for their religion and social practices, is reflective of the national condition in which Mindanao is a semiautonomous region. Dependent upon tropes of exoticism, the Muslim Suite has been both lauded for its stunning presentational style as well as criticized for its flaws in representations of actual people. Perhaps in the face of this quiet but ever-present controversy, it is worth mentioning that in the earliest days of folklorization and the development of Bayanihan, choreographers worked very closely with royalty, the general public, performers, and their research counterparts in order to learn as much as they could about dance and music traditions from the area. These interactions reveal much about how the arts can bring people together even during the most divisive of times and circumstances. It is fair to critique the legacy of those fruitful engagements as an exoticized collection of stylistically altered material; however, folklorization also promotes the logic of de-exoticizing through familiarization. Bayanihan, even with all its flaws, asks audiences to celebrate the fierce independence of the Muslims in a simplified message of national unity despite difference, all colored by a more complicated undertone of what might have been.

Rural Suite

The dances and music of the Rural Suite represent neither past nor present specifically, but rather a mythologized rurality.[21] The music and dance evokes a kind of wonderland somewhere near or far from the city, in a place one might wish to return to if circumstances permitted. Importantly, the portrayal of the countryside directly connects with audience members, some of whom do return to their family homes in the provinces for local festivals and other life occasions. That life in the provinces is vastly different from staged rural life is clearly not the point. Like *furusato* nostalgia for home and the countryside exhibited in Japan, the representation of life in the Rural Suite is a mythologized portrait of a simple agrarian-based way of life (see Yano 2003). Popular dances in this suite include the *"Binasuan,"* in which performers balance glasses of wine in their hands and on their heads in replication of a wedding celebration dance, the "Tinikling," the bamboo dance that some refer to as the national dance of the Philippines, and "Bangko," in which dancers flirt with one another while balancing on stacked benches (see figure 2.3).

FIGURE 2.3. *Bangko* (bench) dance from the Rural Suite (photo from the Bayanihan collection; reprinted with permission)

The equally bubbly music of the Rural Suite, as well as that of the Spanish Suite, is played by the same performers of the Mountain Suite, but formed into a *rondalla*.[22] The *rondalla* is a musical ensemble made up of plucked string instruments brought to the islands by Europeans but adapted over the years into locally made versions. The pear-shaped, flat-backed *banduria* is the primary melody maker of the group, with fourteen metal strings tuned in six courses. Some ensembles are supplemented with piccolo *bandurias*, which are somewhat smaller in size and are a fourth higher in range than the regular *banduria*. The *octavina* and *laud* are pitched identically an octave lower than the *banduria* and can be distinguished from one another by their shapes.

While the *octavina* is waisted like a small guitar, the *laud* is pear-shaped like the *banduria* and sometimes has f-holes. All of the aforementioned instruments are melodic rather than rhythmic in nature, although chords are a possibility, and are plucked with a plectrum. Typically, the strings are plucked rapidly in up-and-down strokes during long notes in a tremolo fashion in order to produce the recognizable "ringing" timbre of the ensemble. Supporting these instruments, the *gitara* (equivalent to a classical guitar, usually with nylon strings) and double bass (formerly the *bajo de uñas*, which is less commonly used) make up the rhythm section. Along with the instruments, Europeans imported the Western tonal system and a repertoire of dance music that continues to be played through myriad versions in folkloric settings (and sometimes at coming-of-age "debut" parties for eighteen-year-old girls). Because of the influence of prominent folkloric groups in the Philippines like Bayanihan, music for most dances has largely been melodically standardized, even on those occasions when the music was composed specifically to accompany the dance in staged productions.

The folk dance for boys and men called "Maglalatik" is an interesting example of a real dance tradition coupled with composed music (or arranged from fragments that are never quite revealed as borrowed) that has become a standard in the folkloric tradition. In this dance the performers wear empty coconut halves strapped to their bodies and rhythmically hit their own coconuts and those of others with coconut halves held in their hands in an oblique depiction of a battle between Christians and Moros (Muslims). This time, however, the battle is not for land or souls, but rather for *latik*, a tasty residue left from boiling coconut milk. In some performances the Moros are differentiated from the Christians by costume, wearing red trousers and long-sleeved black shirts, while the Christians are garbed in blue trousers and white shirts. In dances with older boys, the torso is bare and the trouser legs are rolled up for both groups. (Most versions of this dance in the United States do not differentiate Moros from Christians in their costuming, and the original meaning is lost is a swirl of friendly and competitive acrobatics.)

According to Reyes Aquino, the music for the dance observed in Laguna consisted of a steady rhythm played by two bamboo sticks and guitar accompaniment. She does not describe it further. Aquino introduced a version of "Maglalatik" composed by renowned Filipino composer Francisco Santiago (see chapter 1) that has superseded the original accompaniment and is used in most folkloric performances (Aquino 1996: 55). Santiago's "Maglalatik" contains distinct musical sections that change with the shifting choreography of the narrative, but whether the music suited the dance or the dance changed with the music is undocumented. In either case, the result as codified in Reyes Aquino's book is a well-integrated performance in which musical and kinetic elements feel as if they organically support one another.

The introduction serves as a buildup of excitement before the warriors come into contact with one another, relying on a pedal point and a repetitive rhythmic theme that rises steadily in pitch. Followed by an interlude in which the music remains static and only chords are played in order to highlight the sounds of the dancers, the music shifts to a lively polka that makes use of the original rhythmic theme. During the first sections of the dance, meant to depict warfare, the dancers hit the coconuts on their own bodies as well as on the bodies of the other dancers. While the percussive sounds help in the enactment of war, the music is immensely playful, echoing the humor inherent in a battle over *latik*. From part I to part IV, the music changes key in each section, from G to D to C, and the sections are not held together by any particular musical theme.

Part IV, however, does have a very interesting musical theme. Extracting the first and last notes of the first three measures, we find the melody of "Bahay Kubo," a very common children's folk song about a hut dwelling and the variety of vegetables growing around it. While "Bahay Kubo" is normally sung or played in a moderate triple time, part IV of Santiago's "Maglalatik" converts the melody to fit into duple time, inserts passing notes, and challenges the listener to recognize the already familiar (see figures 2.4 and 2.5).

In part V of the dance, the narrative calls for reconciliation between the Christians and the Moros, and the composer displays this with a return to the original key and a metric switch to triple time. As the feeling of the music levels off from a lively duple meter to a more walkable triple meter, the dancers also settle into a circle around which they waltz congenially. Since Reyes Aquino had previously described this section as a *paseo*, or walking

FIGURE 2.4. Section of Santiago's "Maglalatik" that resembles "Bahay Kubo" (transcription by author)

FIGURE 2.5. "Bahay Kubo" (transcription by author)

dance, the change is not surprising. While the melody as written feels rather stilted in the first half of the section, the return to a triple meter moves the music into a kind of folkloric comfort zone, since many folk songs in the Philippines are in triple time. During the last half of this part, the music shifts to the relative minor and flows into the familiar lyricism of a Filipino love song—a "joining together" of some kind.

The arrangement of this music played by the Bayanihan *rondalla* under Lucrecia Kasilag and recorded in the album *Bayanihan Dance Company, Volume* 1 (Monitor Records 1993) is quite similar to the piece transcribed in Reyes's book but with some interesting adaptations to performance. The lively introduction is almost twice as long as written, giving the dancers more time to move across the stage, but at the same time reducing the original tension buildup of the music. Instead of rising to a final relatively static iteration, the theme rises in pitch as written but must then start again at the lower tonic during a repeat. The change makes for less effective drama in the music, but this is balanced by the visual excitement of dancers entering the stage. Following this, the chords of the interlude are played staccato and dampened with the hand as the dancers mark time by stamping each beat with bare feet on the stage. During part III, instead of taking the repeat of II exactly as written, the *rondalla* modulates from D back to the key of G, high-lighting an awkwardness in the original score that pitted part III in D with part IV in C. The transition from D to C is less palatable in simple tonal music such as this, and a key change from G to D, back to G, and then to C would be preferred. As the musical director of Bayanihan and leader of the rondalla, Kasilag opted out of the quirky modulation.

By keeping faithful to the idiom of Filipino folk music and by paraphrasing "Bahay Kubo" in the subtext, "Maglalatik" has stretched the boundaries of folk music to include those pieces that have known composers. So much a part of the culture that produced the folk music from which he found inspiration, Santiago was able to add to the tradition by creating a piece that joined the folk repertoire and, perhaps ironically, is often not credited to him in program notes. In turn, Bayanihan canonized his music in a standard music and dance form that is the model for many folkloric groups that followed.

The standardization of folk music and dance in the Rural Suite, and the parallel process of constructing a national repertoire, has another ironic aspect. A static tradition is, of course, the opposite of what the Rural Suite, in all of its rigorous effusiveness and touristic appeal, hopes to portray. While the stateliness of the Spanish social dances seems to imply the following of prescribed steps, the Rural Suite is a stylized enactment of a particular folk aesthetic that celebrates spontaneity, joy, and a connection with nature. The women and men are ever smiling as they flit through the dances. In contrast to the Spanish Suite, there is a childlike quality to the interactions between men and women in which playfulness trumps sexuality. While I think it hyperbole to suggest that this folkloric portrayal conspires to hide ugly truths about life in the rural lower class, I do think the presentation relies on stereotypes that support the status quo. The clear class differences between the Spanish Suite and the Rural Suite enforce hierarchical structures that rely on a narrative of an elite ruling class empowered with a sense of order and rationality and a large underclass of the nation's "children" requiring that rule. The double-edged sword of Bayanihan's folkloric theme of unity is that the nation is indeed one, but the members of that nation are not necessarily equal.

Bayanihan's president, Helena Benitez, affirmed the theme of unification through staging when she wrote, "It is symbolic of our peoples and serves as both an inspiration and reminder—that our national unity has for its base, cultural diversity that requires sympathetic understanding, sincere appreciation and a continuous search for beauty and goodness in each of these diverse sectors in order to bind and strengthen our nation" (1987: 7). Taken from a contemporary point of view, the Philippine nation is significantly shaped by diaspora and by the sheer number of overseas workers who are employed abroad but still call the Philippines home (and their monetary remittances are crucial to the economy of the nation). Yet, Benitez's vision of the role of the folkloric in authoring and strengthening nationalism, or at least the idea of nation, still holds great significance. There are innumerable folkloric groups based on the Bayanihan model in Filipino communities all over the world. The very real solidarity and sense of cultural pride they engender through social gatherings and events within and external to their own ethnic community are nothing short of a practice of national belonging, however far-flung and variegated that nation might be.

WHEN I BEGIN DOING RESEARCH on the Cultural Center of the Philippines (CCP), I meet with the renowned Filipino composer, ethnomusicologist, and educator José Maceda at his home. After I tell him my topic, he sighs with disapproval. What I ought to look at, he states firmly, is the music of China and Japan. A couple of months later, one of my consultants begins our interview by pointing out that from above, the plan of the CCP resembles a toilet. Throughout my fieldwork, the intermittent dismissals and more common irreverence toward the CCP is revealing, especially when contrasted with the formal and laudatory literature of the monumental national institution of the arts. As it turns out, the CCP is meaningful in complex ways for many of my consultants. It provides an excuse for people to talk about their art and their feelings on Filipino society. It is a window into the world of cultural politics. It also gives some a chance to tell me that there is no such thing as Filipino national culture, followed by an explanation of what might and might not be suitable for consideration if there were such a thing.

By 1998, the building is showing its age, and it is closed entirely one day a week to save on costs. It is dark and quiet most of the time, with old carpeting and a dull smell of dampness that seems a constant in the tropics. I never encounter anyone in the galleries, though the library is often beset with students in the afternoon. One day I watch over the railing as the Ramón Obusan Folkloric Group, a resident music and dance company, rehearses in the lobby. Perhaps the main hall is being fumigated, a regular occurrence for auditoriums.

Many different kinds of shows take place at the CCP. I attend the afternoon matinee of a new *sarswela* (music theater), and students are brought in for free to make up the rest of the audience. They chatter throughout, and the girls swoon over the male lead who happens to be a pop music star. In one evening concert of art music, former First Lady Imelda Marcos emerges as the unplanned entertainment during intermission. She is obliged to rise from her seat and wave when a spotlight descends upon her. She is still striking, despite her age and her ignominious ouster from the presidential palace. At a pop music gala, then-president Gloria Macapagal-Arroyo strides down the aisle several minutes into the program, almost hidden within her flanking entourage. She does not get a spotlight, perhaps because she is moving too quickly, or perhaps because she lacks the glamour associated with the former First Lady. The last production I see there is *Miss Saigon*. I am impressed by the retrofitting of the main hall to accommodate the demands of the foreign producer, but feel guilty after viewing the musical, since many of the artists I have met were displaced from the CCP entirely during the preparations and run of the show.

The CCP has always been a place of battles, big and small, for it has served since its inception as an arena for political power plays and national-level cultural debates. Moreover, the CCP still exudes a certain aura. Like the remarkable "Coconut Palace" next door that Imelda Marcos constructed for a papal visit in 1981, the CCP has survived the notoriety of its beginnings, though not without permanent scars.[1]

CHAPTER THREE | Consolidating a National Present
The Cultural Center of the Philippines

THIS CHAPTER EXPLORES THE CONFLUENCE of nationalism and state patronage at the Cultural Center of the Philippines (CCP) from the late 1960s through the 1970s, including the first years of martial law in the Philippines.[2] The CCP, as a state-run and state-funded institution, has acted as a prism for the nationalization of culture by serving as venue, moderator, and patron. Local arts have been elevated as exemplars of national diversity, while international arts have been sanctioned as part of the national heritage, not only from a history of colonialism, but also through a rhetoric of modernity and progress. The vision of official nationalism is subject to the narrowing lens of survival, focusing cultural nationalism on justifying the state's claim to power and jurisdiction over the whole of the nation. In a postcolonial nation-state like the Philippines, the noncolonial state is, in essence, the culmination of a nationalist movement and therefore is already ordained as a legitimate arbiter of nationalist ideology. Yet, long after the echoes of revolution have faded, the state must maintain the façade of naturalness and "rightness" in the minds of its followers. The deliberate conflation of nationalism and propaganda in nation-states is a hegemonic project that overlaps conceptions of state and nation to give the sense that the constitution of one is integral to the other. In public ceremonies, the government makes use of potent symbols, such as the flag and anthem, to equate nation and state. Likewise, the institutionalization of culture, a modernist strategy of objectification and a way of controlling the construction of a national narrative, creates a forum for the declaration and performance of official nationalisms. García-Canclini's cogent observation applies well in this case; modernity is "a simulacrum conjured up by the elites and the state apparatuses, above all those concerned with art and culture, but which for that very reason makes them unrepresentative and unrealistic.... They acted as if they formed national cultures, and they barely constructed elite cultures, leaving out enormous indigenous and peasant populations" (1995: 7). Hence, the CCP should be seen as part of a larger, elitist effort by Imelda and Ferdinand Marcos to legitimize their regime through the establishment of a national patrimony to which they were intrinsically tied.

The CCP as envisioned by Imelda Marcos would be both a national and nationalist institution, substituting for a ministry of culture. It would absorb national-level performance companies like Bayanihan and the Philippine Madrigal Singers and provide opportunities for nationalist composers. These artists, while finding a home and patron in this center for arts, had to contend with the desires and needs of the Philippine state, personified by Imelda Marcos. Significantly, the CCP would not only reveal her ideas about art and culture, but also prompt significant debates about the role of the arts in society and how they relate to the specificities of the Philippine circumstance. So it is that the history of the CCP is a testimony to the rise and consolidation of power of the country's most infamous ruling couple, and any examination of the institution must begin with the stories of Imelda and Ferdinand Marcos.

Imelda Marcos as Patroness of the Arts

While neither a new idea nor a unique vision, the CCP owed its creation and preliminary evolution to Imelda Romualdez Marcos, the wife of the sixth president of the Third Republic of the Philippines, Ferdinand Marcos. She remolded the position of First Lady into a real political force, achieving not only sensational wealth and influence, but also the official titles of minister of human settlements and governor of Metropolitan Manila. Along the way she earned the apt nickname the "Steel Butterfly." On the one hand, she regularly appeared in public attired in resplendent *Filipiniana* gowns, including the distinctive butterfly-sleeve dress native to the country. On the other hand, the nickname encapsulated an obdurate will cloaked in feminine charm.

From poor beginnings, Imelda crafted a stunning emergence on the Manila social scene during the 1950s. She was quickly crowned Miss Manila, though according to some stories, Imelda actually lost the contest and achieved her goal only after a tearful and persuasive visit with the mayor of

Manila to reverse the decision of the committee. She kept up her public profile by appearing in magazines as a beauty queen and attending parties with a variety of prominent escorts. Her romance with Ferdinand became legendary, partially based on its swiftness (reputed to be eleven days in the making) and partially on embellishments added as the years progressed that gave the story shades of an epic romance (Hamilton-Paterson 1998: 148). In the meantime, Imelda had been studying vocal performance at the Philippine Women's University to round out her already considerable appeal in the public sphere. Her practice of singing during campaign rallies is remembered by many Filipinos from those years and is often invoked as one of her great appeals to the crowds eager for entertainment. She proved to be a remarkable counterpoint to the ambitions of Ferdinand Marcos. With their combined talents, the two staged an impressive campaign for the presidency of the land.

Ferdinand Edralin Marcos, born 1917 in the province of Ilocos Norte, was an ambitious and brilliant man. But before graduating at age 21 from the University of the Philippines law school ranked at the top of his class, he was charged by the police with the assassination of a political candidate who had, a few years prior, overcome his father in a local election. Delivering his own defense with an oratorical facility that would serve him well as a politician, he gained acquittal and attained a kind of celebrity status. In the years to follow, during the Japanese occupation of the Philippines, Marcos claimed to have led a guerrilla contingent called the Maharlikas. While his war record remains controversial, Marcos used these stories, along with commissioned books and even movies, during his campaigns for political office. In 1949 he won a seat as congressman in the House of Representatives, and a decade later he became a senator. He would later serve as Senate president before triumphing as president of the Philippines. By his side stood Imelda Romualdez Marcos.

In a country where politics is more often a play of personalities than a clash of ideologies and platforms, Imelda's ability to woo the masses was more than a slight boon. Traveling from province to province, she sang songs from the localities in their appropriate languages and awed the people with her elaborate Filipina gowns and statuesque appearance. During her speeches and interviews, Imelda Marcos announced that if he were elected to the presidency, she would complement her husband's efforts toward the achievement of national goals. She put forth two intertwined missions for the betterment of the Filipino people, with the first being a social welfare program. The second was the construction of a cultural center for the development of the Filipino soul, a project she believed was just as essential to nation-building as economic development. She may have initially spoken of the need for a national theater at a proclamation rally in Cebu City as early as 1963 (de la Torre 1985: 66). Years prior to that, plans had been discussed for a Philippine American Cultural Foundation, but it had never come to fruition. In any case, it is important to note that while the idea of a cultural institution to serve the nation was not Imelda's alone, her assertive efforts were responsible for bringing the CCP into existence. She envisioned the center to be a showcase of Filipino artistic expression and a landmark of architectural beauty that would foster the arts of present day and preserve the heritage of the past.

"Culture," "the arts," and "heritage" are terms that can refer to a wide variety of practices and artifacts. Imelda Marcos's center would encompass the "high arts" of the West as well as the "traditional arts" of the Philippine localities, and all would be integrated together as part of Philippine culture. Given the Philippine government's attempts since the country became a republic in 1946 to hold the archipelago together as a unified nation under state power, the amalgamation of diverse arts could be understood as a nationalist imperative concerned with time (history) and space (regionality). As for Imelda's "high arts," only in Manila were resources available to support a Western-style orchestra or ballet company; hence, the cultural center would be an institution to develop and house these arts. In conjunction, the CCP would promote "cultures" from the outlying regions, either with performances by practitioners or re-creations of these performances in a staged show (as exemplified by groups like Bayanihan). Certainly, the CCP had the potential to be comprehensive in its programming, accommodating not only Western "high" arts, but also traditional Philippine arts, popular presentations, and performances from any part of the globe. It could be a venue as much as a patron to the arts, but if the Philippine government ran it, what would be its goals and its limits?

Similar ideas about building a cultural center had been bandied about for at least twenty years but without accomplishing anything on a practical level. Existing theaters of the day, such as the Philamlife Auditorium, were not adequate for very large audiences, and in any case were not considered to be national showcases. Moreover, none purported to be institutions charged with cultural promotion. Undoubtedly, then, the desire for a national theater and national institution for the arts was agreeable, at least to the elite social class for whom such pastimes were financially possible. There certainly were those who saw Imelda as a political role model, and her goals as both viable and valid. Estefania Aldaba-Lim, official advisor to Mrs. Marcos in community services and cultural affairs, had charitable recollections.[3] She remembered Imelda Marcos as being little concerned with her image—at least during the first presidential term—and that she made regular checks on the workers building the CCP. "Her industry tended to stimulate the people working with her. The people benefited because for their good were these projects we dreamed up and rushed. Of course, they became known as her works and rightly so." It was only later, Aldaba-Lim said, that Imelda's motivations toward the arts became political (Joaquin 1996: 123, 127). Despite this opinion, Imelda Marcos's actions were subject to debate from the start.

Land Reclaimed Unearths the Opposition

It became clear after Marcos won the presidential election of 1965 that Imelda planned to follow through on her plans. Four months into the presidency, the First Lady announced groundbreaking ceremonies for the cultural center. Finding a home for her dream center within the traditional environs of Manila would be difficult, since the city was already chockablock. Instead, she set her sights on a valuable tract of land reclaimed from Manila Bay in 1961 by Henry Stonehill. The area surrounding the bay, a natural indentation that in past days had provided a perfect harbor for trading and war ships, had not only historical import but also represented international commerce. It was in this bay that the U.S. Admiral Dewey unceremoniously junked the Spanish Pacific Squadron in 1898 to start the Spanish-American War in the Philippines. At the mouth of the bay, the island of Corregidor is well remembered as the last bastion of U.S. forces in the Philippines during World War II and an important target for recapture upon their dramatic return. In times of peace, the bay has provided a picture postcard setting, from when Roxas Boulevard rumbled with its first cars to the new millennium installment of a gargantuan shopping complex called the Mall of Asia. It has long been a place for city dwellers to view the fabled sunsets over the water.[4] The setting presented a marvelously dramatic backdrop for the center. Just three years prior to construction, Stonehill had been deported for fraud, and the government had seized the land, paving the way for the new center.

The plans for the cultural center building, designed by the accomplished Filipino architect Leandro Locsin, were originally intended for the R.P. (Republic of the Philippines)–U.S. Cultural Center proposed in 1964. According to Carunungan, "It was to have been a monument to the friendly ties between the Philippines and the United States," but due to disagreements over how to spend the money made available for the project, construction was aborted (1969: 2). It was not until Imelda adopted the idea with her plans for the CCP that Locsin's designs could be realized. Imelda commissioned studies of modern theaters located in other parts of the world, such as Los Angeles, Sydney, and Tokyo (Ellison 1988: 89). She also called together the first organizational meeting to hammer out the philosophical concept of the center. According to a number of speeches she gave during the construction of the CCP, Imelda intended for the CCP to house all the arts, from visual to literary to performing. She also meant for the CCP to symbolize her quest to uncover the beauty of the Filipino soul as expressed through art, and furthermore that this symbol be up and running in an obvious fashion by the time the next election year arrived. Thus, the CCP was a personal project whose construction and image were intertwined inextricably with Imelda's vision and ambition. With haste, Imelda called for the simultaneous reclamation of more land from Manila Bay and ordered the pile-driving for the main building in May of 1966. While the concrete was being poured, Imelda was busy soliciting collections from art aficionados to house in her future center. Not surprisingly, many contributed. After all, not only was she the First Lady of the land, but Imelda was also masterfully persuasive, with a belt full of political tools to help her get her way. But her aggressiveness was not always appreciated. As James Hamilton-Paterson wrote in his biography of the Marcoses, "While building progressed and she was exploring the thrilling bounds of her omnipotence Imelda was also acquiring a reputation for arrogance and grandeur" (1998: 225).

The building proved to be an extravagant expenditure. "Back in 1966, the center's price had been announced at just below $4 million, but by Christmas of 1968 it was learned that it had already cost more than twice that amount, with only three-fourths of the work completed" (Ellison 1988: 90). The funds for the construction of the CCP came from a variety of sources. During a 1966 state visit to the United States, Imelda cemented her role as patroness of the arts by managing to obtain coveted tickets to the grand opening of the Metropolitan Opera House at Lincoln Center. And it was Imelda who gained the favor of President Lyndon Johnson with her charm and attractive appearance. During one evening of the visit, Imelda sang "Dahil Sa Iyo (Because of You)," her signature love song from the campaign trail, directly to President Johnson. The results of her efforts were astonishing, and, one might find, amusing.

> "Bravo," cried a radiant LBJ, standing to applaud, as did Washington's
> society columns. IMELDA STOLE SPOTLIGHT, declared the
> Washington Post. The Washington Star thought her worth two stories,
> with photos. Betty Beale, chronicler of the after-hours doings of
> Washington's powerful, acclaimed Mrs. Marcos as "talented, beautiful

and aristocratic." A longer story appeared that day written by Ymelda Dixon; Imelda Marcos, displaying her mastery of flattery, suggested that she might change the spelling of her name, because "'I' sounds so egotistical." (Bonner 1987: 55)

In the end, her husband was successful in pushing for money from the U.S. government. Marcos made away with $45 million in economic assistance and $31 million for veterans of World War II who had fought on the American side (Ibid. 1987: 53). On top of all this, Johnson committed $3.5 million for the cultural center, money that was supposed to have come from the veteran's package. Because this would have cut into her husband's appropriations, Johnson reached into his political bag of tricks and found the money in an obscure Philippine claim from years past for veterans' education benefits in the sum of $28 million. Johnson confided to Imelda Marcos that he would guide the appropriation through the proper channels and insisted that it be used only for the center. After checking in with her husband, she agreed to $3.5 million (Seagrave 1988: 192). Even with this vast sum of money, the amount was not nearly enough to accomplish what Mrs. Marcos envisioned, due to the enormous percentage of funds lost in kickbacks and other forms of corruption. Just as she had during the campaign, Imelda set her sights on the Philippine wealthy to support her plans. According to one of her biographers, "Before any of her parties, for an anniversary, birthday, or holiday, she warned guests to bring their checkbooks, expecting each to make donations—not only to the Cultural Center, but to a host of other rarely precisely defined charity projects" (Ellison 1988: 89). While on the one hand it appeared that a good part of the CCP was going to be financed privately by Manila's wealthiest families and not by public expenditure, it seemed clear from the start that the CCP would serve only the well-to-do. As such, rather than the Robin Hood that she claimed to be, Imelda merely played the role of queen, siphoning from her feudal-lord subjects a bit of what they had already squeezed from *their* peasant tenants, in order to construct a monument too intimidating and expensive for the poor to enter.

The exorbitant and almost unbelievable amount being spent on the CCP raised vehement protests, initially from politicians of the opposition party, but also by private citizens and members of the freewheeling Philippine press. One Filipino journalist voiced the opinion of many when he queried, "Is she really sincere in her desire to help the Filipino artist and find for this artist a home for his art? Or is she doing all this to promote herself to the people, since, as everyone knows, she is her husband's 'secret political weapon'?" (Carunungan 1969: 2). Even members of the wealthy, the target group for a center of this nature, showed their displeasure. Long considered to be an oligarchic country in which the wealthiest families are also the most prominent political power brokers, opposition to the Marcoses came in a variety of forms. In one example, desiring to irk the First Lady, Eugenio Lopez, Sr. (the father of Ferdinand Marcos's vice-presidential running mate) opened the Meralco Theatre in 1967 to steal a bit of the shine off of Imelda's cultural crown jewel (Hamilton-Paterson 1998: 304).

Among the most vocal politicians, Senator Benigno "Ninoy" Aquino became the rallying voice against the CCP and, by association, Imelda Marcos. He argued that the cultural center and its board had not been created by law, and that, therefore, Mrs. Marcos's handling of funds was nothing short of illegal (de la Torre 1984: 23). His colorful rhetoric opposing the use of funds for Imelda's center was very public, but it was his great fervor that was said to have stung Imelda enough to fuel a very long-lasting grudge. Ironically, Aquino was close to both Ferdinand and Imelda Marcos, and the friend/enemy dynamic of their relationship was not atypical among the confined echelons of the monied and powerful in the Philippines. In fact, Aquino was Marcos's fraternity brother (Upsilon Sigma Phi) at the University of the Philippines, as well as a cousin-in-law to and former suitor of Imelda, though that flirtation had been short-lived. Roque Ablan, an old friend and fraternity brother of Marcos and Aquino, summed up their peculiar relationship as secretly quite close. "In 1969 Ninoy gave a speech condemning Imelda for the wastefulness of her new CCP Project. The joke is, it was Marcos who edited the speech for him, writing his comments on Ninoy's draft like . . . 'Sock it to her!'" (quoted in Hamilton-Paterson 1998: 293).

Private citizens also attacked the center using legal means, carrying the debate from the streets and private salons to the courts. Executive Order No. 30 officially created the Cultural Center of the Philippines on June 23, 1966, stating, "The Cultural Center of the Philippines is a trust for the benefit of the people for the purpose of preserving and promoting Philippine culture in all its varied aspects." It appeared that EO 30 blatantly disregarded another piece of legislation made during the time of President Macapagal (1961–1965). Republic Act No. 4165 had created the National Commission on Culture (NCC) whose purposes were noticeably similar to those of the CCP.[5] The Marcoses dismissed this complaint, asserting that RA 4165 did not preclude the creation of the cultural center but rather allowed the establishment of institutions such as the CCP that could execute the overall goals of the NCC. The difference was a matter of politics and, much more important, credit.

In another legal maneuver, Manila lawyer Ramón A. Gonzales filed a lawsuit that questioned the center's legality as an outgrowth of an executive order. He argued, "Only Congress can legally create the trust for the operation of the Cultural Center. Thus, the Center must not be allowed to open in its present personality" (Carunungan 1969: 2). To this, the judge replied that the executive branch could work separately from the legislature and that the center's trust would be in the persons of a board (*Manila Chronicle* December 9, 1969: 13). Gonzalez was legally stymied, and the center continued as a project of the president and his wife. The dismissal of the Gonzales case came as no surprise to the public. One journalist wryly summarized, "There is really nothing which is legally impossible for a government that is determined to do its thing. Administration apologists can easily turn out press releases claiming that the creation of the Cultural Center is well within the bounds of law. No matter. The more important objection raised by Senator Aquino is that the Center was built at a cost ridiculously out of proportion to the more pressing needs of the country" (Salazar 1969: 14). Clearly, underneath the legal aspects of the case simmered pragmatic and moral questions. Did a country as impoverished as the Philippines need to spend such a gargantuan sum of money on a cultural center while people continued to starve in the streets of Manila and in the countryside?

By the 1960s, the rate of economic growth in the Philippines had reversed itself and slowed to a decline. Agricultural frontiers that had attracted the landless throughout the 1950s had disappeared, and food production in the 1960s could not keep up with rapid population growth. Provinces outside of the largest cities were themselves densely populated, and without employment, migrants began streaming into Manila. Because of this, and because there were more people than jobs available, unemployment rates increased while wages decreased. This situation was exacerbated by reforms in 1969 by the International Monetary Fund that caused wages to drop 10 percent in only two years (Wurfel 1988: 60–61). The economic policies favoring protectionism, touted as nationalist in the previous decades, combined with the slowdown in manufacturing and rise in population to lower the GNP per capita (Tarling 1992: 160). Imports of machinery and other types of industrial equipment, conversely, increased from 10 percent in the 1950s to around 20 percent by the mid-1960s, while exports struggled to keep pace (Dolan 1993: 175). Moreover, even when the industries controlled by the elite were thriving fantastically, their workers did not receive the trickle down benefits of profit.

With such lack of employment and opportunity, many Filipinos expanded their net globally and took advantage of relaxed immigration laws in North America. This pattern of working overseas was to continue to expand, and limited contract work for construction began under the Marcos dictatorship.[6] Until the present, the prevalence of overseas workers has shaped both the economy and society of the Philippine nation. It is in this context of mass migration and the constant movement back and forth of people and money that globalization and the Philippines are often considered. In fact, the term *diaspora* has been applied to the Philippines primarily because of mass migrations forced by economic needs that the country cannot sustain internally. At the same time, globalization should also be understood as a process of continuous contact of people, things, and ideas within the region; the irrevocable impact of multiple colonizations; and the explosive spreading of information through technology from radio to television to the Internet. From this perspective, globalization is nothing new, even if rates of transference have increased exponentially. In the Philippines, nationalist music, literature, painting, and all other artistic and performative media express this transnational point of view. Likewise, the larger debate over the role of the arts in the Philippine nation, spurred by the extravagant expenditures on the CCP, was also broad-ranging and based in cosmopolitan, or perhaps Western-influenced, perspectives. The philosophy that arts comprised the soul of a society helped validate the need for the center and Imelda Marcos's attention to it, and supporters needed only to look to the West for idealized models.

In defense of the center and as a larger statement of ideology about the arts, the first president of the CCP, Jaime Zobel de Ayala, commented on the need to nourish the arts at all times and not only during periods of prosperity. He began a speech before the Rotary Club of Makati-West by quoting John F. Kennedy, "I see little of more importance to the future of our country than full recognition of the artist. If art is to nourish the roots of our culture, society must set the artist free to follow his vision." Then, continuing in his own words, "Art, like virtue, is its own reward; it is inevitably degraded if it is justified in utilitarian terms.... Many of us have long held the hope that facilities be provided which will make the enjoyment of the arts available to a greater number of our people. I, for one, have always believed that the arts are not only for the privileged few—the highly educated, the sophisticated or the affluent" (de Ayala 1969: 21). The hunger of the soul and the hunger of the body were pitted against one another in the battle over the CCP, and the elites held ground on the issue of the arts as paramount for the still young nation.

More than theoretical, the question of government funding for the arts is especially critical in a country like the Philippines that cannot avail itself of as many resources as more wealthy nations. For Filipinos, the CCP posed a difficult scenario, as for some, the basic problem of physical needs not met seemed to outweigh the need for a national theater. Furthermore, even if one were to agree that culture could not be measured in utilitarian terms but was vital nonetheless, it was unclear as yet whether the CCP's programming would be broad-based enough to serve the wider good. There were those who argued that the money could have been better spent constructing a national theater for performing arts and then enriching the National Museum or National Library instead of creating an entirely new cultural center. Situated as it was in Manila, the idea that there could even be a national center revealed the urban bias of those in power. Yet, the urban sprawl of Manila and its environs could also be seen as the place most in need of a revived and perhaps manufactured traditional culture.

In many societies, that which is deemed traditional culture is perceived as a psychologically stabilizing factor for the individual and society at large in opposition to the destructive effects of urbanization. For instance in Puerto Rico of the 1950s, "Operation Serenity" promoted a romanticized version of the traditional past "to provide a sense of spiritual balance to a society threatened by the rapid social change caused by the new economic policies" (Davila 1997: 34). In such a role, the support of a particular kind of culture could be viewed as integral to a healthy economic movement of development, and therefore funding must be devoted to it. And yet despite what could be read as positive intentions to protect the populace, in this case, the people in government held the power as arbiters of taste and culture.

In the case of the CCP, the government and the elite were funding a cultural center whose agenda, beyond Imelda's passionate rhetoric, remained to be seen. After all is said and done, it would be misleading to pretend that the debate of the CCP involved the general population. While argument served politicians and discussion was rampant in the parlors of the "Haves," the "Have-Nots" of Manila had to have been more concerned with feeding themselves and caring for their families. While the majority of poorest Filipinos live in the countryside, there were and are a vast number of urban poor in cities as well. In Manila, they live in slum areas or as squatters without electricity or running water. Despite many having a high school education and/or technical skills, most are underemployed, informally employed, or not employed at all. Thus, the inauguration of the CCP, a glamorous "must-attend" of the social elite, was little more than a distant flash of light as glimpsed from the shanty of a squatter family by the bay.

A Second Term Won, the Center Unveiled

Foreshadowed by the bloody elections of 1967, Marcos won his reelection in 1969 through killings, coercion, vote buying, and other methods of tampering on a massive scale. He spent millions of dollars to determine the outcome, desiring not merely to win but also to thoroughly dismantle the ambitions of his opponent from Cebu, Sergio Osmeña, Jr. (Bonner 1987: 76–77).[7] His campaign included an array of propagandistic media artifacts extolling Marcos's virtues, including a Hollywood-style movie about his supposed heroism as a guerilla during World War II and another biography. In the end, the rigged result was overwhelmingly lopsided, with Marcos garnering some 74 percent of the vote. The fraud had been perpetrated with a heavy hand, but the need for it reportedly left Marcos despondent. According to the investigative reporter Sterling Seagrave, "Ferdinand could falsify the ballots, but he could not change the realization that he had really lost" (1988: 219). In the meantime, Imelda Marcos, assured of the stability of her position, kept focus on her personal projects. The Marcoses had become a kind of monarchy of the land, both charismatic and feared. The folklorist Francisco Demetrio contextualizes their position in the Philippines with a personal anecdote about a well-known popular music group arriving in Manila and failing to meet with Imelda Marcos at the presidential palace. Newspapers reported the slight as an egregious affront to Filipino hospitality. "The interesting point was that the people identified disrespect to the First Lady as disrespect to the entire country. And why? Because she was the wife of the President. And for them the President represented the country. In other words, their concept of the President was that of a King" (Demetrio 1978: 288–289).

The same year that Marcos held the inauguration for his second term, the Cultural Center of the Philippines opened to the public. It was September 8, 1969, and as is common for houses, buildings, and cars in the Philippines, the building was blessed to keep away evil spirits. The presiding priest recited an invocation printed in the inaugural day program that likened the Son of God to a "work of art." He asked for blessings on the "noble edifice by which we hope to preserve and transmit the cultural heritage of our people," and prayed that the CCP would "reflect, re-echo and reveal the goodness, truth and beauty" of God. Afterward, those present proceeded through the halls as each important room was sprinkled with holy water.

The center contains a main theater designed to seat 2,000 people, a small experimental theater in the basement with 440 seats, a restaurant with a bar, offices, recording rooms, rehearsal spaces, and dressing rooms. Also on the grounds, the Museum and Art Gallery complex included the Painting and Sculpture Hall, the Colonial Art Pavilion, the De Santos Pavilion specifically housing that family's art collection, the Filipino Muslim Pavilion, and a Library for Art and Music. Finally, under pressure from Mrs. Marcos, the

Folk Arts Theater sprouted up in a shocking seventy-seven days with seating for 10,000 people and in time for the Miss Universe pageant. Currently, the Folk Arts Theater has two stated cultural goals: to preserve, promote, and develop the traditional folk arts of the Philippines; and to encourage the presentation of contemporary and popular theater in the hope that it may eventually become the folk arts of this generation. The enormous capacity has indeed turned the space into a venue for popular music concerts as well as other large-scale ballets, plays, and folk dance exhibitions.

Carlos Francisco designed the logo for the CCP, a design of three Malay-script Ks arranged in a triangle containing the acronym for the motto of the center. The letters stand for the words *katotohanan* (truth), *kagandahan* (beauty), and *kabutihan* (goodness). This KKK quickly calls to mind a similar acronym, the KKK of the insurrectionists against Spain at the end of the nineteenth century. The long version of their name, Kataas-taasang, Kagalanggalangang Katipunan ng mga Anak ng Bayan (Most High, Most Venerable Society of the Sons of the People), is normally shortened to Katipunan, and their insignia includes the letters KKK (de Viana 2006: 21).[8] More than their limited historical role, the Katipunan are representative of revolutionary Filipino nationalism as an ideology, sentiment, and character-defining trait of the nation. While many adjective nominalizations in Tagalog begin with the letter K, the parallel between the CCP logo and motto and Philippine nationalism is quite obvious. The nationalist intent of the CCP, then, has clear ties to the longer nationalist tradition of the Philippines, giving it symbolic validation as a cultural actor and not just a venue for performance.

Beyond the motto, the more concrete goals of the center (written after the establishment of the center and not before) also exhibit a nationalist thrust toward the promotion of Philippine arts and provide for an international presence:

(1) to invite foreign artists to perform and exhibit in the Philippines
(2) to sponsor and assist local performances
(3) to establish branches in all regions of the Philippines
(4) to draft and implement plans: (a) to provide enabling scholarships for young talents to undergo intensive study locally and abroad; (b) to assist music, dance, drama, and art education efforts; (c) to promote research and related activities in the area of indigenous music, dance, and folk traditions and the collection, preservation and dissemination of resulting materials together with commissions for composers, choreographers, and playwrights to experiment on native themes as the basis

of larger works of Philippine identity; (d) to organize and present cultural groups and assist in the staging of plays, concerts, operas, dance exhibits; (e) to hold annual competitions for young soloists and young choral and instrumental groups in association with established sponsors; (f) to manage annual rondalla and grand-choral contests; (g) to conduct playwriting and verse-writing contests; (h) to perform commissioned works; (i) to tour performing groups through the provinces and schools; (j) to publish, record, and video-tape for archival purposes, and for presentation by radio and television programs for the greater national audiences. Such are the activities of the Cultural Center of the Philippines.[9]

Imelda Marcos titled herself active chairman along with Harvard-trained businessman Jaime Zobel de Ayala (later to become president of the CCP) as executive director. The Board of Trustees, established by Imelda during construction of the CCP, included Marcos crony Juan Ponce Enrile, a Harvard-educated lawyer; Father Horacio de la Costa, a Jesuit scholar with a Ph.D. from Harvard; I. P. Soliongco, a professor at the University of the Philippines and columnist for the *Manila Chronicle*; Andrés Soriano, Jr., a businessman trained at the Wharton School; another businessman named Ernesto Rufino; and Antonio Madrigal, a businessman from a prominent Filipino family. Antonio Quintos, a practicing lawyer and executive director of the Cultural Foundation of the Philippines, served as the deputy director. The director of the new museum, painter Roberto Chabet, received a grant to study curating in the United States. Finally, Lucrecia Kasilag (see chapter 1) began her stint with the CCP as the theater director.[10] From the aforementioned list, it becomes apparent that the initial guidance of the CCP came not only from prominent Filipinos in business and from the arts, but also that many of them had some education in the United States. While in and of itself, this kind of training does not imply that the center would be run following a particular American model, the backgrounds of some members of the administration point to at least some kind of influence from life abroad.

Right from the opening, the center was subject to cries of elitism. Artists who feared that the mere architecture of the CCP would be too intimidating a complex to attract the general (read poor) population were also to be disappointed by the expense of programs (see figure 3.1). "While [Imelda] made public promises of discounts for the poor, her $1 and $2 tickets still exceeded most Manilans' daily wage" (Ellison 1988: 92). Without access, what good could the center accomplish for the poor? A writer for the *Philippines Free*

Press quipped, "The masses have not become, and will not become, cultured just because, hallelujah, the Cultural Center is here" (Salazar 1969: 14). From a broader perspective than ticket price, not only was the center inaccessible to the masses, the debate itself seemed to matter only to the intellectual and cultural elite. Nowhere is there evidence of massive rallies by the poor to protest the expenditure of money on the CCP (although one might assume government spending was certainly a ripe topic of conversation among pedicab drivers waiting for fares or over the dinner table).[11] All the letters pro and con appearing in the dailies were written by artists or members of the cultural community belonging to the middle and upper echelons of society. The voice of the regular "man on the street," or "Juan de la Cruz" as he sometimes is called in the Philippines, was noticeably absent. On opening night, artists marched outside in protest as scores of Manila's socialites shuffled through the lobby marveling at the grand architecture and sumptuous decor of architect Leandro Locsin's building. To counterbalance the protesters outside, Imelda allegedly paid her own picketers to carry picket signs inside and outside that praised her and the center. Journalists commented that "placard bearers in work clothes moved about the fashionably gowned guests" (Carunungan 1969: 2) as if nothing could be more natural underneath the ornate capiz and glass chandeliers.

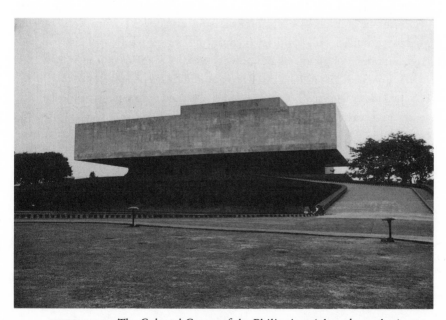

FIGURE 3.1. The Cultural Center of the Philippines (photo by author)

United States ambassador Henry Byroade remarked, "That center makes our Kennedy Center look cheap. The Filipino architects did a good job" (Ellison 1988: 92). He was joined that night by then California governor Ronald Reagan and his family, all of whom stayed at Malacañan Palace, the official residence of the Philippine president. Notably, Richard Nixon did not make the trip. By this time, Nixon had succeeded Johnson as president of the United States. He too gave Marcos his support, primarily to maintain a grip on the Philippines as America's greatest ally in Southeast Asia, renewed as a critical region for the United States during the Vietnam War. The Philippine military had been defined and developed under American rule, and Filipino guerilla fighters (with or without Marcos, depending upon one's point of view) had fought alongside the United States during World War II. Even after colonialism, the military relationship continued, with the United States funding the government through rent for their military bases in the Philippines and through aid to support the Philippine forces. The two nations shared a Mutual Defense Treaty and an annual joint exercise called Balikatan. As public relations between the two countries became less publicly intertwined, the mutuality in military could no longer be counted upon. In 1959, the Military Bases Agreement shortened the term originally allotted to the United States, so that either nation could end the agreement after 1991, while in 1965, the Philippines passed amendments to allow for greater jurisdiction over the bases in criminal and civil matters (Dolan 1993: 276). Consequently, by the time Marcos was in power, both Johnson and Nixon could not be assured of Philippine assistance in the Vietnam War. Indeed, Marcos promised only limited nonfighting forces while still insisting on large amounts of financial aid, much to the chagrin of the Americans. Although a U.S. governor seemed too low-ranking a personage to stand in for U.S. president Richard Nixon, Reagan's presence did manage to validate the center in a way that only foreign influence could and in a way that Imelda craved (ibid. 93). Moreover, the relationship between the Reagans and the Marcoses borne this night was to have far-reaching implications in the future of the dictatorship. For others, however, Governor Reagan's solution of smashing protests at Berkeley with National Guardsmen made him a darkly appropriate choice of U.S. representative at the opening of the Marcoses' CCP (Carunungan 1969: 2). In any event, on inaugural night, Imelda appeared nonplussed that Nixon did not grace her affair and proceeded to extend the warmest hospitality to the Reagans.

Blissful in her element, Imelda gave a stirring inaugural speech to dedicate the building. Excerpts of the speech are included here in order that her own rhetoric reveal her intentions and her beliefs.

Should this building stand the test of time so that our children's children, unto the tenth generation, will one day gaze at its beauty, the future shall call us fortunate. But more important than this, is that, until the dust of its last brick shall have been washed away by the ocean tides, his Center shall serve as a shrine of the Filipino spirit. It shall be our Parthenon built in a time of hardship, a spring-source of our people's living conviction on the oneness of our heritage....

We are young and struggling to understand ourselves, trying to construct the nobler meaning of our race. Our greatest strength lies in being truly what we are; by nature and by grace, one people; by fortune and by fate, Filipinos.... It is the purpose of this Center to enrich the minds and spirit of our people and to foster among other people a true understanding of the Filipino self....

This then, is the charge that we lay upon ourselves today, and upon all who follow us: to keep this Center as a treasure-house of the Filipino soul, that our works in stone and story, in dance and drama, in music and color may remain, for all time, a testament to the goodness, the truth, and the beauty of a historic race.[12]

The rhetoric of Imelda's speech contained more than just sentimental images of the Filipino soul. Her words belie the underlying ideology that the cultural mission of her center could help to unify the Philippines through development of a national-scale cultural identity. A national identity is possible only when one becomes aware of the Philippines as a sovereign nation and only when one can perceive this nation as having identifiable internal commonalities that differentiate it from other nations. While sovereignty on the global stage serves political ends, the internal understanding of Filipinos as a race within that nation relies on a sense of cultural nationalism. While cultural nationalism and political nationalism may be distinguished conceptually from one another, they are not exclusive to one another. The concerns of cultural nationalism—that is to say, what expressions, arts, or traditions are representative of the nation — are subject to politics. Likewise, political nationalism may be performed culturally, supported by the conviction that culture is a unifying force, or described as a distinguishing trait of the national body. Just as they had used folklore such as the myth of Malakas and Maganda (the Filipino Adam and Eve) to serve their own political ends, the Marcoses conflated cultural nationalism with political nationalism in order to more firmly entrench their right to rule.

Ferdinand Marcos realized that the rhetoric of nationalism could be a tool for enriching his own power both inside and outside the country. For instance, in negotiations with the United States over parity rights, Marcos pulled the nationalist card as leverage during talks on renewal of the agreement. The original agreement had been negotiated quite unfairly in favor of American business interests, since the Philippines at the time had only recently ceased being a colony and a commonwealth of the United States. Instead of renewing the agreement, Marcos ensured that the percentage of a business run in the Philippines that could be owned by an American dropped from 60 to 40 percent, giving majority ownership to Filipinos. As many Filipino businesses were granted to Marcos's cronies, none could say for sure whether nationalism or cronyism was the stronger motivation (Hamilton-Paterson 1998: 312).

The Marcoses simply provided another voice to the long running and deeply felt debate on Filipino nationalism. As revealed earlier, Filipino nationalists, from scholars to politicians to composers to choreographers, had long grasped the connections between nationalism, culture, identity, and the battle against colonial mentality. Furthermore, they understood the actual diversity of the islands and how problematic forging a national identity could be in the face of divergence and a history of schism. In a treatise on cultural nationalism in the Philippines, Hosillos noted a "paradoxical quality," arising from the diversity of the nation itself. She furthered that Filipino nationalism has always been directly related to elite conceptions garnered from Western concepts, including patronage of the arts (Hosillos 1970: 307–314).

Imelda's actions make it clear that she understood in her own way how purveying nationalism would enhance her role as the ultimate patroness of the Filipino arts. On the one hand, she tried to ensure herself a place in history not only through the shaping and "elevation" of Filipino culture, but through her Perón-esque projects for social welfare as well.[13] The idea that she could lift the soul as well as heal the body had great appeal to her personally as well as for political reasons. Still, her ideas about "high art" and Filipino culture were so imbued with Western ideals that it became difficult to see through her eyes where a colonial mentality ended and where Filipino nationalism began. Everything from cultural performances to the menus for Malacañan Palace fetes displayed a mix of Filipino and Western reflective of the country's past. Yet, the tendency toward seeing the West as superior to the East was often evident. One biographer gives a telling example, stating, "On January 31, 1975, for example, the Marcoses gave a dinner in honour of the delegates of an Afro-Asian writers' symposium. There was a printed program of African, Indonesian, Chinese and Filipino songs, plus Philippine folk dances. The bill of fare, beautifully printed, did not offer much in the ethnic line, however. It ran as follows: Le Consommé Double a L'Essence de

Tomate, Le Filet de Lapu-Lapu Amandine, Chablis, Le Tendre Coeur de Boeuf Cordon Rouge" (Hamilton-Paterson 1998: 339). Imelda Marcos's patronage of international, and particularly Western talent, and the disparity in pay between foreigners and Filipinos, became well known. Anecdotally, one of my consultants recalled with a combination of annoyance and amusement how Imelda would present a Filipino performing group in the same production as a Western one, but that she would get up and talk during the Filipino performance after sitting attentively through the Western one. In effect, Imelda exhibited a colonial mentality that embraced Western culture over Filipino culture.

Would the CCP be able to chip at the mentality through patronage of the Filipino musician and artist? Auspiciously, the opening of the brand new Cultural Center of the Philippines in 1969 was heralded by a production written, composed, choreographed, and performed by Filipinos—the *Dularawan*. The theatrical event was based on a mythical-historical event in Philippine history, with music supplied by an orchestra of bamboo instruments and gongs from the Philippines and other countries of Southeast Asia. The composer, Lucrecia Kasilag, drew from her own collection of instruments gathered during travels around the country and abroad. So varied and, at the time, exotic were the instruments for the *Dularawan* ensemble that the collection began a museum exhibit of traditional Asian instruments, which is still on display at the CCP some thirty years later. Notably, in the liner notes for the recording of *Dularawan*, Imelda Marcos is credited with the idea of using indigenous instruments for the theatrical presentation, and not Kasilag. Attempting to create a new model for the Philippine arts, *Dularawan* experimented not only with musical sound, but also with the very mode of presentation, utilizing two or more artists—an actor, a dancer, and a singer—to simultaneously portray a single character.

The myth, popularly known as the *Maragtas* epic, was first published by an Augustinian priest in 1902 and was supposed to have been based on an ancient manuscript, though there is no evidence that the manuscript ever existed. In the tale, ten chiefs and their families arrived in the Philippines from Borneo after escaping from an evil ruler. Finding inhabitants already there, the Malays exchanged a golden hat and necklace with the Filipino Atis for their lands. The Atis moved into the mountains, and the lowlands became the domain of Malays. As a result, these Malays are representative as the ancestors of lowland Filipinos who became Christianized under Spanish colonial rule. At the same time, the congenial relations between the lowlanders and highlanders exhibited in the tale belie the inequitable relations extant in real-life interactions between the Philippine government and the upland tribal groups. Instead, the staging allowed audiences to relive a national myth as implicated in the washing away of guilt as the Thanksgiving myth of the United States, in which Native Americans come to the aid of beleaguered Pilgrims. As a kind of genesis story, the *Dulawaran* was a fitting inaugural performance for the CCP, where culture could be controlled through institutionalization, and the imagined personification of nation could come to terms with its own difficult histories.[14]

Performances at the Cultural Center, Performers for the Nation

In its first year after inauguration, the CCP included both an international festival and a Philippine festival, both revolving around music. Following three consecutive nights in which *Dularawan* was performed for the express pleasure of invited guests, the CCP presented the Grand Ballet Classique from France accompanied by the in-house Philippine Symphony Orchestra. For the next two months, the halls of the CCP played host to performing groups from India, the Republic of China, the United Kingdom, Japan, and Australia. In addition, the programming choices of soloists from Germany, Israel, and the United States—such as Klaus Hellwig, Mindru Katz, and Eugene Istomin—revealed a penchant for classical pianist virtuosos. Because the performances in the first month were so strongly dedicated to international artists, critics of the CCP renewed their arguments against the center and against Imelda Marcos. They declared that the CCP was "hardly intended for the advancement of Philippine culture, but rather to entice international artists with whom Imelda wanted to cavort" (Bonner 1987: 71). As active chairman of the center, Imelda involved herself with programming enough to ensure her role as the First Lady of Culture. She saw herself as a visionary and a worker, tirelessly arbitrating between government and community to promulgate a national cultural program. She wielded influence over the board and involved herself with invitations to foreign artists and special events at which she would be present, but the CCP's administrative staff handled the day-to-day affairs, management, and regular programming.

The Philippine Festival opened with another presentation of *Dularawan* in October, followed by two symphony concerts of works commissioned from Filipino composers. In November the center featured an original ballet entitled *Mirinisa* with music and choreography also by Filipinos, and in December the festival closed with a commissioned *sarswela*. The first concert of the Philippine Festival featured Alfredo Buenaventura's "Philippine Panorama"; Lucino Sacramento's "Violin Concerto in E Minor"; and Sister Maria Rosalina

Abejo's "Oratorio Pagtubos." Three days afterward, the second symphony concert showcased Abejo's "Panahon" song cycle; Rodolfo Cornejo's "Third Piano Concerto"; and Felipe de Leon's "Awit ng Buhay," a symphonic drama for voice and orchestra. This rash of commissioned works by Filipinos was unprecedented in Philippine history. In later years, one journalist would observe with approval, "Some 17 symphonies and 18 chamber works have been commissioned by the Center during the five-year period of the program. According to the CCP, these activities have been programmed to generate participation from the grassroots level and to discover, assist and develop talents and create greater opportunities for individual and national self-expression in cultural affairs" (Atabug 1978: 20).

Hence, the Philippine Music Festivals were an ideological boon for musicians and professional Filipino vocalists. While some could argue that the medium of presentation was Western in form and that the music was essentially Western-based as well, the use of Filipino themes by native-born composers lent a sense of nationalism to these symphonic affairs. In presenting commissioned works by Filipino composers as the crux of the Philippine Festival, there existed a clear message of nationalistic pride in the performing arts. As we have seen, nationalism itself is never a simple affair, and in the 1960s there was no escape in discourse from Marcos-era politics. The Philippine Music Festivals at the CCP could evoke pride in Filipino identity through the achievements of prominent composers, while at the same time promoting the Marcoses as caretakers of a narrowly defined national culture of the Philippines. According to conventional wisdom, which was already conventional in the early days of the CCP, Filipino culture is a blend of East and West, reflecting a history of colonialism, trade, migration, and assimilation. Sometimes certain aspects of a performance piece might be identifiable as primarily Asian or Western, though even these assertions were open to debate. For instance, a journalist reviewing the ballet *Mirinisa* observed that it was Asian in its hand movements and "occidental" as a ballet. Yet, "above all, *Mir-i-nisa* is Filipino—neither western nor eastern, but Filipino, distinctly Filipino" (Hernandez 1969). That one might distinguish East from West is not uncommon, even if the exercise can be somewhat arbitrary in its methodology. That one might distinguish Filipino from "Oriental" or even from Western highlights a certain cultural ambiguity that has enriched the archipelago throughout its history but that often confounds cultural critics.

In its first decade, the CCP presented such a wide variety of artists and genres that it would be a fallacy to conclude that, even as a national institution with the patronage of the state, the center was only a tool for propaganda. A better overview acknowledges state influence in regard to funding,

Imelda Marcos's personal interest in particular artists, and the everyday inter-play of hundreds of individuals who ran the institution and those who per-formed in it. Because the various venues of the CCP were open to anyone who could pay, as long as they were not particularly oppositional to the Marcos government, the role of class in society is as much a factor as politics. Furthermore, as in most arenas of Filipino society, "getting in" was often a matter of knowing the right people. In this scenario, the composer or musi-cian was left to negotiate micro- as well as national-level politics in order to gain the prestige of performing at the CCP. Once inside, there was no obliga-tion for the performer to pursue a nationalist agenda, nor even a state-promoting one.

Sometimes performing at the CCP was a matter of pride—a chance to prove one's mettle as an artist by gaining access to a national venue. A young artist at the time, the classical guitarist Michael Dadap described how impres-sive the CCP was at the time of its building.

> When the CCP came along, I thought it was the greatest thing to hap-pen to the cultural scene in the Philippines. At the time, as a student, I felt the sentiment that the CCP could not really reach out to the common *tao* (people) was very valid. But luckily at the time the economy was very good. I was able as a student/professional to see con-certs of great guitarists, but very few Filipinos. There were rumors at that time that if you were a Filipino artist that you were treated differ-ently. Not much has changed. But anyway, we were "gaga" over the architecture. (2000)

Ding Pajaron commented wryly that others who professed political opposi-tion to the Marcoses were still drawn to the center. "When Imelda Marcos asks you to perform, a lot of artists are dying to have the opportunity to per-form" (2000).

In contrast, another artist asserted, "The Cultural Center tended to impose its wishes on the artists enjoying its patronage, thus constricting their activ-ities and virtually dictating upon them" (Lanot 1969: 20). Many artists were never invited to the CCP as a consequence of their statements against the Marcos government (and some of these same people took positions of power at the CCP after the Marcoses left the country). Yet, for avowedly apolitical and politically ambiguous artists, the center offered the chance to participate in a national forum for the arts in hitherto unprecedented ways.

While the performances at the CCP in its first few years, and even in years to come, were quite diverse, the Marcoses were able to commission a number of songs favorable to themselves and their social and political programs throughout the years. For instance, Lucrecia Kasilag composed "Sa Inang Bayang Pilipinas (For the Motherland)" for the inauguration of President Marcos's second term in 1969. The song appeared again during the inauguration of the Cultural Center of the Philippines, effectively tying the office of the presidency to the CCP through music.

Martial Law and the Birth of the New Society

When Marcos assumed the presidency for his second term in 1969, he presaged the change of the coming years in his inaugural address by warning, "The next few years will lay the basis for a reformation—a revolutionary reformation of our international and domestic policies—of our political, social, legal and economic systems.... It is our destiny to transform this nation; we begin by transforming ourselves first."[15] Within three years, the nation would be placed under martial law, Marcos would become dictator, and the New Society would supersede the Third Republic. It began with several months of unrest among students and the socialist and communist political Left, lasting from January to March of 1970 and known as the First Quarter Storm. In the next two years the violence continued, including the assassination of candidates from the opposition party (in a rally that Benigno Aquino would miss) and a series of bombings. Marcos decried the anarchy. Critics blamed Marcos for creating the conditions under which he could assume more power.

Marcos declared martial law at 7:30 P.M. on September 23, 1972, appearing on television and on the radio to announce Proclamation No. 1081 (it had actually been signed two days beforehand). That previous night, the military raided various sites in the city to round up thousands of anti-Marcos politicians, including Benigno Aquino, student activists, Communists, journalists, intellectuals, and any others who posed some kind of threat to the status quo. And yet, surprisingly to outsiders, martial law in and of itself was not immediately disagreeable to many Filipinos. The historian Stanley Karnow points out that Filipinos at first showed little consternation over the declaration of martial law, since order seemed to prevail. "Virtually nobody mourned the closed legislature.... Nor was there much indignation over censorship of the press, which had formerly been sensational to the point of licentiousness.... The prospect of sound, honest government suffused citizens with a new sense of civic virtue" (Karnow 1989: 381). Yet, like many failed promises, martial law's benefits soon gave way to the underlying corruption of the Marcos regime, and what had at first appeared to be a boon revealed itself as smokescreen.[16] With the military at their beck and call and a variety of cronies lapping up the largesse, the Marcoses continued on their political junket for the next fourteen years until the People Power Revolution of 1986.

During the early part of the 1970s, construction continued around the main building of the CCP, and Imelda's ceaseless efforts to create landmarks in her name became a popular joke that labeled her as afflicted with an "edifice complex" (Lico 2003).[17] In addition to the many buildings of the CCP complex, she ordered the construction of the Philippine Center for International Trade and Exhibition (Philcite), the Coconut Palace, and the Film Center. The Film Center has been notorious since its very beginnings because, like the Folk Arts Theater, it was quite hastily constructed to meet a deadline—in this case, the first Manila International Film Festival—but with tragic consequences. "The speed of the project was so hectic that serious corners were cut in its construction. On the fateful night of November 17, 1981, the newly poured top floor collapsed onto shift workers sleeping below in the auditorium. To this day nobody is certain how many workers died in the Film Theatre and it is said that many are still there, entombed in its walls and floors" (Hamilton-Paterson 1998: 346).[18]

Meanwhile, work in the CCP building itself continued. In 1971 the Little Theater of the CCP located below the main hall was inaugurated with a production of Virginia Moreno's *The Onyx Wolf*. Speaker of the U.S. House of Representatives Carl Albert and his wife served as sponsors for the new hall. A more intimate and practical space for smaller groups, the Little Theater served an important function for the members of the community who did not require the cavernous main theater with its split-floor orchestra lift and large capacity seating. Instead, the Little Theater was to become a home for many local productions and cultural programs sponsored by the CCP, from lecture demonstrations and solo recitals to film showings and music-drama pieces. Over time, the theater also became home base for Teatro Pilipino, an ensemble culturally significant for its pursuit of native works and foreign plays translated into Filipino.

The year 1972, the same year that Marcos declared martial law, was a banner year for the CCP: a total of 272 performances took place and a concerted push toward cultural preservation and promotion began developing. Given more freedom to pursue their own ends, the Marcoses were no longer hamstrung by the checks and balances (weak as they may have been) imposed by traditional government in the Philippines. On October 15, 1972, Marcos signed Presidential Decree No. 15 declaring the CCP a nonmunicipal public corporation. This decree separated the CCP from the Office of the President, but the complex was still to be funded from the public treasury. Seeking other ways in which to fund the arts, the CCP administration opened the five-star luxury Philippine Plaza Hotel in 1976 to coincide with the IMF-World Bank Conference held at the Philippine International Convention Center, also a part of the CCP land. In addition, throughout the decade the CCP engaged in a number of private investments with questionable "loans" to businesses that were not uncovered until the Marcoses lost power in 1986. As an example, the CCP invested 4 million pesos (almost $92,000 in 2008) in a private Philippine company called Blackgold that was supposed to promote Filipino artists. As it turned out, the nephew of President Marcos was a member of the board of directors of the parent company of Blackgold, darkening the transaction of money from Imelda's CCP as ethically questionable (A. L. de Leon 1986: 14). During the 1970s, the murky financing of the CCP followed the general trend of other Marcos controlled institutions. Serving as either a front for Marcos and his cronies in some cases or as a legitimate investing corporation in others, the money flowed behind an opaque veneer.

The Marcoses had another use for the CCP in 1972. As the year drew to a close, just a few months into martial law, Imelda Marcos sponsored a gala fashion show to be held in the main auditorium. Featured in the program were two new pieces by Filipino composer Felipe de Leon that gave tribute to the Marcoses' "New Society." Entitled "Bagong Pagsilang" (meaning "new birth," but the translation is often given as "March of the New Society") and "Bagong Lipunan" (Hymn of the New Society), the songs became staple nationalistic pieces in schools across the country during martial law.[19] In a book entitled *Mga Awit Sa Bagong Lipunan* (Songs of the New Society), written by unnamed propagandists, Imelda Marcos is extolled in three full pages at the beginning. The first page declares in very large print, "Mrs. Imelda Romualdez Marcos, First Lady of the Philippines, PATRONESS OF THE ARTS," all underlined with a flourish. The following page contains a black-and-white picture of Imelda in a formal *terno* (Filipino traditional gown) with a young violinist, while the facing page displays a message from her with her signature on the bottom. It reads, in part, "Music reflects the yearnings and aspirations of a people. It is the language that unites the feelings of the community, no matter in what form or nuance it may be expressed" (1974: 7).

The notes for "Bagong Pagsilang" describe the tune as "energetic, contagious and full of optimism, reflecting the ideals and objectives of the New Society" (there is no citation as to who wrote the notes in the book). Commissioned by Imelda Marcos, the march first premiered in 1971 as part of the First Lady's "Green Revolution" project, a social initiative urging Filipinos outside of rural areas to plant their own gardens. The piano and

vocal score is a 6/8 march marked "Con spirito," and the left hand is dominated by open octaves (no chords) outlining the duple time. In the second
section of the song, de Leon uses the same strategy he did in "Awit sa Paglikha
ng Bagong Pilipinas (Song for the Creation of a New Philippines)," the
anthem written during the Japanese occupation, quoting musical snippets
from the national anthem of the Philippines. The lyrics by Levi Celerio read
as follows:

> Ang gabi'y nagmaliw nang ganap
> At lumipas na ang magdamag
> Madaling araw ay nagdiriwang
> May umagang namasdan
> Ngumiti na ang pagasa
> Sa umagang anong ganda
>
> May bagong silang
> May bago nang buhay
> Bagong bansa, bagong galaw
> sa Bagong Lipunan
> Nagbabago ang lahat tungo sa pagunlad
> At ating itanghal
> Bagong Lipunan
>
> English translation:
> The evening has completely ended
> And the whole night has elapsed
> Dawn is celebrating
> There is morning to behold
> Hope now smiled
> At a glorious morning
>
> There is a new birth
> There is a new life
> New nations, new movements
> In the New Society
> All is changing towards prosperity
> And let us display
> New Society[20]

In "Bagong Pagsilang," the musical aesthetics of the catchy and stirring
march signify martial and patriotic attributes that are easily legible to

Filipinos, first, because the band tradition has been well established in the Philippines since the Spanish colonial period. Bands have long been commonplace, despite the cost of instruments. Second, people recognized the name of the composer, and he had, by this time, already written a large array of recognizable songs crafted in traditional styles (see chapter 1). Third, de Leon inserted a short bridge near the end of the piece based on the opening theme of "Lupang Hinirang (Pambansang Awit ng Pilipinas)," the national anthem of the Philippines (see figures 3.2 and 3.3). The reference is clear: the New Society is equated with traditional patriotism, and patriotism is made synonymous with nationalism. While one might find the music to be an oddly rousing choice for the inauguration of a fashion show, the event as a whole was specifically timed to relieve tensions arising from the imposition of martial law through spectacle. Of course, the public would not be invited to attend. At the same time, coverage in the press would have allowed the common person to observe from afar the activities of the well-heeled upper class, with reportage serving as proxy for spectacle. The fashion show featured Filipino talents, but also, and perhaps more important, the ability of the Philippines to stage spectacular events in a world-class showcase like the CCP. The need to validate the nation through state sponsorship of the arts is also evident in the institution of national awards.

Also in 1972, the National Artist Award (*Gawad Artista ng Bayan*) was created by Presidential Proclamation No. 1001 as the highest national recognition of Filipino artists in the fields of music, dance, theater, visual arts, literature, film and media arts, and architecture and design.[21] Though the national award was to be conferred by the Republic of the Philippines as a whole, Proclamation No. 1144 (May 15, 1973) designated the board of trustees of the CCP as the National Artists Awards Committee. Nominees for the award are judged on their creation of a significant body of works that

FIGURE 3.2. Beginning melody of the national anthem of the Philippines, "Lupang Hinirang" (transcription by author)

FIGURE 3.3. Passage from "Bagong Pagsilang" (transcription by author)

has consistently displayed excellence, promoted national cultural identity, and enjoyed broad acceptance nationally or internationally. The nominee's reputation is further validated if he or she has received other awards in the past. Presidential Decree No. 208 of June 7, 1973, granted a special fund for the recipient of the National Artist Award, including a cash award of 10,000 pesos, a life pension of 2,000 pesos per month, medical and hospitalization benefits, life insurance through the Government Service Insurance System, and the expenses of a state funeral. The money for such expenditure was to come from a special account in the annual General Appropriations Act, beginning with 500,000 pesos from the National Treasury. By earmarking public treasury money for certain lifetime expenses of an artist, the award was at least one measure of the state's mandated sponsorship of the arts. Moreover, since very few could attain such an honor, the conferment of national prestige on an individual was unprecedented. The CCP became the source of a variety of awards, with the National Artist Award at the pinnacle. Unsurprisingly, choosing awardees invited heated debate, political wrangling, and personal power plays. While on the whole, the awards have been distributed in predictable ways, a few have fueled controversy, appearing to have been furthered by the personal agendas of people in power rather than judged on merit alone. The CCP International Artist Award certainly fit into this category.

On June 14, 1973, Imelda lionized the place of foreign artists at the CCP with the institution of the CCP International Artist Award. Like its domestic bedfellow, the award was justified as a practical and tangible recognition of the place of all types of arts in Philippine society. Moreover, it recognized and accepted foreign influence in Philippine culture without the ambivalence of native-oriented nationalism. Significantly, the International Artist Award made a strong antinationalist statement amidst the very nationalist rhetoric often employed by President Marcos, particularly with its first selected recipient. Van Cliburn, an American pianist who played at the CCP on numerous occasions, became the first recipient of the International Artist Award. I do not mean to question Cliburn's musical abilities by pointing out that he was one of Imelda Marcos's favorite pianists and personal visitors. But, beyond his relationship with the First Lady, how is one to assess his individual role in contributing to the cultural heritage of the Philippines? To critique the award is not to critique the artists selected for it, but rather to question the personal motivations in both its creation and execution. The International Artist Award might better be understood as a personal gift from Imelda Marcos as well as a small incentive for international performers to make the long journey to the Philippines to perform at the CCP.

That the CCP supported local arts while valuing Western culture as superior was not, of course peculiar to the Marcoses, but endemic in society. Examples of how this bias manifested in an arts institutional setting include anything from programming to compensation. As an obvious example, even the most highly valued Filipino artists were those who specialized in concert repertoires from the West. A columnist for the *Manila Times*, Anna de Leon wrote, "CCP insiders said before Ballet Philippines could mount a Philippine Ballet, it had to have first a series of Western 'classics' such as *Swan Lake* and *Sleeping Beauty* 'to please Madame,' referring to Imelda Marcos." In the same article, Professor Doreen Fernandez of the Ateneo de Manila University is quoted as saying, "There certainly is a pro-western orientation in many of us. But patronage from the high places of government definitely influenced this orientation in the audiences" (A. L. de Leon 1986: 13). In 1977, when Marcos celebrated his birthday, the biggest cultural event of the year featured foreign luminaries including the dancers Margot Fonteyn and Rudolf Nureyev, and the favorite houseguest of the First Lady, Van Cliburn. By elevating these figures as luminaries above their local counterparts, the Marcoses implicitly supported colonialist cultural trends and gave foreign artists higher cultural "weight." The higher valuation of the West could also be seen in the practice of paying visiting musicians in American dollars while local soloists were paid in Philippine pesos. Though this appears to be a very pragmatic method of payment, it also contributed to perceptions of inequity. Not only was the peso worth less due to exchange rates, but even if the currencies were more equal, the gross amount was still lower for the Filipino.

Still, the CCP did offer opportunities for Filipino artists and, as a national institution, provided validation that no other existing venue in the country could. Artists interested in achieving national prominence, even as a jumping-off point for international touring, could use performances at the CCP as one measurement of their success. As we saw with the inaugural presentation of *Dularawan*, Imelda, in cooperation with the administration and staff of the CCP, supported not only the work by local artists but the idea of Filipino art as well. As Lucrecia Kasilag stated, "The First Lady, Imelda Romualdez Marcos, has been very solicitous about our local artists. 'What you would spend on mediocre foreign artists, allot instead for local talents who need support,' she advised us" (Mananquil 1979: 17). Furthermore, the CCP promoted local arts with a variety of important programs that were established during the first decade. As enumerated in a newspaper article from the late 1970s, the CCP conducted the National Music Competitions for Young Artists (NAMCYA) and Philippine Music Festivals in which commissioned musical works of leading Filipino composers were performed.

NAMCYA, which began in 1972, managed to reach even distant parts of the Philippine Islands with a goal of "discovering" young musical talent through competitions, festivals, and workshops. Because the organization was itself based in Manila (and was intimately connected with the CCP), all "discoveries" were brought to the capital for the final rounds of national competition. While the main categories of competition are choral performance, solo voice and instruments, family ensemble, and chamber music, the idiom can be either Western or Filipino (indigenous or folk), leaving room for a variety of performances and genres. The implied meritocracy and regional equanimity of such an arrangement has contributed to NAMCYA's sustained success throughout the years.

In the five years following the declaration of martial law, the CCP presented 1,254 performances (Atabug 1978: 19). Yet even while the artistic output maintained a high level of productions in terms of numbers, the CCP continued to have trouble attracting a diverse audience. By the end of the decade, the president of the CCP, Lucrecia Kasilag, still dealt with the same difficulties initially experienced by the CCP. The *tao*, or "regular people," had to weigh even the lowest of ticket prices against the cost of food for the family, and the common perception that one had to dress up merely to enter the building inhibited many from coming to shows there. In both justifying the efforts of the CCP and also encouraging more to attend productions there, Lucrecia Kasilag reflected that CCP ticket prices were even cheaper than those for the cinema. She asserted that the Folk Arts Theater attracted more of the "masses," due to lower ticket prices, and that this would carry through to the CCP as well. Nevertheless, she was also critical of the attitude of Filipinos who, if they had the money, would be quite willing to buy tickets to a popular music concert but not one by a classical artist. She blamed this on mass media and the lack of music education (Mananquil 1979: 17).

Kasilag's thoughts on cultural uplift rather than simply music education are illuminating in regard to the institutionalization of culture and the molding of a modern vision for national arts.

> The upper income groups, having been more exposed to culture will naturally be more appreciative of cultural shows than those in the lower income group. But now, 10 years after the CCP opened, we believe there is now a greater consciousness in culture among our people. Our peoples' tastes have been raised, and there is a marked increase among theater goers. I think we are experiencing a renaissance now. We give free shows in the town plazas.... Thus we arouse the rural

folks' curiosity and their desire for the finer things in life. We present shows to lift the audience's level of taste. (ibid.)

The "finer things in life" promulgated by CCP performances included Western arts and Philippine arts ranging from "traditional" to "high." When Lucrecia Kasilag served as president and artistic director of the CCP, the productions reflected not just nationalistic programming but also a great variety of presentations stemming from the artistic visions of many different people. One journalist described the atmosphere during the 1970s in the following way: "[Kasilag's] fellow artistic directors for music, drama, the dance and the visual arts never suffered for lack of independence. That may have given rise to *prima donna* complexes, but overall it was a lively and creditable season she managed from year to year, even if a bit lopsided in favor of the international and the Western, a criticism that grew apace with the years suffered under the Marcoses" (Salanga 1986: 14). Thus, while the CCP is forever linked to the Marcos regime, gaining entrance to its hallowed halls depended greatly on the influence of the president, artistic director, and department heads at the institution.

Moreover, working against a thesis of a single iteration of official nationalism in the arts, the CCP offered its venues for a fee, paving the way for a mishmash of nonpolitical presentations, from restagings of Broadway productions to individual recitals. It was a desirable venue, after all, because performing there bestowed national legitimacy on artists. Many artists knew, too, that access to the CCP could be garnered with the right connections. The notion of "institution as venue" rather than "institution as hegemonic filter" confounds easy summaries of the CCP as a nationalist establishment but gives a more realistic portrait of cultural politics at a national-level organization. Part playground for Imelda when she came calling with foreign dignitaries and personal guests, part long-awaited bastion for the cultural elite, and part patron for Filipino artists, the CCP was and is not beholden to any single master or ideology. Historically, music at the CCP has been both evidence of and agent of the cultural politics that surround the Center and were pervasive in much of Manila society as well. While analogies between social movements and musical production at the CCP can only be painted in broad strokes, the image that emerges reveals much about Filipino identity and Philippine national identity. An even closer scrutiny of certain historical moments and musical events shows myriad ideologies, personalities, and political agendas in contestation and confluence.

Pundits and regular people often point out that politics in the Philippines is a game of personalities more so than ideas. In a wide field of colorful personalities, the Marcoses remain the most notorious both for their length of stay in the national spotlight and the extravagance of their excesses. During their regime, the Marcoses—much as most public figures do—defined official nationalism according to their own agenda in order to fuel a larger goal of institutionalization. The modernization and centralization of industries reflected the modernism of the arts as a commodity that naturally was the purview of the elite, but that also could be cultivated and spread to the masses in the name of cultural nationalism. Significantly, the Marcoses used the CCP as a symbol of their patronage over the arts to legitimate their authority, supported by the mandates of the Philippine constitutions that guided the development of the nation-state.

THEY SIT, COMPOSED AND CONFIDENT, at the front of the St. Hugo of the Hills Catholic Church in a semi-circle, hands on their laps, all attention turned to the choirmaster, Mark Anthony Carpio. He signals them to begin with a deep breath and slight rise of his body and then blends back into the group, ceasing to direct in ways that are easily discernable to the audience. The voices of the Philippine Madrigal Singers (also known as the Philippine Madrigals, the Mads, and the Madz) fill the capacious hall with the "Pater Noster," the Lord's Prayer texted in Latin and composed by a Filipino named John August Pamintuan. Their singing is warm, faint, and gentle at the start, but it builds in volume and intensity, causing an electric sensation to radiate on the surface of my skin. They mesmerize the audience with the sheer precision of their execution—with silky harmonies and perfect intonation, the power of dynamic changes, the crystalline tones of the high sopranos, and the synchronicity of diction and phrasing. Their performance skills extend to facial expressions and body postures, communicating the appropriate emotions for the songs in the repertoire. From art to popular music, their command over the repertoire is prodigious. In tonight's program, the "Pater Noster" is followed by an impressive variety of pieces, including "Revoici venir du printemps" (Claude Le Jeune), "Jagdlied" (Felix Mendelssohn-Bartholdy), "We Beheld Once Again the Stars" (Z. Randall Stroope), "Kaisa-isa Niyan" (Nilo Alcala II), "You Raise Me Up" (Rolf Løvland and Brendan Graham), an adaptation from the "Flower Duet" (Léo Delibes), and "Circle of Life" by Elton John. The audience is particularly enchanted by the recognizable Filipino pieces of the second half, such as "Ano Kaya Ang Kapalaran" (Francisco Santiago), "Cebuano Medley" (arranged by Eudenice Palaruan), "Dahil Sa Iyo" (Mike Velarde), and "Leron, Leron Sinta" (traditional folk song arranged by Annie Nepomuceno). The witty and often challenging arrangements breathe fresh life into the standards, while the familiarity of the tunes evokes both nostalgia and a temporary sense of community among the audience members. In contrast to the mostly somber and focused countenances of the first half, there is smiling and nodding from the audience with each familiar tune of the second half. A few even hum during the simpler parts, and the intermittent rhythmic clapping during lively moments sparks a higher level of energy. The level of engagement and participation in the second half reveals the functions that a visiting group from the Philippines can serve in a diffuse diasporic community.

The audience has come from all around the southeast region of Michigan to the church in wealthy Bloomfield Hills, not only because Filipino performers are a rarity here, but also because the Philippine Madrigal Singers are highly regarded. Some may have come from even greater distances, because the sponsoring organization is a statewide association for Filipinos in the medical field. The event brought together a loosely knit community of Filipino Americans (as well as a healthy sprinkling of non-Filipinos), gathered together for many different reasons, including to express affiliation with the home country, to expose American-born children and spouses to something of the Filipino arts, to fulfill community and organizational obligations, and to play host to the performers. For expatriates who have been away from the country of their birth for a long period of time, visits like these can bring up many feelings of nostalgia and pride.

In his short story "The Day the Dancers Came" (written in 1955 and published in 1967), the famous Filipino writer Bienvenido Santos describes the space of home created in the mind of an elderly Filipino in America after watching a performance of folkloric musicians and dancers from the Philippines. He records the show for himself, and even the playback of sounds moves him. But for him there is only a distance – from home, from memories, and from the young dancers who refuse to engage with him. He is a *manong*, a Filipino man who came to work agricultural or menial jobs in the United States and grew old apart from his family and community. Times have certainly changed. Filipino Americans have established diverse communities, far different from those of the male-dominated workers of the early twentieth century. Even without the constant travel back and forth of relatives and friends, Filipino goods are often available in Asian markets and through several enterprising Internet sites. But the space of live performance, where community gathers together in one space and for one period of time, is a collective affirmation of ethnic identity. In a multicultural United States, Filipino Americans are not quite homeless, but there is a lingering tie to another idea of home—the one I have acknowledged my whole life but experience only as a visitor.

There is added anticipation for their arrival here, because this particular group of performers has just recently won first place at the nineteenth Grand Prix Européen du Chant Choral. Having earned the laureate a decade earlier in 1997, the Madrigals' grand prize in 2007 marks the first time that an ensemble has won the competition twice since its inception in 1989.[1] The popularity of the Philippine Madrigals vaults beyond their superb performances; they are also highly valued for their international cachet, earned through competition victories abroad. While Filipino communities in different countries are often welcoming of visiting performers like the Loboc Children's Choir and the Bayanihan Philippine Dance Company, the Philippine Madrigals have the prestige of consistently being considered one of the finest vocal ensembles in the world. As former member Leo Mascarinas reflected, "To a certain extent, it may in fact be this success on the international stage that the audience would like to vicariously experience" (2007).

The experience is, indeed, a performance full of meanings to unpack. At times, it is all about the musical sound, the disembodiment of voices, and a kind of transcendence for the audience. At others, it is about the idea of a shared homeland. The Philippine Madrigals have sung their way into our collective experience, into our memories, and even into the transnational imaginary.

CHAPTER FOUR | # Embodying the New Society
The Philippine Madrigal Singers

The only true and viable foreign policy of a sovereign nation will always be, and should always be, nothing more than an outward projection of what the nation is at home in the first place.

José Laurel, Jr. (1956)

THE PHILIPPINE MADRIGAL SINGERS ARE a fascinating example of a self-professed nonpolitical ensemble that has been overtly nationalist at times, has gone through the process of nationalization, and has represented both the nation and the state in performance. They are a secular group whose repertoire celebrates the hybridity of the nation, ranging from archaic European polyphonic pieces to contemporary compositions by Filipino composers, and their very formation is closely linked to the internationalist and transnationalist tendencies of the modern Philippine nation. The Madrigals served as role models for the Marcos regime's vision of its own brand of modernity, the New Society. Yet, though they benefited from transformation into a national company, the choirmaster and members have long been insistent about the group's separateness from politics in general and the dictatorship in particular. Because the idea of the Philippine nation is not always equivalent to the nation-state, singers within the group have a history of both pride and ambivalence regarding their roles as international ambassadors.

The negotiations of performers within structures of dominance and within the processes of institutionalization are palpable throughout the development of the Madrigals, and the forces of tension between public art, political manipulation, and individual agency become apparent through an examination of the group's history.

While Bayanihan (see chapter 2) also underwent nationalization and has represented the Philippines all over the world, there are some obvious differences between the two ensembles. As performance genres, dance accompanied by instrumental music and choral music have different effects in reception, primarily because the latter has explicit text. The Philippine Madrigals sang nationalist songs, sometimes with texts that were supportive of the state, while Bayanihan encapsulated a national cultural tradition by formulating a standardized repertoire with the veneer of tradition. The trope of preservation and Bayanihan's close relationship with the state may be read as nationalist, but the music and dance material obscured political undertones. Even when instrumental and vocal music are closer in genre and performance context—for instance, folk dance music at a school as compared with a choral group's rendition of an arranged folk song—folkloric dance in the Philippines references the populist, while the arranged folk song is much more overtly professionalized. This may be only a matter of perception, but that perception is not unfounded. Folk dances are still performed by indigenous people, old-timers, and even people in rural areas. Folkloric dance in the Philippines is taught in gym classes to all students (or at a certain age, all girls) or in folk dance clubs, and Spanish-era dances like the *Rigodon de Honor* are regularly performed by teenage boys and girls during coming-of-age parties for young women. Choral music is neither a required physical exercise nor a life cycle event. While singing may be ubiquitous, vocal music in parts requires a skill set for participants and teachers that is less common, sometimes has religious associations, and is held to a high standard that many groups find hard to achieve. This difference is evident in diasporic populations of Filipinos for whom the formation of folkloric dance groups is much more commonplace than choral groups (especially outside of church).

Another important difference is that Bayanihan's collection of music and dance, constructed as a modernist strategy to recoup tradition, seeks to make ties with an imagined past, while the Madrigals and their mixed repertoire link Filipino music practice to modernity and internationalism. The command of a European art music repertoire spanning several eras, where individual pieces are deemed iconic of a certain age and then recontextualized in the imminence of live performance, is a modernist accomplishment. Elena Rivera Mirano affirmed this when she said, "I can probably say that the Madz became a part of the Marcos apparatus that sought to project an image of the Philippines as a modern nation. The sophisticated and difficult repertoire was deliberately crafted to appeal to global, cosmopolitan audiences and the group sought to shine in 'international competition' venues" (2008). It is their connection to European singing practices, songs, and their repertoire of new Filipino choral compositions that projects the image of the Madrigals as modern artists.

European-style choral singing in the Philippines has a long history that begins with the Spanish introduction of liturgical music to the archipelago by the Augustinians, Franciscans, Jesuits, Dominicans, and Recollects. The first choirs were made up of boys who learned a variety of musical functions for masses, including instrument performance and the singing of polyphonic chants. Group singing by the congregation served an important role in making religious conversion palatable inside and outside of church settings and remained a strong tradition throughout Spanish colonization. In secular settings, informal serenaders sang *harana* in two or three parts for courtship or to celebrate birthdays and other special occasions. More serious groups sang as part of music clubs and societies (see Bañas 1975). In the 1860s, publications indicate that Spanish schools, including those for native children, had at least one songbook called *Pequeño método teórico-práctico de solfeo y colección de cánticos sencillos para los niños de las escuelas elementales de Filipinas* (Little method for solfège, theoretical and practical, and collection of simple songs for the children of the primary schools of the Philippines) (Cainglet 1981: Volume 1, 136). By the late nineteenth century, professionalized choruses could be found in the musical theater *sarswelas* and in opera productions (see Canave-Dioquino 1998). During American colonial rule, group singing continued in public schools for the first time as part of music education (Evasco 2001: 50). In addition, more opportunities for choral singing emerged in the twentieth century with the rise of programs and schools devoted to music training, including the music department of St. Scholastica's College, the Conservatory of Music at the University of the Philippines (founded in 1916), and the Academy of Music of Manila (Santos 1998: 869–870).

As secular choral singing developed in academic institutions and in musical societies, it inculcated Filipinos with a sense of value for trained singing that separated musical production by regular people for functional and social reasons (including religious) from music as an art form to be appreciated for aesthetic reasons alone. Whether the singers were professionals or, much more likely, passionate amateurs, glee clubs, choirs, and other organized singing groups in the Philippines have always been quite popular. In the decade before the Madrigal Singers, the Mabuhay Singers, who formed in

1958, pioneered the choral music aesthetic in popular recordings, releasing more than 100 albums in multiple languages used throughout the Philippines. In line with the Mabuhay Singers, Filipino choral ensembles strive for the same musical goals as other choirs that have developed with Western influence the world over, including good ensemble, precise intonation, tonal blending, expressiveness, and clear diction. Unlike examples such as protest music or Protestant Tonic Sol-fa singing in which enthusiasm and ideology is desired over quality (McGuire 2006: 123), joining a choral ensemble in the Philippines generally has meant accepting training and undergoing rehearsals in order to achieve what have become measurements of musical competency that are standard in choral groups the world over.

These standards are fostered in education and through models, and they are also enforced by international competitions for choirs. Not only are regulations in place to ensure a certain uniformity among groups, but also a sense of proper aesthetics is heavily imposed through judging. Thus, while religious and secular choral singing in the Philippines has developed through its long hybrid history, the modernist standards of professionalism applied to touring ensembles are a relatively recent imposition wrought by international exposure. Equally important, these international competitions reflect an impulse of globalization, in which borders are crossed and connections are made through the "universal" act of singing, while at the same time, nations are reified through an insistence on categorization, labeling, and an institutionalized affection for markers of locality (for instance, costuming and the use of native songs). The groups are expected to represent their nation, and the people of their home nation expect much the same thing. Beyond the quaint idiosyncrasies of national ethnoculture, the group may also embody something of the national character, and it is here that the intrusion of politics becomes more obvious.

A choral group may impart political ideals in performance as well as serve as a political tool in domestic and international arenas. Yet, this does not necessitate homogeneity of political opinion among the members of the group, nor even a direct expression of support for the state by the group as a whole. As pertains to the first, a self-selection process takes place in which potential members come to realize the priority of singing over political ideals and other competing agendas. This may not change their points of view, but it creates an atmosphere in which one is encouraged to treat rehearsal and performance space as distant from real-world problems and distractions. In addition, the membership changes over time, so that no single political ideology can be said to govern the group when viewed over several decades. Consequently, while at any given time personal opinions in regard to politics may move one way or another along the political spectrum, this average is completely masked by the public face of the group as a whole. On the surface—and if one considers that the surface is not superficial and is, rather, the exteriority of the performed self—the Madrigals are politically neutral. Yet, as a national group, the Madrigals cannot escape politics. Still, a careful balancing act has allowed them to transcend connections to any particular political body. They are imagined representatives of the national culture and therefore the nation itself. Of course, the ways in which the Madrigals are imagined as symbolic or metaphoric of the nation at large depends upon who is doing the considering and during what time period. All this said, it becomes clear that the Philippine Madrigals offer an acutely vivid case study of the ebb and flow of political purchase between the state and a nationalized musical company.

The Birth and Cultivation of a National Company

Andrea Soledad Ofilada (later Veneracion) was born in 1928 and began piano lessons at the age of 4. She followed the example of her mother, an accomplished pianist and vocalist with training from the University of the Philippines Conservatory of Music. Veneracion received her own degree with honors in piano in 1950 and spent two years teaching in Guam before returning to the Philippines to get married. Her musical background extended from playing into singing with techniques she developed as the piano accompanist for the Philippine soprano Jovita Fuentes (whose credits include debuting in Puccini's *Madama Butterfly* at the Teatro Municipale de Piacenza in Italy). Veneracion continued her musical studies and in 1960 completed a second degree, this time in voice. Encouraged by Eliseo Pájaro, founder of the League of Filipino Composers, Veneracion left the Philippines to work toward a master's degree in voice at Indiana University under the auspices of a Fulbright scholarship. She excelled in her training as a soloist, but she was also attracted to ensemble singing (Evasco 2001).

While attending Indiana University, she joined the campus madrigal choir without any prior experience in the genre and found the experience revelatory. Madrigals, though they may not have been completely foreign to the Philippines as a result of the infiltration of European genres throughout the colonial years, were not sung and were hardly known in the twentieth century, even in university settings. In its history, madrigal has referred to two distinct musical genres—a secular poetic piece of fourteenth-century Italy and another secular song of Italy in the sixteenth and early seventeenth centuries that spread to the rest of Europe in the late Renaissance. Both were generally sung alone, though madrigals did sometimes have instrumental accompaniment during the time periods of their widespread popularity (Arnold and Wakelin 2008). In contemporary madrigals, two easily identifiable features are typical: *a capella* group singing and polyphonic texture. Though there is a variety in the texts, settings, and contexts in which they are sung, madrigals are still a specific genre of music. This specificity should be contrasted with the development of the repertoire of the Philippine Madrigal Singers, which quickly extended beyond madrigals, despite the name of the ensemble.

Before returning to the Philippines in 1963, Veneracion took advantage of monies granted to her by the University of the Philippines to attend operas in New York and Europe in order to enhance her grasp of the many aspects of live performance and to be able to bring that knowledge back to the Philippines (Evasco 2001: 39). Yet, as history has shown, Veneracion did not make an impact on the development of Philippine opera in expected ways. Instead, she precipitated the rapid growth of Philippine choral music through what had begun as a sideline for her—madrigal singing. The original ensemble comprised faculty and students at the University of the Philippines, including Evelyn Mandac, Vina Dominguez, Elmo Makil, Johnny Ramos, Imelda Ongsiako, Noly Laureola, Susan Lim, and Raquel Dadap (ibid. 2001: 49). This gathering differed from other choral groups in its relatively small size. They met informally in hallways and classrooms and perfected their technique while poring through an unfamiliar repertoire of classical music, sacred music, and even a small number of Filipino pieces (Veneracion 2000). In the early going, reading through the music together fostered collegiality through a musical medium that was familiar as a vocal genre and yet novel in the nuances of its performance. As they became more formal in their practices and found venues in which to showcase their singing, the ensemble took on a name, the University of the Philippines Madrigal Singers.

The original sixteen members made their formal debut in 1963 during that year's school convocation ceremony. In it, they sang just a single piece by Filipino composer Hilarión Rubio, "Pinagkawing-kawing" (Evasco 2001: 51). The Madrigals quickly expanded their repertoire due as much to the expectations of Filipino audiences as their own creative impulses. As Leo Mascarinas, a member from 1972 to 1973 and again between 1977 and 1982 mused, "I don't think madrigal singing per se is popular among Pilipinos, at least not in terms of the works of Monteverdi, Dowland, etc. I believe it is the recasting of familiar Pilipino tunes, be it folk or pop, into the madrigal idiom that has expanded the audience for choral music" (2007).[2] As time progressed, the selections of the groups continued to expand into existing Filipino choral music as well as a variety of other arrangements, some of which were commissioned exclusively for the Madrigal Singers.

Finding Filipino music for the group to tackle often meant gently compelling composers to put pen to paper, since merely sifting through the files of the university music library revealed limited material. Most Filipino composers had written or were currently writing for the symphonic repertoire or for solo voices, and Veneracion could find only three or four extant pieces of choral music for her group (Veneracion 2000). Consequently, she needed to tap into her musical network, and over time composers became enamored with the possibilities. The role of the Madrigals as musical catalyst has expanded the field of Philippine choral music in tangible ways. Veneracion recalled that the core of arrangements for the Madrigals grew through arrangements by her friends and by the students of some of the singers who were composition majors. They would ask their network to arrange certain pieces, until the repertoire grew into the hundreds. Along with a larger scope came a higher valuation of the music itself, and Veneracion had to stop sending free copies to newer ensembles that followed her own. The arrangers deserved compensation, and in the development of this compact, the Madrigals became owners of those arrangements (ibid. 2000).

Filipino composers took to the madrigal genre easily, and several members of the League of Filipino Composers have become well known as arrangers for vocal ensembles. Lucio San Pedro (see chapter 1) in particular contributed a large number of arrangements to the UP Madrigal Singers repertoire, though he did not write exclusively (nor even specifically) for them. Veneracion described the situation.

> [San Pedro] wrote many songs during the Marcos regime. Because I worked for Folk Arts Theater at that time and we were also choral resident for the CCP (Cultural Center of the Philippines), most of the works that he made, we would be the first ones to sing. So it was not really necessarily written for us, but written for the Cultural Center, and we would premiere it. There was one piece that he wrote, and he asked me if we would sing it. We were the ones to sing it in competition and we won. (2000)

Several Madrigals from the past, familiar with the group's polyphonic style and progressive approach to Filipino music, made their own contributions.

As their repertoire grew and the skills of the group sharpened, they reached audiences of greater diversity and number. Veneracion, as leader, took charge of finding engagements and made it policy in the early days to sing anywhere that they were invited. "Filipinos are not really concertgoers," she insists. "You have to develop an audience. That's why we were willing to sing anywhere we were asked to sing. We sang at the garbage dump. We sang in Tondo" (2000).[3] This egalitarianism begs the question, to what end would music serve people whose lives consisted of scraping out the most meager of livings? Are songs merely momentary diversions—sensual and visceral escapes from the vagaries of daily survival? One former member of the Madrigals stated what many believe, that Filipinos as a people sing in order to counter the difficulties of life. Likewise, experiencing the act of singing by groups like the Madrigal Singers, and likely even singing along with familiar tunes, may offer an emotional, vicarious release through the transcendent quality of performance. Even their idiosyncratic performance style–one that the ensemble has retained over the decades—seems to bring order to chaos. Instead of standing with a conductor, the members sit in a semicircle with Veneracion on the far right, cueing songs with the most minute of head gestures. The preciseness of their performances crystallizes long before coming onstage, and they are as crisp as a military drill team. They embody the strength of individuals that is heightened by a controlled surrender to the group.

Thus, for young audiences, the singers may easily become role models of a sort, and membership in the ensemble something for which to strive. Talent and commitment, and not the lightness of skin color or economic background, are the most important factors for belonging. This is not to say that there are no barriers for the poorest of the poor who may never have any opportunities to breach the social and academic walls that traditionally enclose the Madrigal membership.[4] But the Madrigals generate a feeling of kinship by tapping into the communal feeling of Filipino-ness as a national abstraction. They represent the heights in artistry and performance that Filipinos are capable of, and in performance they seem to elevate familiar folk songs into "high art." If radios blare the everyday music of both near and far to the common *tao* (people) of Tondo, then a visit by the Madrigals represents that which is out of the ordinary and that which is homegrown but somehow heightened. Perhaps, most important, their performances are live and therefore can create connections between members and audiences, even if they are fleeting. This power to move people and to serve as role models to aspire to would prove tempting for the state, leading to the eventual co-optation of the group through the process of nationalization.

During these years (1972–1986), the Madrigals maintained a close relationship with the Marcos dictatorship. A former Madrigals soprano from 1969 to 1970, Elena Rivera Mirano, described the growing ties between the singers and Imelda Marcos just prior to the declaration of Martial Law in the following way.

> I was a junior in English and Comparative Literature at the College of Arts and Sciences. At the time, unlike the College of Music, which was considered quite conservative and apolitical, the AS was the hotbed of student activism. It was an honor to have been invited to join the Madz as they were the only Philippine choir that had travelled abroad at the time, and they had carried off their first world tour quite well. UP was proud of them. Imelda was still in the background then but had recognized that they were of international caliber. Because of this, we were able to sing at a state dinner at Malacañan Palace once, but it was considered an honor to be invited to sing at the Palace for any president and any occasion. The association of the group with the regime, therefore, was not very strong at that time and the Madz were not yet the court musicians at her beck and call that they would become later... a year or two later, I noticed that the group was being called back increasingly to sing at the Palace.... Then came Martial Law and I severed my ties with the group completely. During Martial Law, the relationship between the Madz and the Palace intensified. The UP community, particularly the more progressive sectors, became increasingly critical. (2008)

Leo Mascarinas recalls that Imelda Marcos not only enjoyed hearing the Madrigals singers and having them participate in events at the presidential palace, she also likely saw the political value of co-opting a cultural group from the University of the Philippines.

> The choir was known to the First Lady as the group had performed on several occasions at the Malacañan Palace. Perhaps it was serendipitous that a Madz favourite, Fabian Obispo's arrangement of "Dahil Sa Iyo" (which possibly defined the Madz style), was Imelda's signature song in prior election campaigns. Professor [Felipe] de Leon's son, Magdangal (now a justice of the Court of Appeals), was a member of the Madz at that time. The UP tag in the group's name was key. The University of the Philippines was the hotbed of student action (against the Marcos regime) and it was most convenient that a UP group (the Madz) was doing its own action in a more positive way. (2008)

But UP was also a historically nationalist institution—state-funded and home to some of the most prominent intellectuals of the country. The president of UP from 1962 to 1968, Carlos Romulo, instituted symbols of official nationalism throughout the campus, including unfurling the Philippine flag over the administration building for the first time (Gaerlan 1998: 214). And during the early years of martial law, UP president Salvador Lopez attempted to secure at least some measure of academic freedom by allowing the discussion of ideologies against the Marcos dictatorship in campus classrooms but not officially supporting these points of views in any other way (ibid. 242). As the institution walked the political tightrope, so too did the Madrigal Singers. Yet, despite the more apolitical intentions of Veneracion and many of its members, the group became entangled with the Marcos regime, a reputation that would be difficult to shed.

Coming of Age in the New Society

At the end of 1975, the year before the Madrigals won their first international competition, President Gerald Ford of the United States came to the islands as part of a tour of Asia to solidify relationships with allies in the wake of the Vietnam War. President Marcos publicly interpreted the visit as American approval for his government and for martial law (1972–1981). This visit also marked the well-known conversion of Secretary of State Henry Kissinger into an admirer of Imelda Marcos, whose notorious charms served as her primary tool of diplomacy (Bonner 1987: 153–156). The year 1975 was certainly good for Imelda Marcos. Before it was over, she had gained even more official power with her appointment as governor of Metro Manila and had been proclaimed one of the ten richest women in the world by *Cosmopolitan* magazine. Throughout that year, she traveled the globe and provided great exposure for the country (ibid.). From Asia to the Middle East to Latin America, Imelda served as a model for the Filipino as cosmopolitan, all the while promoting a confidence among Filipinos that they were on the same level as other countries. This self-assurance would be supported well by the success of the Madrigals a few months later with their competition victories in Poland and Hungary.

Yet, the domestic picture seemed much less bright. While life had never been easy for the majority of Filipinos who lived in poverty, their incomes actually declined in rural and urban areas from the 1960s to the mid-1980s, even though the per capita income appeared to rise; the elite continued to be the beneficiaries (Boyce 1993: 4). Likewise, the "green revolution" of rice production, meant to provide more food for the country and for export, proved most profitable for the Marcoses and their cronies. In addition, excessive borrowing caused external debt to explode, with economic effects that have lasted beyond Marcos's own life and into all succeeding presidencies (ibid. 10). Critics of the state recognized the damage to the nation wrought by cronyism and corruption, and their protestations were only partially suppressed. Hence, the public mood had a negative tinge that belied stage slogans and presidential speeches.

Though martial law had been declared with the chaos and violence of the First Quarter Storm as the declared provocation (along with a series of bombings), it did not end protests by the radical left against the Marcos government. Populated by students—those from the University of the Philippines were particularly active—communist organizations, and umbrella groups like the Movement for a Democratic Philippines, the opposition sought to politicize the whole of the country (Muego 1974: 2). Martial law, rather than dissolve the protests that had plagued metropolitan Manila, actually gave the previously fragmented opposition a common cause.[5] Throughout the 1970s and 1980s, activists were frequently jailed and tortured, and a number suddenly and mysteriously disappeared as the regime attempted to tighten their grip over society.

Of course, the control of bodies is often accompanied by the control of minds through the dissemination and repression of public images of major media outlets. The Marcos government controlled the media during the 1970s and the first half of the 1980s, through bribery and intimidation, but their custody had its limitations. Even those papers owned by Marcos cronies carried articles that were critical of state policies, and outright expressions of opposition thrived throughout the early 1980s (Florentino-Hofileña 1998: 6). Rumors that some of these articles were actually planted by Marcos to give the illusion of free public debate continue to persist anecdotally among people who lived during that period. The media, in other words, remained relatively lively, despite the impositions of a *de facto* dictatorship.

One could argue that the nationalization of media had some positive results as well. Primarily, the state's approach to national culture influenced the indigenization of print and broadcast media. In the mid-1970s, legislative acts launched by the government's Broadcast Media Council (BMC) forced broadcasters to open the airwaves to Filipino music and television programs, including those that were explicitly about perceived traditional culture. As far as radio was concerned, the 1973 KBP-BMC regulation imposed a rule that "challenged the dominance of foreign music and talents. Beginning with one song per program hour in 1975, the requirement was brought up to four in 1982" (E. Enriquez 2003: 32). Pointedly, the nurturing of a local popular music genre like OPM (Original Pilipino Music) does not protect "traditional" music or discourage it; it simply distinguishes radio-friendly popular music made by Filipinos from popular music from the United States, Europe, or other parts of Asia. Most OPM sounded and continues to sound entirely like American and British popular music in instrumentation, form, and style. Many OPM songs utilize English lyrics, though they are not necessarily marketed in primarily English-speaking countries. Whether in Filipino, English, or a mix of both, targets for international marketing remain mostly other Asian countries such as Japan and Indonesia. In sum, the legislation of the state did open up opportunities for growth in the Filipino popular music sector, but it had nothing to do with the age-old debate over Western musical aesthetics and Filipino identity.

In television, the nature of the marketplace becomes even clearer through the travails of explicit "cultural programming," exemplified by the failure of Renaissance Television, an experiment meant to keep traditional culture alive through advanced media. Forcing the networks to present certain programming met resistance, but for a short while, during primetime each night, one hour was devoted to cultural programs. The practice proved to be problematic from a commercial standpoint, and Renaissance Television dropped the broadcast (del Mundo 2003: 18–23). Cultural programs continued to air in different forms, and musical shows were particularly popular among Filipino television viewers. *Concert at the Park* and *Paco Park Presents* gave wider access to live performances of classical, popular, and folk music, while locals like Pilita Corrales and her daughter (*Pilita and Jackie*), Armida Siguion-Reyna (*Aawitan Kita*), Lilia Reyes (*Lilia Reyes and Other Voices*), Kuh Ledesma (*Kuh by Special Arrangement*), and Ryan Cayabyab (*Ryan Ryan Musikahan*) emerged as nationally broadcast stars with their own shows (ibid. 26).

The 1970s also saw the rise of the "Manila Sound," a subgenre of OPM and a marketing ploy used by Vicor's Sunshine music label to appeal to Filipino youth. Songs that fell into this genre generally fit into popular music styles of the 1970s also found in other parts of the world—and particularly the United States—such as disco and rock (Japitana 1982: 6). Lyrics blaring over the radio were in Tagalog, English, or Taglish, a combination of English and Tagalog used in everyday communication. Taglish was especially important in the development of the Manila Sound, because, according to Japitana, "there are not enough words in Tagalog to express sadness, and there is a limited number of words to describe joy" (1982: 6). The hybridity of language and the flexible appropriation of Western popular music styles like rock, disco, and jazz were integral to the development of local Philippine pop music. Japitana concludes that the development of a local popular music was especially critical for young people's perception of being Filipino. "The British have their Liverpool Sound, the Americans have their Motown Sound and Philadelphia Sound. And the Philippines now has the Manila Sound" (1982: 11).

During the late 1970s, groups such as Hotdog, Cinderella, Juan de la Cruz Band, and the folk-oriented Asin (Salt), and pop/rock stars like Celeste Legaspi, Hajji Alejandro, and Didith Reyes dominated the airwaves. Imelda Papin scrapped her way from poor beginnings to success and developed along the way a relationship with the Marcoses. Leah Navarro closed the decade with Nonong Pedero's hit from the 1980 Metro Pop Music Festival, "*Isang Mundo, Isang Awit* (One World, One Song)," proclaiming the same sentiment in multiple languages during the chorus, "*Yo te amo*, I love you, *watashi-wa anata-o aishite imasu, ich liebe dich, iniibig kita, gwa ay di.*" OPM and the Manila Sound were modern, in keeping with Western popular music, and evidence of Filipino international aspirations. If industries could be modernized, could not the very sound of Filipino music represent moderinization through the use of technology in recording? Equally important, if popular music could come into the nation, was it possible for this modern Filipino music to have success outside? It would take a singer with just the right sound to transcend national borders and become commercially popular in a way the Philippine Madrigal Singers never could. This singer was Freddie Aguilar, and he succeeded mostly by virtue of one song.

In the 1970s Freddie Aguilar was honing his skills and developing his stage persona in the bars and nightclubs of Olongapo, the city adjoining the United States naval base at Subic Bay. In 1977 he entered his composition "Anak (Child)" into the first Manila Metropop Song Festival; though he did not win, the song became a domestic and international hit and was translated into numerous languages. In Japan, the song was already a hit in its Tagalog version, but it gained even more momentum when the popular singers Tokiko Kato and Jiro Shigeta remade it in Japanese (Japitana 1982: 19). The song's regretful tone over youthful mistakes and its plea to parents for forgiveness touched international audiences, while the musical aesthetics emulated the popular folk music sound of singers like Joan Baez and many others (including some in the Nueva Canción movement of Latin America).

Yet, even more surprising than Aguilar's rise to stardom was the ascent of the singer and actress Nora Aunor. Discovered while still a teenager after winning a popular singing contest called *Tawag ng Tanghalan* (Call of the Stage), Aunor bucked the long-running bias in media and society at large for fair-skinned stars. Darker skinned, petite, and from a poor background in the countryside, Aunor was a kind of "everywoman," and the public adored her for it. Neferti Tadiar creates an analogy between Aunor's star power to a character she played in the film *Himala* (Miracle), arguing that audiences made a strong connection between the main character's ability to return power to the people and the actress's iconic revolt against stereotype and the hierarchical status quo (2002). She did not evince the same kind of elitism that the Madrigals did by virtue of their professionalism and association with UP and with the Philippine state. Nora Aunor was a singer for the masses who did not have to cultivate an audience so much as make a connection. Just as Fairouz connected to the masses of Lebanon—despite being a female performer in a Muslim country where this behavior is problematic—Aunor was a kind of Other who could also personify the nation through metaphors that appealed to the masses (Stone 2008).

While early political nationalism in the Philippines favored the retrenching of the elite into the upper echelons of power offered by an independent state, public debates over language and the arts, developments in popular media, and mass expressions from student protests to religious movements offered a multiplicity of nationalist articulations. Freddie Aguilar demonstrated the universality of human experience that tied the Philippines to the rest of the world, while at the same time, he proved the international viability of Filipino music. Nora Aunor challenged the prevalent colonial mentality that favored (and still favors) *mestizos* in the public eye and demonstrated racial pride to the masses with whom she shared *kayumanggi* (brown) skin color. They are soloists among the group that is the Philippine *masa* (masses), and their songs benefit the whole.

During the late 1970s and early 1980s, Filipinos needed heroes like Freddie Aguilar and Nora Aunor to focus on, since the country itself was going through a crushing recession. In June of 1978, Marcos declared a period of "normalization," a transition away from martial law that was supposed to liberalize the dictatorship without actually dismantling any of the Marcos power structures. In practice, "normalization" was a process by which the regime could be further legitimized before the world. In 1978 the Philippine government allowed the first elections since martial law was declared, and martial law was officially lifted in 1981.

From the Nation Outward

Shortly before the end of martial law in 1980, Imelda Marcos tapped the UP Madrigal Singers to be the resident choral group of the Cultural Center of the Philippines (CCP). It bears mentioning that during this time, while students continued to be very vocal about the government, the University of the Philippines as an institution maintained close ties with the state. After all,

UP is the national university of the Philippines, founded in 1908 by the first Philippine legislature. In 1981, while the government conditioned the country for the end of martial law, UP inaugurated a new president named Edgardo J. Angara. A lawyer trained at the University of Michigan in Ann Arbor, Angara had the approval of President Marcos and was good friends with Defense Minister Juan Ponce Enrile (Bauzon 1985: 547). University faculty and students wondered whether Angara would threaten academic freedom, especially in light of his support for the Education Act of 1980, a bill that gave the Ministry of Education and Culture the power to regulate and administer the entire educational system (ibid. 548). Throughout the many controversies that plagued UP during the 1980s, the obligation to balance nationalism, academic and political integrity, and dependence upon government support remained an imperative.

The change from university ensemble to nationalized performing artists had a number of ramifications, including an ironic disassociation with campus politics, even though the group maintained strong ties with UP. Remembering back, Veneracion stated, "When the Cultural Center made us the choral resident, Mrs. Marcos asked me, 'Can you not now change the name to Philippine Madrigal Singers? Because now you are national. You are not just university anymore.' For me, what's in a name?" (2000). By calling themselves the Philippine Madrigal Singers rather than the UP (University of the Philippines) Madrigal Singers, the ensemble more easily represented the nation as a whole in international performances. The new name also gestured toward another symbolic reading. Perhaps the most intriguing aspect of juxtaposing "Philippine" and "Madrigal" is the manner in which postcolonial Filipinos take ownership of a European art music genre and, through a mixed repertoire of European and Filipino music, sing themselves into the global marketplace of performance and self-representation. Madrigals belong to the Filipinos, and the Madrigal Singers belong to the Philippine nation. The nation is charged with supporting the performers, while the performers must uphold the values of the nation as ambassadors inside and outside of the country. Leo Mascarinas summarized the appointment, saying, "The designation of the Madz as a resident artist of the Cultural Center of the Philippines was a means by which the government formally and financially recognized the contribution of the Madz in promoting Philippine culture. Although the members were not paid individually, the funds were used for international concert tours. Thus, the government support afforded the Madz to reach a far wider audience and bring the Philippines to the forefront in the choral world" (Mascarinas 2008).

In fact, one of Veneracion's goals in developing the Madrigals to such a high level was to establish the Philippines as an active member of the international choral community. Internationalism became a major element of the Madrigal's identity, allowing the group to transcend Macaulayism not just through the mastery of the musical language of the West, but also through a sense of national pride and the cosmopolitan crossing of national borders (Anderson 1991: 91–93). The Madrigal Singers engaged in an extensive amount of international touring with support from the government and sometimes as official representatives of the nation-state. From China, Indonesia, South Korea, Hong Kong, and Taiwan at the end of the 1970s, they continued on to Bulgaria, Germany, France, Sweden, Finland, the Netherlands, Spain, Portugal, Hungary, Austria, Poland, Italy, Vatican City, Greece, Egypt, Japan, and the United States in the early 1980s. With her talented and determined singers, Veneracion achieved stunning results. Since 1976, the Madrigals have consistently reaped international awards. That year, they took first place in the *Festiwal Pieśni Chóralnej* in Poland and the Béla Bartók VII Nemzetközi Kórusverseny in Hungary, inaugurating more than three decades of competition success. In 1981, the Madrigals triumphantly brought home every available award from the XX Concorso Internazionale di Canto Corale C.A. Seghizzi in Italy, with the exception of the prize for best Italian choir. The ensemble's repertoire showcased technical virtuosity and consummate vocal blending, and their versatility enabled them to compete on an equal level with their European counterparts. In fact, that same year at the Fourteenth International Choral Competition, the group garnered an award from the Union of Bulgarian Composers for the best performance of a Bulgarian piece, singing lyrics that the members had learned phonetically (Veneracion 2000).

Their performances expanded domestically as well. According to Tess Rances, onetime director of outreach programs at the CCP, resident companies like the Philippine Madrigals were sent to outlying provinces throughout the country. "It started during Tita King's [popular nickname for Lucrecia Kasilag] time, but they had just thought of one thing, to bring the performances outside of the institution. They were already being bombarded by the fact, 'Why is it only the Metro Manila people who are able to access shows like this?'" (Rances 2000). Outreach programs were popular among Filipinos, offering national exposure to the artists. Along the way, they were greeted with great enthusiasm and appreciation, with people crowding the venues just to hear them (de Villa 1984: 35). At the same time, the group's success among the masses was strongly event-driven, offering free or low cost live performances by state-supported artists with a positive reputation. That is to say, they were not popular artists like Freddie Aguilar and Nora Aunor who commanded the mass media.

Like the Bayanihan Philippine Dance Company, as resident artists of the CCP, the Madrigals benefited from national monies, recognition, and opportunities to perform at high-level events. The financial boon was particularly important. Despite being called upon to premiere works on a regular basis, the Madrigals did not have money for commissioning pieces directly from composers. According to Veneracion, the CCP could pay 30,000 pesos for the commissioning of a new piece. The official sanction and sponsorship of the CCP has been significant for the continuing development of the Madrigals as well as the tradition of choral singing as a whole in the Philippines. At the same time, with government sponsorship came an obligation to the state, and, even more particularly, the aims and whims of the ruling Marcos dictatorship.

A National Model: Singing for the State or Singing for the Nation?

Examined in the local context, the Madrigals have both contributed to and benefited from the general high regard Filipinos give to solo and group singing. Colloquially, if many adhere to the stereotype that Filipinos are natural dancers, still more would insist that they are a singing people; I certainly have heard both claimed many times (just as they are declared in other countries all over the world). One former member of the Madrigals speculated that it might be "naturally inherent for Filipinos to be good singers."[6] In analysis, it actually matters little whether Filipinos are, as some will press, the best singers in the world. When trying to situate singing in the Philippine milieu, what *is* important is the perception of Filipinos that places value on skillful vocal performance as a national trait.

Singing is meaningful in a multiplicity of ways. The essays collected by Karen Ahlquist in *Chorus and Community* unpack how acts of performance and structures put in place to accommodate choral singing "assert artistic and education achievement, aesthetic merit, and social, national, religious, or ethnic identity" (2006: 2). In addition, whether the choral group is a church or community choir, a state-sponsored ensemble, or a protest organization, singing together establishes a complex web of relationships among people. It is a community-building activity, bonding together the members of a singing group and creating ties with audiences and others who support them. The more popular any such group becomes, the larger their network of support, until it is even possible to consider the artists as exponents of the nation. As experienced by participants, the performative act defines occurrences as concerts, rituals, or some other kind of significant event. In doing so, singing establishes the function of particular spaces that vary from those that are understood as particularly local to those that are emblematic of the nation.

Hence, singing is not only a visceral experience; it also produces meaning on many different levels. For example, Gregory Barz has pointed out in his analysis of East African choral singing that *kwaya* "functions as a microcosm of an idealized social system" (2006: 21). How does such an abstraction occur? In considering the Madrigals, their performance is not meant to be a participatory activity, and conventions restrict audience members from singing along (or at least, from singing loudly). Therefore, the audience may be considered as separate and distanced from the singers, and it is the audience that interprets the network of meanings that circulate in performance. On one level, audiences apprehend the performance as evocative, skillful, or any of a number of factors that relate directly to musical aesthetics. In addition, because the performers are a group, the audience may then admire the teamwork involved. This plays into preconceived notions and positive feelings about how people may work successfully together in more generalized contexts. Metaphors that arise from watching skillful groups such as choirs or sports teams are often functionalist or organic—they are likened to a finely tuned machine or said to perform "as one." In interpreting a Madrigals performance, then, audiences draw upon ways of knowing that relate music to other kinds of group activities, and in that step, they abstract into any number of extramusical contexts. These interpretations will differ from person to person, but existing discourse guides the emergence of particular ideas about the Madrigals.

The specific context in which the Madrigals sing is always already infused with extramusical meaning directly concerning their identity. The Madrigals are regularly billed as singing ambassadors and as representatives of the Philippines with sterling international credentials in the field of music. As a result, it is possible for audiences to transitively interpret musical success as a symbolic triumph for the Philippine nation and for Filipinos as citizens and expatriates of that nation. This leap is not as large as one might imagine when recalling how sports teams in international gatherings like the Olympics come so easily to stand in for their respective nations. Once this interpretive framework has been set up, it is easy to fill in a variety of metaphors that relate the activities needed for successful singing with the positive attributes of a national body.

As such, it seems a natural enough leap that a successful performing group might be adopted by the state and nationalized in order to support and even control the network of meanings that arise from music and its performance. The Madrigals are particularly effective at promoting certain national ideals because of their repertoire and performance practice. They are young and vigorous performers, ideal for representing a new society.[7] They are unique as performers, distinguishing themselves from other choral groups as much as the Philippine nation would want to be distinguished as exceptional. Unlike most vocal ensembles, the members are not seated by section. They sit in successive quartets with one soprano, alto, tenor, and bass making a complete harmonizing unit. In this way, each singer is more sensitive to the blending of the whole, while at the same time, each individual must be strong enough on his or her own to carry a melody without the aid of someone nearby (Mascarinas 2007).

Moreover, the discipline and sacrifices of the Madrigal members, apparent through the professionalism of performance, serve as a powerful model for how citizens might contribute to the national good. The training of singers is especially challenging, requiring personal discipline and sacrifice. Life as a member of the UP Madrigals requires three rehearsals a week on a fixed schedule that accommodates members from the UP School of Music faculty and upperclassmen, as well as members from other schools at the University of the Philippines. To attain a spot in the twenty-member group, newcomers must memorize a copious amount of music during their probation in order to maintain pace with their contemporaries. In addition, under Veneracion, members in training were required to sit next to her on her left side to ensure they were heard, and they had to memorize the titles of the songs in the order of the next concert repertoire to remind Veneracion of the next piece (Evasco 2001: 59, 61). Paz Villanueva, an alto from 1983 to 1990, asserts, "I feel that the importance [of the group] is related to how we have been trained and disciplined by Professor Andrea Veneracion, our conductor. Her intensive training and discipline created that much recognition given to the Philippine Madrigal Singers and the kind of respect and laurels the group still reaps in the international music world" (2007).

The perfect semicircle, practiced postures, and unity of voices are indicative of order—an order that is not reflective of everyday culture, but rather contrasts sharply with the general looseness Filipinos display in regard to time, movement through space (with driving being a prime example), and social interaction (where etiquette is expected, but flexibility and compromise is valued). The order results from the discipline of the Madrigals and relates to their success, thereby serving as an idealized model of an orderly Filipino society, enforced publicly by curfews, military presence, and other coercive means.[8] This message of allowing the state to establish order and the cooperation required of the populace was touted vigorously during President Marcos's New Society of the 1970s. Leo Mascarinas voiced this philosophy, recalling,

> "Sa bagong lipunan, disciplina ang kailangan (In the New Society, discipline is needed)." That was one of the most popular slogans that could be heard on radio and TV. To a Madrigal Singer, discipline was imperative. Even before "time management" became a buzzword, the Madz had already been practicing it. Being a Madz entailed dealing with the demands of a heavy workload involving singing, studies, work and family. The Madz became more and more a fixture at command performances at the palace and at various other government functions. There would be times when we'd be with each other more often than our own families. Looking back, I am amazed myself at how we were able to manage all our activities through an optimal use of time. As an example, the students among us would study during the waiting times before performances. It's incredible that several Madz were scholars and graduated with honours at a significantly higher ratio than the average UP student population. (2008)

Other musical and performance aesthetics that correspond with positive national traits include a unity of sound in which individuals contribute to the overall good of the chorus; the blending and equality of men and women; and the parity of European and Filipino musics sung with equal respect and care. Interestingly enough, the Madrigal Singers employ the group aesthetic and dynamic in a way that both respects and suppresses individuality. Veneracion is proud to claim that every member of the group would succeed as a "first-rate soloist" (Evasco 2001: 65), and indeed, the solos in performance are exquisite. At the same time, those who succeed in becoming members of the group know expertly how to blend with others in sound and in appearance when the ensemble sings as a whole. Singing groups exercise a cultural propensity toward consensus and achievement over individual desire. Much like the *bayanihan* value in which members of a community band together to help one another, ensemble singing stresses the importance of membership, responsibility to others, and the coincidence of individual and group needs. The musical personality of combined individuality and group mentality found in madrigal polyphony extends to the performance practice of other types of pieces in the Madrigal Singers' repertoire.

In tandem, the Philippine state has found it advantageous from an economic standpoint to promote the islands as a friendly destination for tourists. The personality of the Madrigals, as enacted by the individuals and group as a whole, relates well to tourist brochures that praise the Filipinos as an amiable and hospitable people. Former member Regalado T. Jose summed up the desired national personality in the following way:

> I think the Mads (I use Mads, the earlier version used by my generation; the "z" replaced the "s" in the 1990s) projected a particular identity that was beneficial to the government—that projection included wholesomeness, warmness, sincerity, friendliness, and similar such traits. So the Mads were very useful to the government in the presentations for foreign delegates. Personally, I tried my best to exude such a manner; I think most everyone of us did so as well, and had great fun doing it too. In this sense we were like ambassadors of good will. (2008)

Jose further mused, "I guess we would consider ourselves nationalistic, in the sense of bringing honor, prestige, and friendship to our country" (ibid.). When they were invited to perform at state and diplomatic dinners, which occurred on a regular basis, the Madrigals would present a song or two from the guests' home country, often learning and memorizing the music only hours beforehand (ibid.). Likewise, when the Madrigals traveled abroad, they took care to always include international songs, designed to showcase their programmatic diversity as well as their appreciation for the hospitality of host countries.

The practice of learning so many foreign songs has resulted in a wide-ranging repertoire that corresponds well with the globalized history of the Philippines and the self-perception of Filipinos as cosmopolitans (from overseas workers to the globe-trotting elite). Significantly, it was not just that Filipinos were traversing the globe and learning from and about others. The Madrigals achieved what a rare few groups and individuals from the Philippines have managed to do—the spread of Filipino art in international circles. In Singapore, for instance, officials designated Philippine composer Francisco Feliciano's "Pamugun" as a mandatory contest piece, but only after it had gained exposure through performance by the Madrigals (Mascarinas 2008). The domestic and international success of the Madrigals had as its only parallel the famous Bayanihan Philippine Dance Company, and both groups have been extremely important in developing the interior and exterior "face" of national culture.

It is undeniable that at times the Philippine Madrigal Singers acted as the voice of the state, not only as national ambassadors, but also through the performance of state-sanctioned music. Leo Mascarinas recalls how the voices of the Madrigals became a part of the mainstream Philippine soundscape, if only for a short time.

On the airwaves, Prof. Felipe de Leon's "Bagong Lipunan" and his other compositions on the same nationalistic theme were being played. Unknown to many, the voices that they were hearing were those of the UP Madrigal Singers. I would say that if ever there were an all-time "top of the charts hit" of the Madz, "Bagong Lipunan" would be the one. As with most propaganda, it is believed that constant repetition would be a driving force in fulfilling the end. How did the Madz get to be the ones singing the New Society songs? To my knowledge, these are a few reasons: The Madz were simply regarded to be the best, especially with a most successful 1969 premiere world concert tour followed by a cultural mission at the 1970 World Fair in Osaka. It was only in 1974 that another choir, the UP Concert Chorus, embarked on an international tour, albeit only to the US. (2008)

Imelda Marcos commissioned "Bagong Lipunan (New Society)" (the title is often translated as "Hymn of the New Republic") at the beginning of martial law in 1972, and it continued to be taught in schools and to be heard regularly for the next decade. According to a songbook of nationalist songs promoting the New Society (*Mga Awit Sa Bagong Lipunan*), both Marcoses enthusiastically approved of the work, with President Marcos remarking, "These songs very well express what I have conceived of the New Society. I am confident that these will tame the restless hearts of some of our countrymen who have bitterness and hate in their hearts" (1974: 13). The lyrics of "Bagong Lipunan" that so moved the Marcoses are as follows:

> Ang bayan ko'y may dangal
> Puri't kagitingan
> Dagat, bundok ay sagana
> At kay yaman ng lupa.
>
> Pilipinas, sa piling mo
> Maligaya ang buhay ko
> Bagong Lipunan ang dapat,
> Malaon nating hinahangad.
>
> English translation:
> My country has honor
> Praise and courage
> The seas and mountains are rich
> And the land is wealthy.

Pilipinas, by your side
My life is happy
A New Society it should be,
For so long we have yearned for this.

It is understandable that, based on their prolonged ties with the Marcoses and their having sung and recorded New Society music like "Bagong Lipunan," some labeled the Madrigal Singers a "Crony Choir" (Evasco 2001: 148). Most members of the choir soundly disagree with the disparaging and pointedly accusatory nickname. According to Veneracion biographer Marjorie Evasco, the Madrigals took an egalitarian approach toward performance. Their "activism" consisted of singing for all audiences possible, no matter where they were and no matter their political attitudes (2001: 90). At the same time, the state remained their greatest patron. This patronage included official monies as well as the privileged position of being called upon to represent the best of the nation at command performances. One consultant, a bass with the Madrigals, recalled singing at State Dinners and functions almost every week. At the same time, his colleague, Leo Mascarinas, felt that singers could separate politics from performance in subtle ways when he stated that he did not feel that command performances at Malacañan Palace signified allegiance to the Marcos regime. "After all, the Madz have done it at the request of whichever president was in power after Marcos. . . . Inasmuch as we were inappropriately labeled as a 'crony' choir by some parties, we always believed we were doing it for the country" (2008). While critics might argue that such a passive approach is merely acceptance of the political order, others could maintain that under dictatorships, there is always an implied threat to national performers who do not commit to any requests asked of them by the state. Elena Rivera Mirano described the situation by saying, "It was distasteful to be associated with the Marcos regime but just as difficult to refuse them. Many groups just stayed away from the palace eye and heaved a sigh of relief when we were left alone. But OA [Andrea Veneracion] was already part of Imelda's 'in' circle by then and the Madz benefited greatly from this association" (2008).

Others dealt with politics on a very personal level. While it would have been a touchy situation for the Madrigals as a group to keep a distance from the Marcos government and to refuse invitations to sing, even mundane strategies could make the difference between collaboration and the pragmatism of survival. Regalado Jose related with some mirth that he always presented a joyful self when singing but that he showed a very quiet resistance with certain types of music. "During the last Marcos years, some 'propaganda' music would be included which a number of us did not like (including myself) but we went along with it anyway; I just didn't smile during those occasions" (Jose 2008). The varied responses of members of the Madrigals reveal that the relationship between music and politics is a decidedly complicated one. How performers approach politics on an individual basis and as members of a nationalized group is not as simple as collaboration versus opposition, but can be better understood as a constant negotiation. That individuals can clearly make a distinction between nationalism and support for the state reveals an elastic space in which balances of power can be manipulated, even when performers are under duress. Likewise, while authorities of the Marcos-governed state worked to shape the symbols of national culture, there was a limit to the influence they exerted over the repertoire and performance of the Madrigals. The relevance, longevity, and balance achieved by the ensemble over the course of several administrations is partly due to the survival instincts of its leadership and members, but is even more a measure of the group's consistently high level of artistry and focus on music above all else.

THE BUS RIDE WAS LONG, lasting all night on a straight shot to Washington DC from Boston. My mother had asked me if I wanted to join her, so that we could march together in front of the White House to protest former president Ronald Reagan's unwavering support of the Marcos regime. Ninoy Aquino had been assassinated after returning to the Philippines to run for president in a "snap election," and his wife, Cory Aquino, surprised many by taking his place. Both had lived in the Boston area for quite a while, since Ninoy Aquino had been exiled from the Philippines for political and health reasons, and the students and parents of my Filipino school sang Christmas carols at their home. The Aquino family had been members of our community, and even those of us who did not know them well felt something personal when hearing the news of his death and her entry into politics.

So, following the instructions of the organizers, my mother and I dressed in yellow, the color of Cory Aquino's Laban party, and packed some food for the road trip. Neither my mother nor I had ever been particularly involved with U.S. politics. She voted regularly but never campaigned and rarely talked about politics in the home. She joined the group partly for the cause, partly out of a sense of *pakikisama* (smooth relationship) with other Filipino American community leaders, the fact that she had met the couple several times before, and, as it was for me, for the pure excitement of it all.

Upon arrival, I felt like I was a part of something much bigger, something that extended overseas to the people in the Philippines who were actually putting their lives at stake. We marched, chanted, and looked aggrieved for the press, but the most rousing aspect of the experience to me were the songs. More than once we sang "Bayan Ko (My Country)," a patriotic *kundiman* known by most Filipinos. I knew it too, having learned the words phonetically at first during Filipino School. Plus, as long as I could remember, we had kept the score in the piano bench at home. One of my older brothers could play it before I could, so I learned how to play it too. Whenever we did, my mother would remind us to play with feeling, as if our mechanical struggles were doing a disservice to something special.

That one day in the nation's capital, I am not sure I really believed the words, really felt that it was *my* country longing to be uncaged, since my country of birth is the United States. Nevertheless, the music moved me then, just as it has always moved me. I believe my sense of profound affect is similar to that experienced by many who have personal memories related to the song as well as an understanding of its iconic standing over decades of Philippine nationalist history. More than twenty years later, when I play the song with my *rondalla* in concerts, I know it has lost some of its contextual power. But when we play it well, and when we allow our bodies to rise with the dynamic swell and our faces to brighten with the onset of the major mode and the shift to a higher register, it seems we can always make someone cry. It's just that kind of song, with just that kind of history.

| # Reviving the Spirit of Revolution
Songs of EDSA

T HERE IS A WIDE, BUSY highway called Epifanio de los Santos Avenue that arches around metropolitan Manila. Like many organizations and places in the Philippines, an acronym more comfortably stands in for the name; in this case, the street is commonly referred to as EDSA. It is traveled daily, the mundane route of commuters and other erstwhile travelers. Yet, EDSA carries a great deal more weight after 1986, since it became the site of three bloodless revolutions to overthrow the existing heads of state. Because the revolutions are so closely associated with the place in which people gathered, they have been recorded in history and popular memory as EDSA or EDSA I, EDSA II (or EDSA Dos), and EDSA III (or EDSA Tres).[1] It is the first of the three, EDSA I, that is the most well known throughout the world. Also called the People Power Revolution, the 1986 movement to remove Ferdinand and Imelda Marcos is a critical event in Philippine history. It displayed a nationalism that cleaved nation from state and tied Philippine modernity to other democratizing movements around the world instead of to the local regime that touted modernization and enacted dictatorial powers.

This chapter examines the events and the music of the first People Power Revolution to illustrate how musical nationalism can reject the legitimacy of the state. In doing so, participants sang songs that aligned their goals with the revolutionary nationalisms of the past. When patriotic anthems turn against the state, while still vigorously extolling the nation, the separation between the two is made palpable through group expression. There are fascinating dialectics in musical expression during these moments, where patriotism is both for and against order in society. Likewise, the musical affect of protest songs served both provocative and pacifist means, as street concerts and radio broadcasting inspired people to action as well as kept them under control. Music appeared in many guises during those heady days, and in the aftermath, remains as one of the most important memory bearers of the event. Music was also the soundtrack to a televised revolution, where Filipinos performed the redemptive qualities of humankind and renounced the temptations of violence, rewriting their own history of revolution in the process.

Anthemic songs take on heightened importance during times like these, for they derive their strength from communal performance, shared belief in symbolism, and the particular conditions surrounding their use. While every nation has a national anthem as part of the trappings of state, other songs may become anthemic through conditions and use. For many U.S. citizens, "America the Beautiful" is as anthemic as "The Star Spangled Banner," and to some, the former is preferable in text and melody (including ease of singing). Paul Nettl, in his exposition on national anthems, remarked that anthems share the following characteristics: relatively simple melodies that can be sung by most people, meaningful and moving lyrics, and ties to a nation's past. Beyond these, anthems do not need to have musical traits that are closely associated with one place or people, though language is usually the most obvious marker of locality. National anthems may be hymn-like or march-like in character, and both are symbolic of the time in which they were written and a projected characteristic of the nation as a whole (Nettl 1967). During times of social upheaval, anthems like the U.S. civil rights song "We Shall Overcome" and the Filipino *kundiman* "Bayan Ko (My Country)" share the characteristics of performance by an aggrieved group, meaningful lyrics, and emotional arousal. They are not national anthems of the country, but rather, they become oppositional statements against the official nationalism of the state. As passionate statements made communally, these anthems have the added power of transcending the mundane use of national anthems sung at the beginning of school days, ball games, and after the last showing of a movie in a Manila cinema.

The profound social experience of musical affect that occurs during the singing and reception of these anthems can be framed from a phenomenological perspective as a culturally conditioned experience that draws from collective knowledge and relies upon the contingencies of performance. Performance is itself imminently meaningful, not merely through text and musical literacy, but also through shared social knowledge of history and context. Thus, reception is itself a kind of performance one is expected to engage in, and the visceral response to music making offers a heightened sense of empathy and embodiment. Audiences who might sit quietly during other types of performances often find themselves singing or humming along with anthemic songs, a behavior that is acceptable and even encouraged. Others are overcome by an emotional response that is expected and often anticipated. The social and emotional engagement engendered by moments of musical performance is, thus, part and parcel of an active and activating nationalism.

The Televised Revolution

At least for a short time, the February 1986 People Power Revolution in the Philippines served as an iconic model for peaceful change and a people's fervent pursuit of democracy. American television followed the development of the revolution from its beginnings in 1983 to newly installed President Corazon Aquino's triumphant appearance before a joint session of the U.S. Congress in September of 1986. In that same year, she also made the cover of *Time* magazine. Emblematic of the times, "a grinning Jane Fonda acknowledged the people power revolt by flashing the Laban sign (an 'L' made with the index finger and thumb indicating support for Aquino) during the Oscars ceremony" (Lim 2006). People Power had impacted American mainstream culture. It seemed that at the revolution's apex, the Philippines as a country had enthralled her former colonial master with her people's quest for democracy.

The revolution has since undergone a multitude of deconstructions that illuminate the causes behind it, the little known events that occurred during it, U.S. involvement, and its legacy.[2] Many of these later writings cast a pallid light on EDSA, but at the time of its occurrence, it captivated international media and was powerfully symbolic. The uprising, ostensibly against Ferdinand Marcos's dictatorship, attracted so much interest from worldwide media that Americans with little or no knowledge of the former U.S. colony could follow the developments of the revolution on their home television sets.

As politically sophisticated observers were already aware, the U.S. government had a large role to play throughout the period before, during, and after the revolution. Following almost fifty years of colonial control, the U.S. government continued to exert great influence in the Philippines at the presidential level as well as through educational, military, and social institutions. Moreover, the cultural legacy of the colonial years and uninterrupted influx of American goods and media caused many to doubt that the paternalistic bonds had ever been severed.[3] The Filipino populace, and especially the opposition, recognized that the Marcoses had the support of the Reagan administration despite years of martial law and regular complaints of human rights violations. In the end, the demise of the Marcos presidency occurred *despite* American support and with only the last-minute withdrawal of that support in favor of a new president.

Both in the Philippines and abroad, most observers knew that Marcos's opponent was Corazon "Cory" Aquino, who projected herself to the public as a devout housewife-turned-politician. This image stood in sharp contrast to both Marcoses, perceived as profoundly corrupt, and so the battle emerged as nothing less than a polarity of good versus evil. Along the way, Cory (her followers referred to her by her nickname) often invoked the memory of her martyred husband, Benigno "Ninoy" Aquino. He had returned to the Philippines on August 21, 1983, to run for president after years of exile in the United States. He barely made it onto Philippine soil, shot fatally on the airplane steps while disembarking at Manila International Airport. His killing appeared to be an obvious retaliation for returning to the islands, but rather than put an end to the political rivalry, the assassination transformed Aquino into a martyr. International reporters who had flown with Aquino from the United States to the Philippines witnessed his death as it occurred. Their versions of the shooting and the subsequent gunning down of his alleged assassin by the military contrasted with the official disavowal of any involvement by the Philippine government.[4] The event proved to be catastrophic for the Marcos regime, as the political significance of President Marcos's longtime political nemesis magnified tremendously after his death. The tragic events triggered the rise of Corazon Aquino as a saintly mother figure upon whose image the populace could rally. Her reputation for religious faith, bolstered by the martyrdom of her husband, contrasted starkly with the excesses and corruption of Ferdinand and Imelda Marcos's dictatorship.[5]

In the meantime, political activists prepared a steady stream of protests in the form of street theater and "lightning rallies" in which a group would gather for a minute or so in a busy location to denounce the Marcos government with slogans or signs (Barrios 2008). By moving in and out of crowded public areas so quickly, protesters were able to elude capture. During longer productions, however, if the messages were not hidden well enough, performers would be imprisoned for their performances against the government. Many activists went to jail, underwent torture, or simply disappeared, but the performances did not stop. In the meantime, "a lively opposition press built an audience and stoked public discontent with the Marcoses by coming out with daring attacks on the government" (Florentino-Hofileña 1998: 6). The government had controlled the media in the past, but also found it convenient to give the impression of a tolerant rule over society. While crony newspapers spread stories straight from the Marcos propaganda machine (including some that deliberately seemed oppositional) more and more outlets for very real complaints appeared after martial law was lifted.

The growing unrest and popularity of Corazon Aquino spurred Ferdinand Marcos to action. During a November 1985 interview on *This Week with David Brinkley*, Marcos announced that the nation would participate in "snap," or early and sudden, elections for the presidency the following February 7, 1986. Though the elections were closely monitored, Marcos engineered another victory amidst accusations of massive fraud and coercion. Feeling that he had settled the political turmoil and solidified his position with his American supporters with this show of democracy, Marcos held another inauguration ceremony for himself and his wife on February 25. But it was too late. By that time, members of the military had already engineered a mutiny, thousands of civilians had taken to the streets, and the United States prepared to cut its ties with the Marcos government. When defeat became glaring, and the crowds were amassed at the gates, former president Ronald Reagan arranged for the Marcoses to escape Malacañan Palace in U.S. military helicopters.

A breakaway group of military officers played a crucial role in igniting the people's movement to the streets, and the resulting standoff would not have ended peacefully, had the rest of the military not defected over the course of the four-day revolution. The Reform the Armed Forces Movement (RAM) coalesced into action several months before Benigno Aquino's assassination in 1983, when eighty officers of the Philippine military turned against Marcos and pledged loyalty to the Philippine constitution rather than to the president (Hamilton-Paterson 1998: 379). These military rebels followed the leads of General Fidel Ramos and the secretary of defense, Juan Ponce Enrile, when they defected on February 22, 1986. At a press conference, Ramos and Enrile denounced President Marcos for election fraud and pledged their support to Corazon Aquino. Ramos then made his way to the military base, Camp Crame, while Enrile headed for Camp Aguinaldo, both across the street from one another in Quezon City. The street separating the two camps was EDSA. The rebels knew that soldiers loyal to Marcos would soon be on their way to crush the nascent uprising, and it is at this point that the involvement of civilians became of paramount importance.

The cooperation between factions of the military, the church, and the civilian population (including leftist groups) was crucial in bringing down the Marcoses. When the military RAM faction finally declared independence from the Marcoses publicly, people had reason to believe that spectacular change was finally possible. The trick for RAM would be in disseminating word of its actions and in encouraging the populace to rally support rather than merely wait out the uprising in their homes. Much of the news and the pleas to get people into the streets to surround the buildings where the military was holed up occurred over the radio. It began with the Catholic station, Radio Veritas. When that went off the air in the middle of the revolution, Radio Bandido took over just hours later. The voice that guided people over the airways throughout belonged to June Keithley, a onetime children's television show host who became the conduit between the mutineer military and the crowds on the streets. Jim Paredes, a member of the group Apo Hiking Society and composer of the EDSA anthem "Handog ng Pilipino Sa Mundo," was one of many musicians to participate in the revolution, and he took a personal role in trying to keep the rebel radio station on the air. When the military forces under Marcos's command bombed Radio Veritas, Paredes called upon civilians to surround the station. Keithley, hearing about his role, instructed him over the airwaves to find her at Radio Bandido, so that they could better coordinate together (Lim 2006).

Keithley, over the airwaves, directed civilians to form a massive human barricade around the rebel soldiers that would block members of the Marcos military from accessing their targets. The crowds at EDSA included a variety of people from clergy to activists to musicians to the simply curious, and among them roamed veteran activists, armed guerillas, and even street toughs.[6] Why were so many willing to sacrifice themselves before tanks and companies of soldiers with guns raised?[7] The feelings of Malou Roa echo that of many others.

> My participation in people power was basically out of a sense of patriotism and support for Cory Aquino. Weeks before the revolution, I had felt a deep sense of hopelessness that we Filipinos could not do anything to help our country regain respectability, and that we had to endure a government and a President we no longer wanted. I felt that this was our last chance to win our freedom, and if Marcos would still be the victor, then we would just have to put up and shut up. (Roa 1986: 31)

Driven by this sense of urgency, thousands left their homes, knowing that they would be in danger. The radio broadcasts guided the people, but the remote voice from an unknown location was not enough in and of itself to support morale and maintain order. Neither did the radio have continuous broadcasting during the long hours of waiting in between the harrowing approaches by the loyal military. Instead, groups of veteran activists and performers attempted to organize the people using techniques of social protest that had been practiced during the preceding years.

Strikingly, music and street performance played an important part of the revolution from the start. The dialectic of power in performance, where musical affect is both harmless and harmful, ensured that the singing of suppressed music would fuel the oppositional fervor while entertainment songs would help to pass the time and temporarily alleviate the anxiety of the precarious standoff between military and civilians. Musicians kept the crowds from dissipating by engaging them. At once an escape and an incendiary, music appeared in many guises during the revolution. Many musicians and other artists had protested against the Marcos regime since the declaration of martial law almost fifteen years earlier, and these performers were already prepared when the EDSA revolution finally coalesced into a mass movement. The composer and popular music artist Jim Paredes affirmed:

> Music is a powerful tool, definitely. A song can easily summarize feelings and arguments in 3–4 minutes. And combining the emotions with rational points is quite powerful.... People were moved by music to do action. The years building up to the EDSA revolution proved that.... When Ninoy was murdered, I made a song called "Di Ka Nag-iisa" which was distributed on cassette clandestinely. The song summarized and encapsulated the feeling of anger and the rising courage that was beginning to stir then. (2007)

Music followed the path of politics and led the way in voicing ideologies for the direction of society. Where some could be disseminated only underground, the revolutionary zone of EDSA became an arena for their free expression.

Songs of EDSA

Elena Rivera Mirano stresses the peculiar variety of songs that made up the soundscape of EDSA.

> I think people were caught off guard by the events and since a lot of the battle was waged on the radio spontaneously, the radio people laid their hands on whatever was available in the studio. Thus as events

unfolded, we had "Bayan Ko" (a kundiman using the *Inang Bayan*, lost paradise theme), "Onward Christian Soldiers" (which must have been discovered in the Radio Veritas library. Strange, *kasi* [because] Veritas is a Roman Catholic Station), "Mambo Magsaysay" (an election jingle from the 1950's extolling the virtues of the US-CIA supported Magsaysay—text goes "Our democracy will die, kung wala si (without) Magsaysay"), the PMA Hymn was rendered with great emotion by military men guarding the radio stations. (2008)

Songs provided entertainment, created a sense of community, and stirred patriotic emotions that guided the purpose of the people. Far from being incidental, artists understood immediately how they could contribute. According to Jim Paredes, "We put up a concert at Radio Veritas on the first night of the revolution. The stage was a massive truck, and all the artists came *gratis*. Our job was to keep the people there to prevent an attack from the military on Radio Veritas. It was such a great night. We were all seriously ready to die as artists doing our jobs, if we had to. . . . The people could have resorted to violence if the military did" (2007). Far from being obscure, the musicians at the revolution were some of the most popular of their day. Jim Paredes's group, Apo Hiking Society (APO), had accumulated a large fan base with OPM hits and live concerts, and his participation in EDSA strengthened his reputation as a politically conscious musician. At the time, however, through the participation of musicians, EDSA "had become an open-air carnival, a fiesta" (Escalante and de la Paz 2000: 56).

Some of the songs used during EDSA showed support for the opposition military and served to encourage other defectors. In the earliest stages of the revolution, they played the Alma Mater hymn of the Philippine Military Academy (PMA) over the radio as a plea from the rebel PMA officers to their mates from the academy to join them (Melencio 1986: 56). When the rebel soldiers and officers moved from Camp Aguinaldo to Camp Crame, surrounded by thousands of civilians but still exposed to military fire from above, "they were cheered by jubilant Filipinos singing 'Onward Christian Soldiers'" (Bilbao 1986: 124). That particular song, highlighted by Elena Rivera Mirano with some bemusement, actually had become popular as a kind of anthem during the years before EDSA that tapped into the religiosity of Filipinos and seemed to apply so well to Cory Aquino's campaign for the presidency. During the revolution, the song bolstered the sense that the military rebels were both heroes and martyrs for the cause against the Marcos dictatorship. The sense of camaraderie between the civilians and the rebel military deepened throughout the days of the revolution, with many feeling that the political cause naturally intertwined with a much more spiritual crusade. One civilian participant wrote, "The tanks kept on rolling down this side street until they were almost upon us. We started to sing religious songs to keep our spirits up. On the fourth hymn, the tanks finally stopped. We stayed there for two hours praying and singing religious songs until the soldiers got tired and finally retreated" (Villaluz 1986: 98).

In the meantime, activists circulating among the civilians also built relationships through the life-altering experience of self-sacrifice. Where once the legal and underground Left seemed to have few in-roads into the middle and upper classes, now there were opportunities for collaboration against the Marcos regime. Maria Josephine "Joi" Barrios, a writer, scholar, and activist during the Marcos era, had a better awareness than most of the civilians of how persistent and determined the Left had been in the years preceding EDSA and how they had helped to prime the conditions for the people's participation in what had begun as a military mutiny. Still, she realized that civilians felt ambivalent about the participation of the veteran activists.

> On EDSA, there were many stages, many performers, because [the street] was so long. I belonged to a street theater group.... We were organized, we were legal, not underground; we were considered to be Leftists. People didn't know exactly what to do. But unlike other people who went on their own, we had to stop ourselves, because we were part of a group. The Left had boycotted the elections, so it was very, very difficult for us to come into EDSA, because people were wary of the Left. How do you join in? The easiest way is to get your artists to perform, because they would be more acceptable; they look nonthreatening. (Barrios 2008)

Once they were able to set themselves up on EDSA, Barrios and her contemporaries had many songs at their disposal for drawing the attention of the throng. Likewise, they knew how to involve the audience, for they had been performing on the streets in an organized fashion over the previous decade. She continued,

> From the point of view of these groups, this was something we had prepared for many, many years before EDSA. We already had our set repertoire. So we had our usual street plays, including the one with the Ilocano Dracula, where Marcos is Dracula. He was wearing a Marcos mask and a *barong*. It was a funny play. We also explored a lot of other forms apart from the Vaudeville form. An interesting form we did was

kilos awit; it means "song with action." A lot of the movements are stylized, very Chinese revolutionary . . . People were watching because they were curious. . . . We would teach four-line songs with actions. Why? Because we don't want the audience to fall asleep. (Barrios 2008)

My Country, Our Song

"Bayan Ko (My Country)," already an anthem, became a kind of theme song for the opposition. It is a part of the recollections of many participants in the lead up to, and during, the revolution. One participant explained, "People kept pouring into EDSA, restive, shouting and singing 'Bayan Ko'" (Melencio 1986: 53). The original version of "Bayan Ko" was composed in 1928 by Constancio de Guzman, with lyrics by José Corazon de Jesus (see figure 5.1). While directed at the U.S. colonial government of the time, "Bayan Ko" followed from the tradition of revolutionary songs used during the late-nineteenth-century war against Spain. The lyrics of the song clearly articulate liberationist nationalism, but the poignancy conveyed by the *kundiman* style of music suppresses militarism in favor of emotion.

> "Bayan Ko"
> A.
> Ang bayan kong Pilipinas
> Lupain ng ginto't bulaklak
> Pagibig ang sa kanyang palad
> Nagalay ng ganda't dilag
> At sa kanyang yumi at ganda
> Dayuan ay nahalina
> Bayan ko, binihag ka
> Nasakdal sa dusa
>
> B.
> Ibon mang may laying lumipad
> Kulungin mo at umiiyak
> Bayan pa kayang sakdal dilag
> Ang di magnasang makaalpas
> Pilipinas kong minumutya
> Pugad ng luha ko't dalita
> Aking adhika, makita kang sakdal laya

English translation:

"My Country"

A.

My country the Philippines
Land of gold and flowers
With love from her palms
Beauty and splendor are offered
And to her tenderness and beauty
Were foreigners attracted
My country, you were conquered
Charged to suffering

B.

Even a bird that is free to fly
Cage it and it will cry
More so will a magnificent country
Desire to be unchained
Philippines, my beloved
Nest of my tears and torment
My desire is to see you truly free.

Like many composed *kundiman* (a genre examined below), "Bayan Ko" is in binary form, where the A section is in a minor key, and the B section is in the parallel major. Though it seems like a simplistic musical device, the

FIGURE 5.1. Melody of "Bayan Ko" (transcription by author)

change in mode is quite serviceable in shaping the musical sound to the meaning of the lyrics and evoking sentiment in performers and listeners alike. The A section is brooding, lending a melancholy air to the animated melody. The lyrics begin with a description of the country, in a poetic manner similar to that in which a man might describe his beloved maiden. Likewise, the melody starts quietly in a low register and rises in pitch as the textual descriptors become more heartfelt.

The second half of that section begins with a repetition of the melody, echoing the tenderness of the beloved country described in the lyrics. As the lyrics describe the incursion of outsiders, the melody rises higher than before, as if to cry out. The music and the lyrics descend toward the end of the section in pained resignation. Section B opens in earnest. Not only has the mode changed to major, but also the very note that demarcates this change (the third in the scale that has now been raised) is the highest note the melody has yet reached and is the first of this section. The stretching of the melodic ambit matches well with the text in which a bird may fly, and the overall effect is naturally rousing. Perhaps more important, listeners who know nothing about the mechanics of music can hear the change from section to section easily through the key change.

Interestingly, the song has had various incarnations since its composition. By the time Joi Barrios learned the tune, an additional two stanzas had been added, though she could not say exactly when this occurred. She suspected the change happened during the Marcos years, when many songs became part of the Left's repertoire of protest music and "Bayan Ko" had a resurgence in popularity (Barrios 2008).

> Ang bayan kong hirang
> Pilipinas ang pangalan
> Perlas ng Silangan
> Sa taglay niyang kariktan.
> Ngunit sawimpalad
> Sa minimithing paglaya
> Laging lumuluha
> Sa pagdaralita.
>
> Kay sarap mabuhay
> Sa sariling bayan
> Kung walang alipin
> At may kalayahan
> Ang bayang sinisiil

Bukas ay babangon din
Ang silangay pupula
Sa timyas ng paglaya

English translation:
My chosen country
Pilipinas is the name
Pearl of the East
Because of her innate beauty.
But she is unfortunate
In her ideal for freedom
Always in tears
In her misery.

How sweet to be alive
In one's own country
Where there is no serfdom
And where there is freedom
The country that is suppressed
Tomorrow will rise in revolt
The East will turn red
For sweet freedom[8]

In discussing the various versions of the song and its multiple emergences in Philippine history, Barrios stated, "The key here is the East turning red. This had meanings from the turn of the century" (2008). While many would assume that *red* refers to Communism and influences from China, red was also associated with the nineteenth-century Katipunan rebels fighting against the Spanish colonial government. Barrios continued,

{The change in lyrics] happened in the early 1970s before Martial Law was declared....

It opens differently and it ends differently; two stanzas at the beginning and two at the end. Remember that "Bayan Ko" was written in the 1920s. What they would do during the Japanese period, when they wanted to recruit people into the army, they would have a play. And a person would play *Inang Bayan* [Mother Country] and other actors would pretend to be soldiers. The people would go on stage and free her from the Japanese soldiers, and then they would sing "Bayan Ko." (2008)

During the 1986 People Power Revolution, people sang a slightly, but meaningfully, different version of "Bayan Ko." As with the addition of the two verses, it is unclear exactly when this new lyrical change occurred and who perpetrated it, though it was certainly deliberate. Antonio Hila remarks that the line *"Kulungin mo at umiiyak"* from the original version was altered to *"Kulungin mo at pumipiglas"* (2004: 32). Through that lyrical switch, the caged bird would no longer cry when caged; instead, the bird would struggle to escape. This alteration is obviously significant in that it recasts a Filipino sentiment of fatalism, *"bahala na* (so be it)," into a much more active stance against adversity.

That the song has transformed over time is not particularly unique. Joi Barrios and the Filipino historian Francis Gealogo explained that through their years of participation in political groups, they could actually date activists by the versions of a song that they sang. In their experience, they knew which group people belonged to based on whether they sang lyrics that came from the 1950s and 1960s or from a later date. When groups underwent schisms, songs became markers of identification as much as they had always been political anthems. One group would sing a song with one set of lyrics, while another would sing the same song with very different or slightly different text, and in this way it was clear to which organization a person belonged. With resigned amusement, Barrios sighed that there were even more versions in currency that she does not know but is supposed to be able to sing when she checks in with contemporary activists in the Philippines.

"Bayan Ko" has had sustained popularity since the first People Power Revolution, primarily because it has become so loaded with meanings throughout its historical tenure. Always patriotic, the song is nationalist in a way that denies the supremacy of any state over the legitimacy of the nation and its body of citizens. Yet, in its journey through time, "Bayan Ko" has also served to legitimate the state following the fall of Marcos. Beginning with Corazon Aquino, "Bayan Ko" began shedding its revolutionary overtones for a more general sentiment of nationalism. The song became one of many symbols associated with the time period and with Corazon Aquino's rise to the presidency, including the color yellow and the exhortation "Laban (Fight)." During Aquino's 1986 inauguration, "The seventh president of the Philippines wore a simple yellow dress with three-quarter-length sleeves and her trademark yellow-rim glasses. Her first act was to install Enrile and Ramos [leaders of the military rebels] as defense minister and chief of staff.... The new government grasped hands and led the crowd through an emotional rendition of 'Bayan Ko'" (Johnson 1987: 236–237). Even now, diasporic audiences continue to be touched by performances of the song and

moved by the strength of emotions that the song evokes. Those who participated in political movements seem to be especially affected, for to them the
song has many more layers of meaning than just patriotism and nostalgia. It
carries the weight of real struggles, the loss of friends and family, hard-won
victories, and the tenacious hope of the people for the country.

Kundiman, or Songs for the Love of Nation

"Bayan Ko" is a *kundiman*, a genre of Filipino music that for many is strongly
associated with Filipino identity. Popularly described from a metaphysical
perspective, the sentiments of the *kundiman* are felt to have generated from
the soul of the Filipino nation and have as much to do with suffering as with
hope. The *kundiman* is a song of passionate longing and profound love that
translates effectively into patriotic and nationalist music, an analogy made
doubly potent when one compares unrequited love with the yearning for
independence against tremendous odds. Because the history of the *kundiman*
has direct ties to the war against Spain and the age of U.S. colonialism in the
Philippines, it is well worth examining the musical genre in order to understand how it culminated in "Bayan Ko" as an anthem of social protest.

The origins of the *kundiman* are commonly traced to a pre-Hispanic form
called the *kumintang*, though because sources are scarce, the connections
remain somewhat speculative even if the lineage is now assumed. The first
mention of the *kumintang* in print does not occur until the early 1730s, while
the earliest notation appears around 1846, but neither of these sources is
definitive of the genre (Mirano 1992: 29).[9] Musical historians generally claim
that the *kumintang* was a war song, but it more likely had different uses.
Three possible types include songs of conquest, accompaniment for musico-
poetic declamations, and music performed at weddings with dance (See Bañas
1975: 81; Santiago 1957: 6).

If the *kumintang* began its life as a rousing war song, that use gave way
over time to a more plaintive music, perhaps ceding to or merging with the
two other possible types to produce a more multifunctional song style.
Indeed, another broader definition of the *kumintang* could be an archaic
popular song type from the Batangas area (a Tagalog-speaking region close to
Manila). In fact, Bañas contends that "the province of Batangas was formerly
called the 'Province of *Kumintang*' for it was believed that the town of Balayan
there was the original home of this art form. The early Spanish chroniclers
also called the Tagalog regions 'The Land of the *Kumintang*'" (Bañas 1975: 82).
What apparently ties the *kumintang* to the later *kundiman* is the musical

organization of 3/4 meter, though that is clearly an aspect that many genres of Filipino folk music share.[10] According to the eminent conductor, music historian, and composer Antonio Molina (who also wrote his own *kundiman*), the *kumintang* had a characteristic pattern in which the accent falls on the third beat of the first bar and the second beat of the second bar when counted in 3/4 time. Further, he notes that the *kundiman*, often in a minor key, also is always written in 3/4 time and has the same accent on the second beat of the second bar (1977: 2028). This typical beat pattern may more likely apply to *kundiman* that were extemporaneously created, since declamatory improvisation benefits from the expectation of rhythmic regularities in music.

The earliest *kundiman* type should be contrasted with those that were composed in later years as art music and comprise the repertoire with which most Filipinos are familiar (de Leon 1990: 15). Mentions of the *kundiman* as its own song type appear in late-nineteenth-century writings devoted to language and ethnographic description, but it is not clear how long the genre had been in common use before it was documented (see de Abella 1874; de Coria 1872; and Retana 1888). While these *kundiman* may have had a musical-stylistic relationship with the *kumintang*, and though there appears to be a similarity between the terms *kumintang* and *kundiman*, the etymology of *kundiman* is attributed to separate origins. In one theory, the term came from the lyrics "Hele hele nang kandungan; hele hele nang kundiman." In another, *kundiman* signified the red cloth of men who danced to *kumintang* music. Some believe the word is a contraction of the phrase "*kung hindi man* (if it were not so)" found in the lyrics of early *kundiman* songs (Bañas 1975: 82, 84). There is a certain melancholic nature evident in the genre if one were to subscribe to the last of the three explanations, and this fits well with Molina's reverie that "the setting for the early *kundiman* used to be a feudal castle whose bridges made it inaccessible to the enamored swain who had disregarded bad weather and had crossed villages and towns on foot just to reach the window of his beloved" (Molina 1977: 2026). This, of course would be inappropriate to apply to the Philippines, a place replete with churches from the Spanish colonial era but quite devoid of castles (though there remain preserved in Manila the stones of Fort Santiago).

The imagery is a reminder of the *kundiman*'s shared European origins, which are also evident in the genre's musical aesthetics, including the use of the Western scale. Almost always in triple time and utilizing Western harmony, the *kundiman* has a sectional form with different melodies for each section, and often a key modulation between each one (Mirano 1992: 31). Though *kundiman* are commonly sung in a variety of vocal styles, from operatic to popular music voices, the most successful renditions require a performer who can capture emotional nuances, has a wide dynamic range, and who has a feel for the poetic nature of the texts. Felipe de Leon, Jr. (the son of composer Felipe de Leon from chapter 1), insists that the *bel canto* style of Italian singing, the "dark, powerful voice" of the German Lied, and the frivolous pop song voice are inappropriate. Rather, the "deeply felt longing or noble idea" typical of the *kundiman* requires a "'natural' (speech quality), unaffected, warm, lyrical, sensitive and intimate type of voice... for it is capable of conveying the spontaneous, open and sensitive nature of the Filipino" (de Leon 1990: 15–16). While the musical aspects of the *kundiman* have some stylistic consistency, the type of *kundiman* depends upon its lyrics and not on how it is sung. Love songs populate the foreground, but there are also lullabies, laments, and other types that lend themselves well to the heavily emotive style of the genre.

Where the *kundiman* becomes fascinating in regard to politics is in its incarnation as revolutionary music. The revolutionary *kundiman* may date as far back as the Cavite Revolt of 1872, though evidence in support of that is quite scant. This theory asserts that the name came from the red *kundiman* trousers associated with Katipunan members (the revolutionary society that has come to represent the culmination of early nationalism leading to independence from Spain). While typical clothing of the rebels became linked to the songs that they sang, in the end, it was the revolutionary love song that became more prominent and took ownership of the name (Manuel 1997: 19–20). This interpretation of the *kundiman* leads to the speculation that songs extolling love for a woman became symbolically intertwined with the passionate and yearning love for one's country.

The oldest known *kundiman* associated strongly with Filipino nationalism is "Jocelynang Baliwag," also known as the *kundiman ng himagsikan* (*kundiman* of the revolution). Thought of as a kind of prototype for composed art songs in the *kundiman* genre, "Jocelynang Baliwag" is believed to have become popular just prior to the Philippine revolution against Spain that lasted from 1896 to 1898. The lyrics express admiration for a woman—in this case, a person who actually existed named Pepita Tiongson y Lara (R. Santos 2001: 29). In these *kundiman*, as in others, the extreme ardor of the singer for his beloved serves as the primary motif. What differentiates revolutionary *kundiman* from their love song brethren is the coded symbolism in which the figure of a woman stands for the homeland (see Hila 2004). Erotic love becomes transcendent from the mortal realm.[11] The profane is transformed into the sacred, and, for the revolutionary who opposed the Spanish empire as much as the hierarchical strictures of the Catholic Church, nothing could be more pure and sacred than the love of Pilipinas, the motherland. Since the end of the nineteenth century, no music has been as expressive of the Filipino struggle for freedom than the *kundiman*.

Following the wars against Spain and the United States, and during the subsequent American colonial rule, the *kundiman* retained its popularity. Composers expanded on the form, creating a new style that was considered to be art music that was also populist and popular. The "golden age" likely fell between 1902 and 1935, the commonwealth years during which "the Filipinos' intense struggle for freedom clashed with the restraining might of the American military dictatorship," a struggle reflected in the inherent feeling of the *kundiman* (de Leon 1990: 16). Hence, the *kundiman* serves as a musical means for expressing a sentiment that—much like Portuguese *saudade* and Korean *han*—could be described as a collective sorrow. The *kundiman* captures the Filipino experience of the nineteenth and early twentieth centuries, not merely in its lyrics (which are often symbolic in nature), but also through a musical soulfulness. As a significant and meaningful genre, the *kundiman* served as the perfect inspiration for Constancio de Guzman's "Bayan Ko."

Protest from the Stage to the Street

As the *kundiman* increased in popularity among Filipinos, the revived Spanish *zarzuela* became fashionable in the Philippines. Tiongson describes *Jugar con Fuego* (Playing with Fire), a production by the Spanish touring troupe of Dario de Céspedes, as appearing in 1879 or 1880 (1992: 32). A play with songs, dances, and dialogue, the *zarzuela* could range from one to five acts. While Spanish *zarzuelas* often had plots devoted to romantic love, in the early-twentieth-century Philippine context, numerous *sarwelas* developed as vehicles for social commentary.[12] Nicanor Tiongson, scholar and former artistic director of the Cultural Center of the Philippines, has written extensively on the subject of *sarswelas* as they developed in the Philippines. Performed in urban theaters or open-air stages, *sarswelas* were usually performed by commercial troupes with requisite backdrops and props with an accompanying orchestra that played *kundimans*, *balitaws*, *balses*, *danzas*, foxtrots, and other popular songs (Tiongson 1992: 36–37). *Sarswelas* impacted the development of many nationalist Filipino composers, including the notable Nicanor Abelardo, composer of many *kundiman*. Abelardo eventually wrote his own *sarswelas*, beginning with *Lucila*, a collaboration with the librettist Florentino Ballecer. Unfortunately, *Lucila* irritated Filipino critics who panned the contrived deaths of every important character. Abelardo's music, they further decried, was too derivative of Italian opera. The pair's next collaboration, *Akibat*, fared substantially better, perhaps due to its nationalist themes and what critics deemed Abelardo's "modern"-sounding music. Abelardo continued to produce numerous *sarswelas* and other types of art music (Epistola 1996: 28, 30).

While there is a perception outside of the Philippines that U.S. rule had a milder approach than Spanish colonialism, banning and censorship was a common American practice in suppressing Filipino nationalist expressions. According to composer and scholar Ramón Santos, "Works such as *Tanikalang Ginto* (Gold Chain) and *Mabuhay ang Pilipinas* (Long Live the Philippines) of Juan Abad, *Pagibig sa Lupang Tinubuan* (Love for the Motherland) by Pascual Poblete, and *Kahapon, Ngayon at Bukas* (Yesterday, Today, and Tomorrow) by Aurelio Tolentino are but a few of the works whose authors and producers were severely punished and censured by the American colonial government" (2001: 27). Hence, if the writers, composers, and performers of *sarswela* desired to interject nationalistic messages into their productions, they had to combine surreptitiousness and showmanship. As with many types of protest art performed under oppressive conditions, veiled messages, ambiguous language, and other tactics had to become conventionalized so that audiences would understand the messages while authorities could not.

Sarswelas offered clear messages in support of self-government and served as commentaries on political oppression directed at the United States colonial government. José Estella's 1905 production *Filipinas Para Los Filipinos* trained its satirical guns on colonial rule over the archipelago as well as a U.S. congressional bill that prohibited the marriage between American women and Filipino men, since the title may be translated both as *The Philippines for Filipinos* and *Filipino Women for Filipino Men* (Canave-Dioquino 1998: 864). In these theatrical presentations, audiences understood symbolic characters, such as *Maimbot* (Greedy), from Juan Abad's *Tanikalang Ginto*, to refer to the United States. Juan Matapang Cruz's *sarswela* called *Hindi Ako Patay* (I Am Not Dead) featured the villain *Macamcam* (Oppressor), a stand-in for the American colonial government. When *sarswelas* were found by the Americans to be seditious, their composers were fined and imprisoned. Performers, who were sometimes also caught by the American military police, found discreet ways to delight audiences with political messages. Barrios related how a *sarswela* actress in a red dress would find a way during a key moment in the plot to stand beside an actress in a blue dress. Together they joined the colors of the banned Filipino flag. On other occasions, an actress would wait until the military police were not looking, and she would flash a small image of the flag hidden on the back of her fan (2008). The movement was coy, as many fan movements generally are. It was also treasonous.

While the *sarswela* declined in popularity after around 1940, making way for Filipino *bodabil* (vaudeville), the familiar storylines of the *sarswelas* found new life as film musical adaptations (Tiongson 1992: 32). In major cities like Manila, it has been only through state patronage that various productions have continued to appear over the years at venues such as the Cultural Center of the Philippines (CCP).[13] The nationalism evident in the newer *sarswelas* does not have the political edge found in early *sarswelas*, since those were performed during colonialism. Yet, some newer productions still contain pointed social commentary, while others feature popular music stars and serve as light entertainment. Exemplifying the latter generation of nationalist *sarswelas*, *Anong Tamis Ng Mga Sandali Sa Sariling Bayan* (How Sweet Are the Moments in One's Own Country) served as the final offering of the 1969 Philippine Festival. The CCP commissioned this theater production from the composer Colonel Antonino Buenaventura (1904–1996). As audiences expected, the show contained conventional themes of nationalism and romantic love, while at the same time, it upheld the *sarswela*'s prominence as a sublimely Filipino art. Buenaventura, who also served as a conductor and educator, was known in Manila musical circles as a gifted melodist who often included Filipino themes in his works. His "Pandanggo sa Ilaw" (1936), written in a folk song style, had already become so familiar in the Philippines as a folk dance accompaniment that most people did not (and still do not) realize he composed it. Buenaventura spent years studying, collecting, and transcribing regional music of the Philippines and later took leadership over the Philippine Constabulary Band, a résumé that solidified his nationalist credentials and helped vault him to the status of National Artist in 1988. Also taking into account that the *sarswela* is considered to be thoroughly "Filipinized" as a musical theater genre, both the composer and the *sarswela* genre were validated as nationalist. The appearance in 1969 of a new *sarswela* was, therefore, still enmeshed in politics; however, this time, *Anong Tamis Ng Mga Sandali Sa Sariling Bayan* was not at all seditious, instead fulfilling First Lady Imelda Marcos's claims to preserve and promote Filipino arts for the sake of the nation.

The co-optation of the *sarswela* to serve the needs of the state did not diminish its nationalist lineage, but instead tied nation much closer to state. At the same time, smaller scale regional productions endured for entertainment purposes, and street theater with musical numbers arose as underground performances against the state. Barrios commented on the popularity of these productions, saying, "People really liked the songs from protest theater because of the *sarswela* tradition. They really had fun when there was a song" (2008). Street productions, such as those that appeared on EDSA during the revolution, had long been a part of the Left's engagement with culture. Also integral to street performances, a genre known as "songs for the masses" resituated the nation as belonging to the people and not merely the provenance of the state. The tradition has historical ties with the Filipino guerilla fighters during World War II, known as the *Huks*, who developed their own song tradition to sing as they marched and waited, and also to steel themselves for battle during the long months in the Philippine jungles.[14] After the war, the *Huks* continued on as rural Communist fighters against the Philippine state, and their songs were popular expressions for the cause. Kris Montañez explains that revolutionary songs "employ the language of the masses," both in vernacular and in musical style, and that these songs are particularly effective in places where literacy is low and printed materials are difficult to produce. Popular themes included the national democratic revolution, armed struggle, and the revolutionary peasant mass movement (1988: 33). The songs for the masses came from various sources ranging from the larger global Communist movement to reanimated folk tunes to newly composed pieces. Barrios comments that musical inspirations and antecedents have changed over time. "The Chinese influence was more on the songs before Martial Law...our generation was influenced mainly by Latin America and China. We would also draw on the *kundiman*...so a lot of people would write songs along the lines of the *kundiman* or the *marcha*" (2008).

During the period leading up to the first People Power Revolution, the songs of the Communist organizations known as the New People's Army and the Communist Party of the Philippines promoted the National Democratic Revolution and undermined the existing authority of the nation-state as governed by the Marcos regime. Moreover, the underlying ideology of these songs should be read as a kind of supranationalism that joined the Philippine workers and peasants with others in the world proletarian movement. The revolutionaries did not necessarily deny the legitimacy of the nation as an idea, and, in fact, the idea of country was invoked in the very first song of the New People's Army, called "Ang Bagong Hukbong Bayan" (Montañez 1988: 35). Themes of revolutionary songs focused on the eradication of existing class structures that disenfranchised the majority of the nation's population—the proletariat—and allowed the continuation of imperialism. As a result, it is not difficult to tie the sentiments of revolutionary songs of the masses to those found in the early *kundiman* that focused on national liberation from colonialism. As functional music, then, it is not surprising that songs of the masses were used even by the "legal" Left to protest against the Marcos government among the uncommitted urban dwellers. Since, as Barrios described above, those not a part of the Left were quite wary of the activists, these songs were often altered slightly to protect the singers from soldiers and also to appeal to the less radical public. Lyrics mentioning guns or armed struggle were excised, and "socialism" was changed to "democracy." This flexibility, Barrios pointed out, seemed to reflect the performance practices of *sarswela*, where actors and singers tried to convey seditious messages to audiences in front of American military police through coded gestures, language, characters, and the ability to improvise in the moment.

More accessible to nonpoliticized Filipinos, particularly the middle class, folk music with themes of protest proliferated through singer-songwriters like Coritha and Jess Santiago, and the groups Asin and Inang Laya. Heber Bartolome penned a tune meant to awaken the majority to their own oppression and the possibility of their power over a corrupt state. The lyrics to the song "*Oy, Utol, Buto't Balat Ka Na'y Natutulog Ka Pa* (Hey Brother, You're Already Skin and Bones Yet Still You Sleep)" warn listeners that if they remain silent and refuse to become angry, the repercussions are their own fault. These folk singers used popular song to convey their messages in much the same way as folk singers of the United States, and they also experimented with folk instruments (like the *banduria* of the *rondalla*) and traditional folk tunes in order to anchor their music to the national heritage. By the 1980s, folk rock by artists like Freddie Aguilar (including his recorded rendition of "Bayan Ko") had become well known, particularly among the youth, and their presence at EDSA seemed to validate their lyrics of protest. In fact, an appearance at the street concerts of EDSA enhanced many music careers, giving performers wider exposure and the capital of having participated in a historic event (Mirano 2008).[15]

After the Revolution: A Filipino Gift to the World

The song "Handog Ng Pilipino Sa Mundo (Filipino Gift to the World)" arose directly from the experiences of EDSA. "Handog" is OPM (Original Pilipino Music), a general label for music by Filipino musicians that serves as the local answer to imported Western pop music (see chapter 4). Written by Jim Paredes during the heady months immediately following the bloodless coup, "Handog ng Pilipino Sa Mundo" captured the ebullient feelings of the revolution and commemorates the event as a musical artifact of history. "Handog" first hit the airwaves in April of 1986 and became quite popular. A version in English, called "A New and Better Way," with rewritten lyrics, followed and could be heard in both Australia and the United Kingdom. Both recordings, produced on cassette tape, made their way to Filipino diasporic communities all over the globe, and the song became quite well known.

While "Bayan Ko" illustrates the history of conflict with the United States, "Handog" is an assertion of the Philippine nation's rightful place within the global community. Ironically, "Handog" was also a testament to the continuing ties the Philippines maintained with the United States, particularly from a cultural standpoint. After all, the song followed the models of two worldwide hits from Europe and the United States that served to raise awareness and funds for famine stricken Ethiopia. "Do They Know It's Christmas?" penned by Bob Geldof of the group Boomtown Rats, found widespread airplay in 1984 with popular singers that included Phil Collins, George Michael, Sting, and Bono. They performed under the auspices of Band Aid. "We Are the World," written by pop music superstars Michael Jackson and Lionel Richie and produced by Quincy Jones, appeared in 1985. The song featured forty-five performers under the rubric of USA for Africa. The best known, including Stevie Wonder, Paul Simon, Diana Ross, and Cyndi Lauper, were invited to sing lead vocals.

Fifteen Filipino singers, including Kuh Ledesma, Celeste Legazpi, Subas Herero, Noel Trinidad, Gretchen Barreto, Leah Navarro, Ivy Violan, Inang Laya, Coritha and Eric, Lester Demetillo, and Joseph Olfindo, gathered in the studio to record "Handog." The song is catchy and inspiring, beginning with a series of solos and duets and culminating with all of the singers joined together in the rousing chorus. Much like the minor to major tonality shift in "Bayan Ko," the switch from solos to chorus is a simple and effective musical effect for even the most untrained listener. Disparate individuals become a powerful group during the refrain in a manner symbolic of People Power itself. A translation of the lyrics reveals the revolutionary and communal spirit of the times.

"Handog Ng Pilipino Sa Mundo (Gift of the Filipinos to the World)"
I will not allow you to lose freedom
I will not allow it to be taken back now
Our freedom that for so long we desired
I will not allow it to be taken back

Arm to arm, thousands of people
How sweet it is to be Filipino
Together with one desire
Never to be enslaved

Refrain:
Gift of the Filipinos to the world

Peaceful way for change
Truth, freedom, reason
Is possible to acquire without bloodshed
As long as all of us are one.

Observe what is taking place in our country
Together the poor and the rich
Arm in arm nuns, priests, soldiers
This part of the world became Heaven

Do not allow again darkness to rule
The voice of each person gives notice
We are brothers/sisters to the Lord
This we must always remember

Jim Paredes, the composer of "Handog," was a member of the well-known singing group Apo Hiking Society, along with Danny Javier and Boboy Garrovillo. The group's name, shortened from the Apolinario Mabini Hiking Society, takes its cue from Apolinario Mabini, a hero of the nineteenth-century revolution against Spain whose lower body paralysis and keen intellect earned him the historical nickname "the Sublime Paralytic." The group specialized in humor, catchy pop tunes and biting lyrics directed at society, politics, and even the Marcos government, ultimately leading to a crackdown from the state aimed at reducing their popular impact. According to APO's website, they "poked the eye of the powers-that-were with their irreverence and satirical wit. One could count on one hand how many artists were willing to stick their necks out to regain back the freedoms lost under the Marcos regime. At the risk of persecution, they continued their sacred tasks as artists to expose the foibles of the government through concerts, recordings and rallies until victory was won."[16] In fact, APO had been banned from the media for months before EDSA. Despite the government's actions, Paredes states, "The more we were banned, the more people wanted to watch us and see what we would be doing. We were all under the threat of censorship then. That is why anything obliquely referring to freedom, or the struggle against the dictatorship was immediately applauded. It was amazing" (Paredes 2007).[17]

Following the successful release of the song, the Filipino movie director Mike de Leon created an accompanying video for "Handog." It appeared on television for a short time before censors pulled it off the air, concerned that the images of crowds battering pictures of Ferdinand and Imelda Marcos might be too strong. This censorship was a surprising turn of events considering that the revolution for democracy had not only just occurred, but that Filipino independence in general was the subject matter of the video. In any case, of great significance was de Leon's juxtaposition of images of the Philippine-American War against those of anti-Marcos rallies, creating a sense of revolutionary lineage. His movie classicized the Filipino quest for liberation as a national theme. In the video, Benigno Aquino appears next to the martyr José Rizal. Filipino girls hand flowers to soldiers during EDSA, and nuns walk arm in arm before tanks. Corazon Aquino supporters raise their fists during a rally, and a soldier smiles as he makes the Laban (fight) salute of her political party. Communist guerillas marching through the jungle culminate in television shots of the thousands who came out to EDSA. Stills of ethnic minorities and a starving child follow footage of protestors being hosed by the police. And the musicians come together to sing throughout, swaying as they sing until the final chorus fades into a map of the Philippine nation.

Three years after the revolution, in 1989, the Shrine of Mary, Queen of Peace (Our Lady of EDSA), was established at the intersection of EDSA and Ortigas Avenue in Quezon City. The church has come to be known as the EDSA shrine. The church's website states that it "is dedicated to Our Lady who has miraculously interceded to oust the dictatorship in a peaceful and bloodless uprising that is now world renowned as the People Power Revolution of 1986.... With the help of the Blessed Mother and Santo Niño, the people's prayer for a moral leadership was answered. A Holy Ground marker was inaugurated at the EDSA Shrine on February 25, 2001 during the 15th anniversary of the first EDSA People Power."[18] Notably, the lyrics of "Handog ng Pilipino sa Mundo" are inscribed on one of the walls of the shrine, keeping a record not only of historical events, but also of the music that commemorated the first People Power Revolution.

Since the 1986 People Power Revolution, there has been steady critique over the lack of real and substantial change in the country achieved during the Aquino and subsequent presidencies. Graft, corruption, and ineptitude are among the charges directed toward the executive branch of the Philippine state by historians and journalists alike (see Arillo 2000). Fidel Ramos, the primary military leader of the rebels against Marcos during the People Power Revolution, served as President Aquino's chief of staff and then secretary of national defense. He succeeded Aquino as president in 1992 and, despite fears that he would push to alter the constitution to allow for an extended stay in office, he stepped down at the end of his term. In 1998, Ramos watched as the country elected his former vice president (in the Philippines, the president and vice president are elected separately), Joseph Estrada. A former film star who specialized in action movies, Estrada had great popularity among the Filipino lower class that comprise the vast majority of the country's population. Estrada became the president during the new millennium, and it was during his tenure that EDSA Dos and EDSA Tres (the second and third EDSA events) superseded the first People Power Revolution. Still, the original EDSA remains a watershed event in global as well as Filipino history. And, for at least a few moments in time, resistance, hope, and pride uplifted the spirits of thousands and was expressed, and then commemorated, in song.

Conclusion

Celebration and Recapitulation

T HE YEAR 1998 MARKED THE centennial of Philippine independence from Spain, an event celebrated throughout the country and in diasporic Filipino communities around the world. The Philippine state's formal observation of the centennial, through the appointment and funding of a committee to coordinate the year's events, revealed something of present-day political agendas. Taking ownership over the commemoration linked the current government to the history of governments in the Philippines, in particular the first revolutionary state, with special attention to the idea of legacy and legitimacy. The celebration was, in effect, a nationalization of collective memory, an authorization of history, and a shoring up of official nationalism with popular sentiments of patriotism. This connection to the past was, and remains, most rigidly enforced by Section 37 of Republic Act No. 849, demanding that all renditions of the Philippine national anthem "whether played or sung, shall be in accordance with the musical arrangement and composition of Julián Felipe." The punishment for deviation includes fines and possible imprisonment. Ambeth Ocampo, in his 1998 collection of essays called *The Centennial Countdown*, pitted musical creativity and affect against tradition when he decried that "some arrangers and composers have transformed the military cadence into something yawny as a royal or graduation march. Worse, choral groups show off by branching into different voices and counterpoints that discourage the public from singing along" (34). The conservative need to confine expressions of nationalism to an ideal of authenticity justified by a single historical moment is at least some indication of the insecurities over national identity that have plagued the Philippines over the last century.

Even locating the achievement of independence with the declaration of the mythical First Republic in 1898, rather than the granting of independence by the United States after World War II, validates a more potent nationalist history of liberation. While the Philippines extricated itself from United States imperialism slowly and through stages—transforming from colony to commonwealth to nation (and, some would argue, U.S. power is still prevalent even now)—the forming of a nation through an aggressive (albeit momentary) disengagement with Spain at the end of the nineteenth century evokes a much more dramatic narrative that includes the conventions of bloody sacrifice and heroic leadership. While these types of nationalistic celebrations are common to all nations, they take on heightened meaning when present-day emotions can be connected to events of the past.[1] Through a celebration of revolution, the Philippine nation links itself to other nations birthed through glorified revolutions, including, ironically, the United States. As with other nations, the time of revolution produced the first symbols of nation, including the flag and the national anthem. In 1998, as the curtain began its slow close on the twentieth century, expressions of nationalism again erupted into the spotlight through commemorative products and productions, including the Centennial Parade, the Centennial Ball (featuring an opening dance by then president Fidel Ramos and his wife, accompanied by the Manila Philharmonic Orchestra), and a bevy of concerts, books, and musical albums (Urlanda 1998). Altogether, the "stagecraft" and symbolic import of commemorative objects that year offer evidence of Benedict Anderson's "late nationalism," including, most distinctively, a nostalgic penchant for an idealized past (1998: 48). The events and artifacts reaffirmed ties between the present and the past, while also serving as memory keepers of present-day events. Musical performers making recordings and holding concerts during that year had very different backgrounds from one another, and many had experienced the nation's transitions from democracy to martial law and back to democracy. Some had participated actively in protests, while others navigated the political waters with much less tumult. Clearly, individual perceptions about nationalism, even and especially on this occasion, would be diverse and based on the life experiences of the performers and their hopes for the nation's future.

What follows in this concluding chapter are impressions of the 1998 products of a postrevolutionary, postcolonial, and perhaps even postmodern Philippines. Even a cursory inspection of the musical recordings that follow reveals how multifaceted the perceptions of the nation are. Yet, a modernist tidiness materializes in the very act of encapsulating the long hundred years of national change in the Philippines. The struggle to come to terms with hybridity and national identity, present and past, and local and global—embedded in musical aesthetics and performance—is evident in a narrative of the Philippine nation that relies on tropes of modernism to smooth out the disparities of everyday life. These musical recordings, which were widely available for purchase, project their own retellings of a hundred years of the Philippine nation through song anthologies and a populist presentation style.

The CD album *Sandaan 100: 1898–1998* not only bears the stamp of the Philippine Centennial Commission, the governmental group tasked with spearheading and organizing the year of celebration, but it is also endorsed through a message in the liner notes by then president elect Joseph Ejercito Estrada. The collection is straightforward in its distillation of Philippine nation-building, with a strong focus on political leaders and patriotic music, but it is curious in its juxtaposition of simulations and historical recordings. It begins with the Philippine Marine Corps Drum and Bugle Team playing an appropriately martial and succinct instrumental rendition of the Philippine national anthem. Between songs, the history of the Philippines is re-created. The sound of horses and gunfire evoke the 1899 Battle of Tirad Pass, and air raid sirens precede the radio broadcast of U.S. president Franklin D. Roosevelt's 1941 declaration of war against Japan. A ringing bell and wheels along a track represent the modernization of the Philippines through the introduction of Meralco's electric streetcar, while the announcement of Filipino boxer Pancho Villa as flyweight champion of the world is a matter of international pride. Listeners are also treated to snippets of speeches given by former Philippine leaders José P. Laurel, Manuel Roxas, Ramón Magsaysay, Diosdado Macapagal, Ferdinand Marcos, Corazon Aquino, Benigno Aquino, Jr. (the only non-president of the group), Fidel Ramos, and finally president elect Joseph Estrada as a retrospective of the nation's political history. Interestingly, these inclusions ignore the controversy of collaboration during World War II and the dictatorial nature of the Marcos regime.

There are, because of the many interludes, relatively few songs on the album. In fact, the national anthem appears three times, once as an instrumental, again in its English iteration (a rendition rarely found on recordings), and finally as it is presently sung. "Bayan Ko" has two versions, both by performers best known for their folk and protest music. Lolita Carbon of the group Asin sings the first, and Coritha & Erik sing the second (complete with a Hendrix-esque introduction on electric guitar), solidifying the anthem's contemporary dialectic of patriotism and opposition that was at its most fervent in the 1986 People Power Revolution. Jim Paredes's "Handog ng Pilipino sa Mundo" transitions the album to its final series of pop tunes by various artists. The final song is "Maligayang Sentenyal (Happy Centennial)," noted as "the official celebratory song of the Centennial Year," with music by Juan Miguel Salvador and lyrics by Romy Sinson. The text strikes a unifying tone, calling out to the three regions of Luzon, the Visayas, and Mindanao, as well as the ethnic groups of Cebuanos, Chabacanos, Badjaos, Hiligaynons, Iyatans, and "everyone" else to celebrate together as a nation.

The tone of the album, in which history is neatly linear and past transgressions against the nation are massaged into the timeline, is strikingly similar to that of the period of reconciliation immediately following the People Power Revolution. If there is something vaguely postmodern about the collection of sounds, there is also something poststructuralist about the refusal to impose meaning on their juxtaposition. Listeners are left to their own interpretations of how one hundred years of the nation translates into a contemporary experience of collective history, but the apolitical nature of the album is telling. Holding together the ideas and the realities of the Philippine nation has involved a heavy dose of political maneuvering, violence, and compromise, and yet along with all of this has been a consistent desire among political leaders to keep intact an illusion of unity. Many of those who worked with the Americans during the colonial period, the Japanese during World War II, and the Marcoses during their dictatorship were accepted back into the political fold and the national community. In local communities, this may relate to the cultural imperative to compromise and eliminate conflict. But among the elite, this historical propensity towards reconciliation is just another assertion of the strength of political clans and the upper class in controlling the nation.

In 1998, the Philippine Madrigal Singers released an album on compact disc called *Bayan Ko, Aawitan Kita (My Country, I Will Sing to You): A Centennial Celebration*. Like the *Philippine Graphic Centennial Yearbook*, published by Weekly Graphic magazine that same year, the musical repertoire rekindles the fire of the Katipunan revolutionaries who fought against Spain and signed their oath in blood, acclaims the national hero José Rizal, and evokes the poignancy of victories and tragedies intertwined.[2] Both the Yearbook and the Madrigals' album feature the ubiquitous "Bayan Ko (My Country)," the former as an artistically laid-out page devoted to the lyrics, and the latter as a moving choral arrangement. The *Yearbook* ends with two notable articles. The first outlines the lost hopes of the First Republic as a result of American imperialism, a sobering reminder that Filipinos are, in fact, keenly aware of the tragedies of their own national history (Brillantes 1998: 93). The second has a revealing title for the final article in this keepsake document—"Defining the Filipino." In it, the author invokes the common symbolism of East merging with West to define his nation. "We cannot, by wishful thinking, erase our history.... We have experienced many things. We are what we are. Let us not be ashamed of ourselves. Let us not be ashamed of our history. We are Asians; but we have been greatly influenced by the west. We belong to both. In this we are unique" (Bernad 1998: 106–107).

The Madrigal Singers define the Filipino nation through an abbreviated history of national songs that is as effective as it is expected (or perhaps is effective because it is expected). It is hard not to hear the metaphor of national community in the chorus of finely honed and immaculately blended voices. In comparison with other albums of that year, this work by the Madrigal Singers seems burdened more by the solemnity of a historiography that cannot overlook the tragedies of history. The *kundiman* "Jocelynang Baliwag" follows "*Alerta Katipunan*," a Spanish march adopted by Filipino rebels during the revolution (see chapter 5). "Amor Patria," based on the text of a song by the literary character Maria Clara, calls to mind the martyrdom of her creator, José Rizal. "Ang Bagong Lipunan" carries listeners of a certain age back to martial law. Serving as a counterbalance to all of these are two anthemic songs. The first is "*Ako Ay Pilipino* (I Am Filipino)" by George Canseco. The second is "*Isang Dugo, Isang Lahi at Musika*" by Dodjie Simon, and its title translates as "One Blood, One Race and Music." In tandem, both declare that one is Filipino, and that to be Filipino is to belong to one race. Even if there were failures in the revolution, these songs point only to the success of the contemporary nation in giving a large-scale identity to its population. "*Isang Dugo*" has been performed by the Madrigals in concert to rousing ovations, both because the music is well written and because the lyrics impart a long-held promise of various Philippine governments to hold together the diverse nation. The occasion is sealed by the final track on the recording, a short piece called "*Maligayang Centennial* (Happy Centennial)" by Romy Sinson and Juan Miguel Salvador that also praises the unity of the country and its various regions.

Long Live the Philippines! Mabuhay ang Pilipinas! claims the title of "official album of the Philippine Centennial 1898–1998." That is to say, like *Sandaan 100*, it too had approval of and support from the Philippine Centennial Commission. The first song bears the same name as the album and, tellingly, combines English and Filipino lyrics. It is both pop music and anthem, with a chorus belting out "God bless the Philippines!" while a pair of singers emotionally intone *"Pagpalain mo, panginoon, habang buhay* (Bestow your blessing, Lord, for our whole life through)." Featuring music stars like Sharon Cuneta, Pops Fernandez, Martin Nievera, and the group Side A, along with the Concert Chorus of the University of the Philippines, the song captures the populist spirit of the centennial year.

Overall, the collection of songs is a spirited popular culture tribute that is accessible if not profound. Yet, the album does have a few curious inclusions. In one instance, the First Lady of the Philippines at that time, Amelita M. Ramos, plays a piano rendition of former First Lady Imelda Marcos's favorite song, "Dahil Sa Iyo (Because of You)." Mike Velarde, the popular music and film music composer, wrote the music and paired it with text by Dominador Santiago.[3] The song has been popular among many Filipinos for decades and is so well known that it can transcend even Imelda Marcos's use of it. For instance, it was the local song chosen by Nat King Cole to sing in its original language when he played a concert at the Araneta Coliseum in the early 1960s. Further, it is a standard for wedding bands and lounge pianists. As a love song to the nation, it resonates well, but there is a palpable irony in its inclusion in a retrospective of the nation. Here it does bear the weight of its own past, though Ramos may have been deliberately attempting to liberate the song from its ties to Imelda Marcos.

Another number, "Mabuhay Philippines! (Welcome to the Philippines)," resurrects the momentous occasion when the 1994 Miss Universe Pageant was held in Manila.[4] The song served as the opening theme for that show and afterward morphed into a tourism-friendly ditty.[5] After all, if tourist brochures are to be believed, the Philippines is a country brimming with smiling beauty queens. It is a destination for cosmopolitans and, indeed, has a population of cosmopolitans who still manage to maintain the local traditions that distinguish this "Pearl of the Orient." Whatever problems might ail the nation, there is no shortage of beauty to rival that found in any other nation. Indeed, Western-style beauty contests are quite popular throughout the islands, and standards for judging winners are unsurprisingly conventional, favoring tall, slender, fair-skinned young women. Perhaps this translates to success at international pageants, where Filipinas must compete against an army of analogous models from around the world. Imagine, then, the delight and pride over the Philippines' two Miss Universe winners, Gloria Maria Diaz in 1969 and Maria Margarita Moran in 1973. The two confirmed the country's capability in competing on an international level, at least when a very narrow and specific set of criteria is used to determine success. Fortunately, the ability of the women to display a certain standard of beauty, charm, polish, and poise corresponded well with how the Philippine government wanted to present the nation. Unfortunately, the 1994 Miss Philippines did not make the top finalists; in an ironic turn of events, Miss Spain won the Miss Universe title that year, recalling for some the colonial history between the two countries. At any rate, the show began heartily enough with all of the contestants singing "Mabuhay (Welcome)" during the opening credits, occasionally making way for spurts of folk dance by the Bayanihan Philippine Dance Company and the Ramón Obusan Folkloric Group.[6] Its lyrics are in English, opining about the country with delight, "It's the place in the world today, when you're here you'd wanna stay. It's the colorful nights, beautiful sights; it's the warmth of the sun, cool falling rain. There's no place like it in this world." The song evokes such beautiful qualities of the nation, it is perhaps no wonder that Miss Philippines came away with the award that year for best national costume.

The album is frivolous, earnest, touching, and full of meaning. The tracks are not just the music of a nation, they are also the music that celebrates the continuous production of nation. They are commodities based on ideas, and they can be bought either from the music store or, in true Filipino market fashion, as pirated copies at easily accessible outlets. While space has not permitted this book to explore in much detail Filipino and Western pop music and its dissemination in the Philippines, future work on national identity in the global age would certainly need to take into account the popular music marketplace.

The album *Kalayaan: Sandaang Taong Pag-Gunita* is a mixed bag of pop songs and contemporary folk music. Appropriately, the title, *Kalayaan*, means "independence" and "freedom"—military freedom, spiritual freedom, and freedom to fulfill one's own self. The Katipunan revolutionaries under Bonifacio, who named their newspaper *Kalayaan*, also meant for the word to encapsulate the well-being of the Filipino race, implying a return to an age without imperialism and oppression, and a condition of "brotherhood, abundance, and equality" (May 1983: 368). Seven of the sixteen tracks on this compact disc feature the singing duo of Becky Demetillo-Abraham and Karina Constantino-David, who performed for many years under the moniker Inang Laya (Mother of Freedom). More political than either of the albums previously mentioned, *Kalayaan* contains songs of struggle, including Inang Laya's protest piece "Base Militar (Military Base)," a piece that invokes an important nationalist trope. The American military bases Clark Air Force Base (established 1903) and Subic Bay Naval Reservation (established 1901) represented throughout their tenure the continuous grip of the United States on the Philippine Islands. The bases promoted prostitution, damaged the environment with toxic wastes, and infringed on the sovereignty of the Philippine nation. Much nationalist rhetoric was spent on denouncing the military base agreements signed by Philippine presidents until the land and facilities were turned over to the Philippine government in 1991. Likewise, another song on the album by Inang Laya, called "Babae," is an exhortation to Filipino women not to rely on men and to follow the models of women warriors from Filipino history like Gabriela Silang. Their mention of prostitution in the lyrics also recriminates the American military bases, around which the trafficking of women proliferated. They declare, much as nationalist songs of the past did, "The goal is to be free and to be equal."

The album as a whole is a history of revolution, not just against Spain, but also against oppression of many kinds. Linking the continuing colonization of the country to the United States, even after independence, redefines the centennial as merely a marker of time and not as a moment for triumphant retrospection. The modern nation continues to develop unevenly, and the struggles of the past are still present in one form or another.

These music recordings and commemorative publications are not merely artifacts of patriotism. They are also fragments in the long memoir of the Philippine nation. They are a historical record of individual works, but their combination is more about disjuncture than cohesiveness. Do these examples— and, for that matter, do all the case studies in this book—constitute a national music of the Philippines? It is fair to scoff at the very notion of the Philippines having a national music. Yet, it is clear that it was not national music I was seeking all along, but rather the music that would reveal narratives of and insights into the Philippine nation. What I found were competing ideologies between various incarnations of the state and among an array of musical actors. I found that looking back helped to see the present and to construct plans for the future. I found that modernity was not rooted in time but in ideas. And I found that what has become mixed cannot become unmixed, and that it is sometimes important to see things as never having changed. Thus, while the Philippines has a complicated national history that forecloses the dominance of any single cultural narrative about the construction of nation, studies of how music and dance author and authorize nation do tell a story of the importance of the performing arts in nationalism. From gongs to strings to modernist symphonic scores to popular songs, the variety of music in this study has been as thrilling to explore as the material has been difficult to corral. The messiness of it all is a useful reminder of how much more there is to be said and interpreted on the subject, especially as the meanings and relevance of the Philippine nation continue to reconstitute over time.

Introduction

1. The festival was organized and sponsored by the Philippine National Commission for Culture and the Arts, the Developmental Institute for Bicolano Artists Foundation, the Office of the Mayor of Naga City, the Office of the Mayor of Legazpi City, the Cultural Center of the Philippines, the University of Santa Isabel, and the University of the Philippines College of Music.

2. The diplomatic practice of a touring group playing a local piece is not uncommon. In 2008, when the New York Philharmonic performed in North Korea, they connected strongly with their audience through a rendition of the famous Korean song "Arirang."

3. Additionally, in her book *The Star-Entangled Banner*, Sharon Delmendo theorizes that studying U.S. colonization of the Philippines tells a larger story about American conceptions of nationalism and militarism that continue to be relevant in foreign policy, including the "War on Terror" (2004).

4. Foundational studies on the relationship between music and nationalism are too numerous to name, but one could begin with the eighteenth-century writings on German folk song by Johann Gottfried Herder and the various essays of Béla Bartók.

5. See, for instance, the fascinating study of the changing sound of nationalism in China over decades of drastic societal change by Sue Tuohy (2001).

6. Bañas's (1975) and William Pfeiffer's (1976) books have been foundational reference books about music in the Philippines. They are primarily concerned with recording musical genres, certain people, institutions, and musical pieces.

7. Anthony Giddens defines the nation-state as "a set of institutional forms of governance maintaining an administrative monopoly over a territory with demarcated boundaries (borders), its rule being sanctioned by law and direct control of the means of internal and external violence" (1985: 120).

8. In regard to late nineteenth-century Filipino nationalism, Vicente Rafael theorizes that nationalism is not a singular and unproblematic entity. Instead, nationalism was and is "inherently conflictual," and "the means for imagining nationhood may at times be at odds with the very nature of the images that are reproduced" (1990a: 593). Likewise, nationalism as it has appeared in different countries and under different words, is no singular ideology. It is, perhaps, essentially a question of belonging, but this is only one aspect of nationalism (see Shafer 1982).

9. As an interesting aside, historical musicologist Richard Taruskin points out that an early definition of musical nationalism related to the Western art canon was the rejection of German music by people in other nations. Later definitions highlighted the use of "distinguishing national characteristics," but only when considered as a deliberate strategy. These characteristics had to be understood by both the composer and the listeners in order to express and arouse nationalist sentiment, leading Taruskin to proclaim, "Nationalism is an attitude" (Grove Music Online).

10. As one example among many others, Gage Averill writes, "Many Haitian exiles hold nostalgic views of home that have been amplified by the time and distance away from Haiti; reinforced by the indignities of immigrant life and encounters with American racism and xenophobia; and focused by reflexive and purposeful activity of politicians, journalists, and artists (especially musicians)" (2006: 262).

11. I do not diminish the importance of language as a foundation for national culture as described by Herder and others, but national language, particularly in postcolonial nations, is a divisive issue (for the Philippines, see Gaerlan 1998).

12. The preceding material was found on the frequently updated online World Factbook of the U.S. Central Intelligence Agency located at https://www.cia.gov/library/publications/the-world-factbook [September 23, 2008].

13. For outstanding scholarship on Filipinos at the time of Spanish contact, see the work of William Henry Scott, including *Barangay: Sixteenth-Century Philippine Culture and Society* (1994) and *Cracks in the Parchment Curtain* (1985).

14. The Spaniards named the islands after their future king, Felipe II.

15. The use of music as a tool of early conversion is outlined in a variety of music sources and is summarized by José Maceda et al. in the encyclopedic article "Philippines" (Grove Music Online).

16. Regarding the word *ilustrado*, "By definition the term connotes advanced education and learning and this was how the term was used in the late nineteenth century. The close association between advanced education and wealth, however, has led to the application of this term to the 'Filipino upper class,' especially by the early American colonialists and by many scholars today" (Cullinane 1989: 35).

17. According to an eyewitness, a Filipino who served as a member of the Spanish military drum corps, the music played just moments after the execution consisted of a march called "Paso Doble Marcha de Cadiz" (de Viana 2006: 88).

18. See also Scott's *Barangay: Sixteenth-Century Philippine Culture and Society* (1994) for the development of the label "Filipino."

19. The acquisition of the Philippines in the United States' first imperial foray engendered bitter debate at home over American imperialism, with Mark Twain as a prominent voice in opposition. Nevertheless, despite the odd coalition of anti-imperialists, isolationists, and racists who were unwilling to accept brown-skinned people into the nation, the United States colonized the Philippines with an imperialist mission of secularization and cultural assimilation (see Bresnahan 1981).

20. A while back, I was chided by an anonymous reviewer who felt that I was hiding something by not stating at the outset of my article that I am Filipino American rather than Filipino born. I found this perturbing, imagining how it would appear if all articles in ethnomusicology began with author statements about race, ethnicity, and birthplace, no matter what the topic. At the same time, my inclusion of interludes in this book validates that request and further insists that the accident of my birth has less to do with my perspective than the experiences I have had since then.

Chapter 1

1. I had a very similar experience during my first musical tour of the Philippines in 1990. Our *rondalla* was slated to appear on a popular television show, and we arrived in our "traditional" Philippine outfits. We were preceded and followed by the show's regular dancers, fitted with contemporary and revealing black outfits. As the host of the program announced the *rondalla* from the United States, the irony was palpable.

2. According to the program notes for the event, the Philippine Music Ensemble was formally organized at the Philippine Women's University in 1982 and led by Dr. Kasilag. The PME's four sections are the Muslim Gamelan Ensemble, the Angklung Ensemble, the PME Chorale, and the PWU Guitar Quartet. In 1987 they termed their performances "Philensemblia."

3. Here is Agoncillo's quote in full: "The efforts of such heroic musicians and musicologists as Antonio J. Molina, Felipe de Leon, Eliseo Pajaro, Colonel Antonino Buenaventura, Lucio San Pedro, José Maceda, and Hilarion Rubio, to develop Filipino music by the use of folk literature and folk songs as thematic materials have so far failed to arouse popular interest and sympathy. The primary cause of this apathy to Filipino music is the corroding influence of the American popular song hits which fill the air lanes almost twenty-four hours a day. Thus the radio stations, instead of exerting a civilizing influence on the audience, actually encourage vulgarization of the latter's taste."

4. For more on nationalist composers between 1870 and the 1930s, see Santos 2001.

5. Filipino scholars explain the same historical development of the Filipino as a result of colonization with concepts such as *Pilipinolohiya* (Covar 1998) and *Sikolohiyang Pilipino* (V. Enriquez 1984).

6. Viewed in retrospect, early Filipino composers of liturgical music are a part of the nationalist narrative, since the mastering of Western compositional techniques may be framed as a point of pride.

7. Reinhard Wendt also makes ties between religious musical expression for the shrine of Our Lady of Antipolo and nationalist thinking (1998).]

8. Art music composers are not the only people capable of creating nationalistic music. I presume that musicians and composers of any level of musical training created music that praised the Philippine homeland. Music relating to the topic of nation exists in many forms, including the improvised ditty that is forgotten almost as quickly as it is uttered, to folk music whose origins have become obscured by the passage of time. The difficulty in discussing the informal music of the nineteenth century is that there is not enough written evidence.

9. Anderson follows Hugh Seton-Watson's description of official nationalism as a defensive reaction by local governing bodies to the rise of nation-states around them and the fear of marginalization in the global community. I extend the use of the term to mean a proactive strategy in late nationalism that legitimates the status quo of a nation-state.

10. For instance, see Martin Daughtry's 2003 article on the changing national anthem of Russia.

11. Interestingly, the relationship between Nakpil and Bonifacio continued after his execution. Julio Nakpil married Bonifacio's widow, Gregoria de Jesús, also known as the *lakambini* (muse) of the Katipunan (de Viana 2006: 33).

12. Nakpil's hymn resurfaced again in 1904 under the title "Salve Patria," and it was used to commemorate the death anniversary of another Filipino hero, José Rizal (Constantino 1964: 15).

13. Despite the official end date of 1902 upheld by the United States, fighting continued at least until 1913.

14. Other laws meant to repress nationalist expressions included the Sedition Law, the Reconcentration Act, and the Bandolerismo Statute.

15. As a commonwealth of the United States, the Philippines was still not an independent nation. The ten-year period of commonwealth was supposed to serve as a transition period leading up to political autonomy.

16. Religious movements inside and outside of Roman Catholicism, such as the Iglesia Filipina Independiente, featured adapted or localized prayer hymns whose transformation could be interpreted as nationalist.

17. See, as a related example, Bakhle's work on the secularization and classicization of Indian music (2005).

18. Using folk music is among the most common nationalist strategies found the world over. For examples outside of the use of folk music in Western art music, see Degirmenci's examination of the modernist construction of folk music in the Turkish republic (2006), Regev and Seroussi's look at the contemporary tradition of folk music in Israel (2004), Zataevich's role in creating a folk music canon in Kazakhstan (Rouland 2005), and the nationalization of musical arts in Mongolia (Marsh 2009).

19. See Tokita and Hugues (2008) for a discussion of the globalized nature of Japanese music.

20. The national language designated in 1936 was actually called "Pilipino" and was a standardization of Tagalog, the language of the region that includes the capital city Manila. In 1973, the name was changed to "Filipino" to provide more flexibility for the inclusion of words from other widely spoken languages in the Philippines like Visayan and Ilocano. Also significant is that Tagalog contains many borrowings from Spanish.

21. Spanish words were also very well absorbed into local languages, especially Tagalog. As an obvious example, the Tagalog greeting "kumusta (how are you)" derives from the Spanish "como está." In addition, the so-called Chabacano language of Zamboanga is creolized Spanish.

22. This attitude is not at all uncommon in postcolonial settings. As Peter Manuel described in relation to Cuba, "From a purely nationalistic perspective the inundation of foreign pop music was offensive to some Cubans (musicians and musicologists perhaps more so than the ordinary person)" (1987: 162).

23. According to Florentino-Hofileña, "Magsaysay knew how to massage the egos of newsmen while his press secretary took care of their financial needs. And perhaps the clearest proof of his patronage of the media was his appointment of several newsmen to government positions and the elevation of the press secretary post to Cabinet rank" (1998: 8).

24. Translation by Mabini Castro.

25. Cullather makes an interesting case for Magsaysay's use of the U.S. Americans rather than the other way around, an analysis similar to the supposition that foreign music is absorbed and used by natives for their own needs rather than thrust upon or given to them (1993).

26. The issue of nationalism and communist movements in the Philippines is a complex one, and the perception of how nationalism might be expressed by revolutionaries against the national state is highly subjective. Communists might be nationalists, but not all communists are nationalists nor all nationalists communist. "In theory the international aims of communism negated nationalism, but nationalist movements in the region were often useful tools.... To many people in Southeast Asia, communism was the hope of the underdog, promising a fairer society with freedom from foreign domination, land for the peasants, and a better standard of living for the poor" (Tarling 1999: 271). Because these possibilities often overlapped with the agenda of nationalists, the two ideologies could work well in tandem.

27. Other national organizations of note include the National Music Council of the Philippines and the Music Promotion Foundation of the Philippines. The council formed in 1953 in cooperation with the UNESCO National Commission of the Philippines. The intention of the council was to create a national body to help unite musical groups throughout the country, and its objectives were to promote cooperation among artists, revive and conserve folk music, encourage musical events, and publish Filipino music (Bañas 1975: 169–170). The foundation arose from a

congressional act of the republic in 1955 in order to fulfill the government mandate to support Philippine arts on a national scale (see "Music Promotion Foundation of the Philippines" 1966).

28. A handful of musical societies for Filipino composers had existed since the turn of the twentieth century, but they were primarily designed to promote camaraderie among artists and to provide opportunities for the performances of individual works and larger scale productions (see Bañas 1975).

29. Program notes from the 1974 Philippine Music Festival.

30. Pájaro was not alone in his admiration for these European composers. In fact, Ramón Santos writes that one of the most famous Filipino composers of the early twentieth century, Nicanor Abelardo (1893–1934), spoke of Hindemith, Stravinsky, and Bartók, and that the compositions of his final years showed the influences of Schoenberg's Expressionist style (1991: 159).

31. Program notes from the 1974 Philippine Music Festival.

32. Ramón Santos summarizes that it was "a local scenario in which music dominated the spiritual and social life of a community, a common phenomenon in practically every major town and city in colonial Philippines to have developed local music masters....Most Filipino composers and other musicians who eventually gained national prominence—from Adonay, Abelardo, and Buencamino to Antonino Buenaventura, De Leon, and San Pedro—came from similar environments and breeding grounds" (2005: 126).

33. The Spanish spelling was "bandurria." Literature and scores include both spellings, but it is very common for contemporary writings to use the Filipinized "banduria." I use the modern version, since it is the one preferred by my first teacher.

34. Whom the authors choose to write about and how they write about them are as much about nationalism as the subject matter of the writings. A good example of this may be found in Gregory Cushman's article about the historiography of Cuban national music (2005).

35. José Maceda, summed up the situation in the following way: "There are two music traditions in the Philippines—a Southeast Asian tradition, practiced by only about 10 percent of the Philippine population...and a Hispanic tradition known to 90 percent" (1992: 304).

36. There are, for instance, gender implications when using "motherland" versus "fatherland."

37. The effectiveness of this strategy can be found in the number of cultural nationalist movements that rely on the symbolism of the indigenous. *Indigenista* policies in Mexico, for instance, are evident in the works of famous nationalist composers Manuel Ponce and Carlos Chavez (see Pedelty 2004).

38. Neoclassicism in the arts appeared at different times. Although the 1920s marked the beginnings of neoclassicism in music and referred back to the classical period of musical composition, neoclassicism in architecture appeared in the mid-eighteenth century and referenced classical Greek and Roman buildings.

Chapter 2

1. Interestingly, Ricardo Trimillos points out that "Tinikling" was originally a dance song, and even in the published version by Francisca Reyes Aquino, the text is provided. Yet, Bayanihan and almost all other folkloric groups perform it as "pure dance," likely because the inclusion of language would make the dance less accessible for the tourist industry (1999: 146).

2. There are certainly other successful and accomplished groups, including the Ramón Obusan Folkloric Group, the Leyte Folk Dance Company, and the Filipiniana Dance Troupe of the University of the Philippines.

3. As a national dance company, Bayanihan is entitled to an annual stipend from the government and free use of space at the Cultural Center of the Philippines. Already a longtime resident company of the cultural center, this change in title adds prestige.

4. The Filipino *sarswela* (also *sarsuela*) is a music-theater show derived from the Spanish *zarzuela* (see chapter 5). Likewise, *pandanggo* is a localized version of the Spanish *fandango*.

5. Notably, other local derivations of *bayan* also celebrate the spirit of the Filipino people. Take, for instance, *bayani*, meaning "hero" rather than citizen.

6. She used her maiden name Tolentino at the time but is now better recognized by the name under which she published her collection of folk dance and music.

7. Alejandro also observes that Bocobo and Aquino were part of an international movement to establish dance in physical education programs (39).

8. Despite strong anti-Japanese feelings that remained high after World War II, the relationship between the Philippines and Japan have continued to develop. In 1956, the Philippine government signed a Reparations Agreement with Japan that meant the influx of $300 million over the next twenty-five years. Particularly after 1967, foreign investment has been welcomed in the Philippines, and Japanese corporations have been invited to channel capital into the country.

9. Hobsbawm takes care to note that the invention of tradition occurs during any time and place, but, as with nostalgia, occurs more readily and frequently during times of social change (1992: 4). Moreover, *invention* seems too narrow a term, for it implies the creation of "something out of nothing" rather than the more commonly observed elaboration of something into something else.

10. In *topayya* as practiced by the Kalinga, the man with the largest gong (*balbal*) plays a traditional beat followed by the second gong (*kadua*) playing the same rhythm, but one beat after the first. The third gong (*katlo*) plays a beat after the second, and the fourth (*kapat*) a beat after that. The fifth gong (*opop*) plays an ostinato, while the sixth (*anungos*) begins by improvising and then settles into a regular rhythm (J. Maceda 1998a: 916).

11. Details from the preceding paragraph can be found in Hila 1992, J. Maceda et al. 2009, and Maceda 1998b.

12. Maria Clara is very similar to the stereotype of the Southern belle, though Rizal critically depicted her as passive rather than strong "underneath the lace," so to

speak. Like the belle, Maria Clara is a metaphor—in this case, the embodiment of the relationship between Spain and the Philippines.

13. One could argue that music and dance designated for the Rural Suite has much in common with selections found in the Spanish Suite. As an example, one *jota* from the Tagalog region is described as requiring a Maria Clara dress, while another from the Ilocos region uses "peasant costume" (Aquino vols. 1 and 2, 1996). One general difference between these syncretic dances appears to be that those documented from the Manila area are treated as more "Spanish" than those from the outer provinces (Aquino, vols. 1–6, 1996).

14. Entire pieces are not usually in the Phrygian mode, but, as an example, the opening passage of a common *Paso Doble* descends with the chord progression A minor–G–F–E. The typical flamenco cadence is, in this case, actually a progression from the tonic in A minor to the fifth rather·than the fourth to the tonic.

15. Gender roles are enforced similarly in the Mountain Suite. According to Bayanihan's choreographer, Lucrecia Urtula, "It is interesting to note the definition of male and female roles in these warrior societies as reflected in dance. Male movements are characterized by aggressive gestures and stances: a hand poised on the hip, the legs spread apart as though ready to tackle the enemy. The women, on the other hand, carry themselves with regal serenity, often balancing a vertical series of graduated clay pots, as many as five to ten to each pile, without losing their elegance of carriage" (1987: 121).

16. Panopio has described that in rural settings in the Philippines, traditional courtship is still valued, despite actual behavior that may include premarital sex (1994: 200).

17. Again, in this example, nationalism is a very complex subject. Majul reminds readers, "Muslims did not participate in the Philippine nationalist movement which agitated for independence from the USA.... They desired to remain under US tutelage until preparations could be completed for their independence as a Muslim state" (1988: 899). In other words, they promoted a Muslim nationalism that unified the separate Muslim groups and also connected them across Philippine national borders with Muslims of other nations.

18. See, for instance, Bakhle's monograph on nationalism and the construction of an Indian classical tradition (2005).

19. Nick Joaquin challenges the long-held and very popular perception of precolonial Filipinos as seafarers by questioning why there is comparatively so little of Asian culture in the Philippines. He posits that the people in the Philippine archipelago before colonization may have been much more insular than assumed and certainly less well traveled (see Joaquin 2001).

20. For example, see Cadar 1975; Kalanduyan 1996; J. Maceda 1963.

21. Other titles include variations on the word *fiesta*, but perhaps the most ironic I have seen is the "Rural Contemporary Suite."

22. To facilitate costume changes, a solo singer or a duo will entertain the audience with classic love songs. In one number, the dancers mimic a town band comprised of all bamboo instruments called a *musikong bumbong*. The bamboo instruments are clever

reproductions of European band instruments too costly and inaccessible for average Filipinos to acquire. While they mimic the shape of clarinets, trombones, tubas, and so on, the sounds of each are quite different from their progenitors. A hole is cut into each instrument and covered with a membrane, effectively making a large band of variously shaped kazoos. With these instruments, the performers simply need to sing their parts into the instruments, and the result is ingenious, comical, and entertaining.

Chapter 3

1. *Tahanang Pilipino* (Filipino Home) is commonly called the "Coconut Palace," because its building materials showcase coconut shells and wood. Pope John Paul II refused to stay there, because he felt it too extravagant, but *Tahanang Pilipino* served as the presidential guesthouse for years afterward. Currently, it contains a museum but can also be rented for special occasions.

2. For a longer treatment of the CCP, see Castro 2001.

3. Aldaba-Lim, the mother of the Bayanihan dancer Patricia Lim Yusah who appears in chapter 2, was at one time the secretary of social services and development (the first woman cabinet member in Philippine history), president of the Girl Scouts of the Philippines, and recipient of the United Nation's Peace Medal Award.

4. Filipinos often humorously attribute the beautiful sunsets to an effect of air pollution, a tremendous problem in Manila.

5. Despite the similarity in acronyms, the NCC was not the precursor to the NCCA, the National Commission on Culture and the Arts.

6. Hamilton-Paterson is highly critical, bemoaning, "If one wanted a single yardstick by which to measure the abject failure of successive Philippine governments, it would surely be provided by this business of Overseas Contract Workers (OCWs). The Philippines is probably the only nation in the world whose entire economy rests to such an extent on the export of its own citizens, many of whom are the country's best-qualified men and women" (1998: 245).

7. Osmeña was the son of president Sergio Osmeña, Sr., who served from 1944 to 1946 during the Japanese occupation.

8. *Bayan* also translates as "country," which is particularly significant for the song "Bayan Ko (My Country)" (see chapter 5).

9. The goals of the CCP are reprinted in full in Pfeiffer 1976: 138.

10. Imelda Marcos and Lucrecia Kasilag had met on a couple of occasions before the First Lady tapped Kasilag for a role with the CCP. On their first meeting, Kasilag instructed Imelda that her candidacy for Miss Manila was causing too many absences at school, and that if she did not attend regularly, she might lose her scholarship for voice (de la Torre 1985: 80).

11. During my stays in Manila, I have noticed a high level of awareness among the general populace regarding politics. This is, perhaps, due to the large number of daily newspapers containing sensational updates on the latest happenings. It may

also be related to the fascinating nature of Philippine politics in which stories of graft and criminality resemble the most fanciful plots of *telenovelas* imported from Latin America, also widely popular. This awareness does not necessarily translate into social activism, despite the long tradition of activists in the country.

12. The speech is reprinted in full in the program for the inauguration of the CCP, which can be found in the library of the CCP.

13. The comparison between Imelda Marcos and Eva Perón of Argentina is easy to make, in that both wielded a great deal of power during the administrations of their husbands, were extravagant in their expenditures and showiness, were not easily accepted by the elites of their countries, and portrayed themselves as maternal figures over the poor people.

14. For a fuller examination of the *Dularawan*, see Castro 2001/2002, from which some of the previous summary was extracted.

15. The speech in full is available at http://marcospresidentialcenter.com (accessed July 24, 2008).

16. Driving down one of Manila's main thoroughfares, Roxas Boulevard, my cousin recalled that immediately after curfews were implemented, morning drivers caught sight of "socialites" in gowns and suits picking up trash along the road as punishment for staying out too late. He laughed that it turned out to be a false harbinger of equality under the law, for these people were later found to be common folk dressed up by the authorities and paid to act like the delinquent rich.

17. The pun is even more appropriate to Filipinos, since there is no letter "f" in the alphabet. It is common for native speakers of various Filipino languages to confuse the hard sound of "p" with the soft sound of "f" found in English. Furthermore, an entire school of humor in the Philippines is based on the puns that arise from combining English and Tagalog (or Filipino).

18. Superstition has surrounded the Film Center ever since the tragedies that occurred during construction, and after the 1982 International Manila Film Festival the building served only to house offices, including the passport office. This function ended rather abruptly after damage was caused to the site by an earthquake in 1990. Certainly the deaths and following disuse of the building as a cultural and government landmark have been part of the tarnish on Imelda Marcos's legacy.

19. "Bagong Lipunan" appears in more length in chapter 4.

20. Translation by Cristina Castro.

21. The original decree and title of the National Artists Award were both in English. The Filipino translation came about in the 1980s as part of the broader process of Filipinization.

Chapter 4

1. The Grand Prix is the final step in a process that begins the year prior with six separate competitions in different sites around Europe. Victors from these six

competitions receive an invitation to the Grand Prix, and in 2007 the Madrigals came as representatives of the *Concorso Polifonico Internazionale Guido d'Arezzo* in Italy.

2. Other former members echo this sentiment. Regalado Jose attributes the misconception to the popularity of Filipino singing ensembles among Filipino emigrants in the diaspora. "Traveling Pinoy groups abroad give the impression that madrigal singing is popular. Personally, I don't think madrigal singing is so popular among Filipinos. What's really more popular is karaoke, very unfortunately" (2007). Another former member wishing to remain anonymous reflected, "Listening to *a capella* arrangements has fascinated the [Filipino] audience—how singers are able to blend voices, how voices are made to sound sometimes like instruments, etc."

3. Before authorities moved the astronomical pile of refuse to another location, Tondo contained the infamous "Smokey Mountain," a giant heap of garbage upon which thousands of squatters scavenged for goods daily.

4. Especially during the early years of the Madrigals, many of the performers belonged to the University of the Philippines College of Music as either faculty or students. Membership in the UP Madrigal Singers has grown to be very competitive, attracting hopefuls from outside of the university. The ensemble's rigorous standards and screening process do not deter a consistent stream of suitors, and the standards for acceptance and continuing participation in the Madrigals have been consistently high. Veneracion remarked gleefully that when the group is opened for auditions, "Many come but few are chosen" (2000).

5. See chapter 5 for more on protest music.

6. Sometimes it matters when and where one is doing the singing. In the old days, elders would admonish the young for singing in front of the stove, for it was said that it would cause them to marry old maids or widowers (Lardizabal 1976: 107).

7. The unofficial age range of the Madrigals extends from college age to forty, at which time Veneracion quipped, members "perhaps should get on with their lives" (2000).

8. Likewise, the desired order for society and the performance of national excellence are exhibited in the "national songs" of Singapore and their promotion by the Singaporean government. As Lily Kong writes in regard to lyrics and group performances of these songs, "Singaporeans are encouraged to continue to give of their best for their country, to defend it and to support the ruling order" (1995: 452).

Chapter 5

1. Few outside of the Philippines are aware that two more People Power revolutions occurred, the second in 2001 to force former actor Joseph Estrada from the presidency, and the third just four months afterward to protest what had befallen Estrada. EDSA II succeeded in shifting presidential power, deposing Estrada in favor

of Gloria Macapagal-Arroyo (the daughter of former president Diosdado Macapagal). In contrast, EDSA III did not result in any change of the establishment. Populated primarily by people of the lower class who had supported Estrada all along, the mass protest revealed how little political leverage the poor actually had. Read today, the three revolutions on EDSA outline a cynical narrative about politics in the Philippines, a rather far cry from the worldwide approval visited upon the country during the highly mythologized first People Power Revolution in which a well-entrenched dictator was driven from the country by a mass movement without violence.

2. Most sources focus on the events of EDSA in the capital city of Manila. For a collection of essays that deal with events in other parts of the country during that time period, see Kerkvliet and Mojares (1991).

3. Vicente Rafael highlights the linguistic relationship between the Philippines and the United States, as English remains an important language in the Philippines. The revolution through the media was conducted in English and Tagalog. The people came out, "driven there in part by the disembodied voices of the Chinese mestizo Cardinal Sin broadcasting from Radio Veritas and the *mestiza* American actress June Keithley on the underground station *Radio Bandido*. That Sin and Keithley spoke in English mattered less than the fact that their voices were overheard, intercepted by an audience that had become steeped in the techniques of interrupting the circulation of signs from above. By responding to these voices, they showed themselves alert to the workings of Taglish" (Rafael 2000: 179).

4. The murder has not been solved to the dissatisfaction of many, despite two investigations. Pro-Marcos writers believe that the Aquino administration thought it imprudent to absolve the Marcoses (Escalante and de la Paz 2000). A larger majority believe Marcos's main henchman, General Fabian Ver, orchestrated the killing (see Arillo 1986).

5. The events of Ninoy Aquino's assassination leading to EDSA and the ouster of the Marcoses have been documented in numerous sources (see Arillo 1986, Angulo 1986, Johnson 1987, Wurfel 1988, and Hamilton-Paterson 1998.)

6. The participants of the first EDSA revolution generally came from the middle and upper classes. Members of the lower class, the predominant population of the Philippines, did not come to EDSA *en masse* until 2001 during EDSA III. For a pro-Marcos reading of the first EDSA as a movement of oligarchs, see Escalante and de la Paz (2000).

7. Estimates of the total number of people at EDSA range. The Philippine historian Renato Constantino pegs the number at a rather exact 623,506 (Escalante and de la Paz 2000: 82).

8. Lyrics transcribed from an interview with Joi Barrios and translated by the author.

9. According to Canave-Dioquino, mention of the *kumintang* is made by nineteenth-century writers from Spain (1998: 850).

10. Though Santiago, Molina, and Bañas note that the *kumintang* was felt in three beat patterns that relate directly to the *kundiman*, Bañas also stated that the

kumintang could be written in 2/4 or 6/8 (1975: 82). There is no repertoire against which this statement can be tested.

11. One might compare this textual transcendence with the poems used in Sufi music.

12. The spelling differences between "zarzuela," "sarsuela," and "sarswela" reflect the Filipinization of the genre. The final change to "sarswela" did not become more common until later in the twentieth century as part of nationalist movements in language, and older written sources referring to Filipino theater use the Spanish spelling. Consequently, the reader should not assume that references to a *zarzuela* refer only to Spanish productions.

13. Tiongson notes that traditional *sarswelas* sometimes are still performed in areas of the Ilocos region (1992: 34).

14. Huks is shortened from Hukbalahap, which in turn comes from *Hukbong Bayan Laban sa mga Hapon* (People's Army Against the Japanese).

15. As noted in a history of the revolution, those that sang at EDSA had "probably the largest live audience in their careers" (Escalante and de la Paz 2000: 56). Mirano furthers this observation, noting that musicians who participated at EDSA were subsequently able to sign contracts with commercial record companies as a result of their exposure (2008).

16. The APO Hiking Society website is located at http://www.apohikingsociety.org.

17. It is likely due to their sense of humor that APO managed to evade censorship for so long before EDSA. Satire and direct humor is an important defining characteristic of APO's work. In fact, when I asked Paredes about the power of music with the crowds at EDSA, he responded with some mischief that music is indeed very powerful, but followed that with, "It was Pinoy humor that was the balancing force. That's why protest concerts had to have humor as well. Filipinos, in my opinion have a tough time concentrating on being hard-core anything!" (Paredes 2007).

18. The website is located at http://www.edsashrine.com/v2/aboutus.php.

Conclusion

1. Michael Bakan describes a similar phenomenon in the celebration of "Puputan Day" each year in Bali, where heroic martyrdom is symbolic of a "glorious past, and an inspiration for present and future challenges" (1998: 453).

2. Rizal's role has engendered debate, and it seems clear that it was the Americans who helped promote his legend as hero, primarily because he did not advocate violent revolution. "The great puzzle for us postcolonial Filipinos is that when the moment of truth came in 1896, rather than leading the revolution, Rizal allowed himself to be arrested and, while awaiting his inevitable death sentence, condemned the revolution. This seeming contradiction has bedeviled nationalist historians like Agoncillo and Constantino" (Quibuyen 1999: 4).

3. This Mike Velarde is not to be confused with the Filipino charismatic Christian leader of the group El Shaddai who bears the same name.

4. The pageant had last been held in the Philippines in 1974.

5. The music and lyrics were written by Tito Sotto and Anthony Castelo.

6. The Pilipino word *mabuhay* has multiple meanings, including "long live."

Abella, V. M. de. 1874. *Vade-mecum Filipino, ó, Manual de la conversación familiar español-tagalog: Sequido de un curioso Vocabulario de modismos Manileños,* 12th ed. Manila: C. Miralles.

Abueva, José. 1999. *Filipino Nationalism: Various Meanings, Constant and Changing Goals, Continuing Relevance.* Quezon City: University of the Philippines Press.

Agoncillo, Teodoro A. 1967. *Filipino Naitonalism, 1872–1970.* Quezon City:R.P Garcia Publishing.

Ahlquist, Karen, ed. 2006. *Chorus and Community.* Urbana and Chicago: University of Illinois Press.

Albano-Imperial, Guia. 1998. "Lucrecia Reyes-Urtula: Heart of a Dancer." In *The National Artists of the Philippines.* Manila: Anvil. pp. 337–346.

Alejandro, Reynaldo. 1978. *Philippine Dances.* N.p.: Vera-Reyes.

Alzona, Encarnación. 1953. *Rizal's Legacy to the Filipino Woman.* Pasay City: N.p.

Anderson, Benedict. 1991. *Imagined Communities: Reflections on the Origin and Spread of Nationalism,* rev. ed. London and New York: Verso.

———. 1998. *The Spectre of Comparisons.* London and New York: Verso.

Andres, Tomas. 2002. *Understanding the Values of the Metro-Manilans/ Tagalogs.* Quezon City: Giraffe Books.

Angos, Leonilo. 1996. Interview with author. Los Angeles: February 18.

Angulo, Lourdes, ed. 1986. *We Were There.* Manila: Staff Members of Asian Development Bank, Pasay City.

APO Hiking Society Official Website. Available: http://www. apohikingsociety.org. [May 11, 2008].

Appadurai, Arjun. 1996. *Modernity at Large: Cultural Dimensions of Globalization.* Minneapolis: University of Minnesota Press.

Aquino, Francisca Reyes. 1996. *Philippine Folk Dances, Volume 1 and Volume 2*. Manila: n.p.

Arillo, Cecilio T. 1986. *Breakaway: The Inside Story of the Four-Day Revolution in the Philippines, February 22–25, 1986*. Manila: CTA & Associates.

————. 2000. *Greed & Betrayal: The Sequel to the 1986 EDSA Revolution*. Quezon City: Charles Morgan Printing & Equipment.

Arnold, Denis, and Emma Wakelin. "Madrigal." In *The Oxford Companion to Music*, edited by Alison Latham. *Oxford Music Online*. Available: http://www.oxfordmusiconline.com.proxy.lib.umich.edu/subscriber/article/opr/t114/e4142. [July 26, 2008].

Atabug, Sonia. 1978. "The Big Cultural Boom." *Philippine Panorama* January 22: 19–20.

Averill, Gage. 2006. "'*Mezanmi, Kouman Nou Ye?* My Friends, How Are You?' Musical Constructions of the Haitian Transnation." In *Ethnomusicology: A Contemporary Reader*, edited by Jennifer Post. New York and London: Routledge Taylor & Francis Group, 261–273.

Ayala, Jaime Zobel de. 1969. "The Aims of the Cultural Center and Its Relevance to Our Society." *Republic Weekly* 1(9): 21.

Azurin, Arnold Molina. 1995. *Reinventing the Filipino Sense of Being & Becoming*. Quezon City: University of the Philippines Press.

Bakan, Michael. 1998. "Walking Warriors: Battles of Culture and Ideology in the Balinese Gamelan Beleganjur World." *Ethnomusicology* 42(3): 441–481.

Bakhle, Janaki. 2005. *Two Men and Music: Nationalism in the Making of an Indian Classical Tradition*. Oxford: Oxford University Press.

Bañas, Raymundo. 1975. *Pilipino Music and Theater*. Quezon City: Manlapaz.

Barrios, Maria Josephine. 2008. Interview with author. Ann Arbor, MI: January 18.

Barz, Gregory. 2006. "We Are from Different Ethnic Groups, but We Live Here as One Family": The Musical Performance of Community in a Tanzanian Kwaya." In *Chorus and Community*, edited by Karen Ahlquist. Urbana and Chicago: University of Illinois Press.

Bauzon, Leslie E. 1985. "Angara's Toughminded Leadership: The Diamond Jubilee Highlighted by Reform of the University System." In *University of the Philippines: The First 75 Years (1908–1983)*, edited by Oscar M. Alfonso. Quezon City: University of the Philippines Press. pp. 541–589.

Bayanihan [film]. 1962. Directed by Allegra Fuller Snyder. New York City.

Bayanihan Souvenir Program. 1964 World Tour.

Béhague, Gerard. 2006. "Indianism in Latin American Art-Music Compositions of the 1920s to 1940s: Case Studies from Mexico, Peru, and Brazil." *Latin American Music Review* 27(1): 28–37.

Belgica, Evelyn Banzuela. 1966. "Music and the Pilipino." *Musical Journal of the Philippines* 1(1): 38–40.

Benitez, Conrado. 1987. "That Night in Brussels." In *The Bayanihan Experience*. Manila: Bayanihan Folk Arts Center. pp. 10–11.

Benitez, Helena Z. 1987. "A Continuing Mission for All." In *The Bayanihan Experience*. Manila: Bayanihan Folk Arts Center. pp. 6–7.

Bernad, Miguel A. 1998. "Defining the Filipino." In *Philippine Graphic Centennial Yearbook*. Manila: Weekly Graphic Magazine Publishing. pp. 104–109.

Bilbao, Cesar C. 1986. "I Was Ready to Be Teargassed." In *We Were There*, edited by Lourdes Angulo. Manila: Staff Members of Asian Development Bank, Pasay City. pp. 123–126.

Bonís, Ferenc. 1983. "Zoltán Kodály, a Hungarian Master of Neoclassicism." *Studia Musicologica Academiae Scientiarum Hungaricae*, T. 25, Fasc. 1/4: 73–91.

Bonner, Raymond. 1987. *Waltzing with a Dictator: The Marcoses and the Making of American Policy*. New York: Times Books.

Boyce, James K. 1993. *The Political Economy of Growth and Impoverishment in the Marcos Era*. Manila: Ateneo de Manila University Press.

Bresnahan, Roger J. 1981. *In Time of Hesitation: American Anti-imperialists and the Philippine-American War*. Quezon City: New Day.

Brillantes, Gregorio C. 1998. "The Lost War to Save the First Republic." In *Philippine Graphic Centennial Yearbook*. Manila: Weekly Graphic Magazine Publishing. pp. 92–103.

Cadar, Usopay. 1970. "The Bayanihan: How Authentic Is Its Repertoire?" *Solidarity* 5(12): 45–51.

———. 1975. "The Role of Kulintang in Maranao Society." *Selected Reports in Ethnomusicology*. II(2): 49–62.

Cainglet, Enrique Cantel. 1981. "Hispanic Influences on the West Visayan Folk Song Tradition of the Philippines, 2 Volumes." Ph.D. dissertation. University of Adelaide.

Canave-Dioquino, Corazon. 1998. "The Lowland Christian Philippines." In *The Garland Encyclopedia of World Music, Volume 4: Southeast Asia*. New York and London: Garland. pp. 839–867.

Carunungan, Celso. 1969. "Mrs. Marcos' P50 Million Gift to the President and the People." *Weekly Nation* 5(5): 2–4.

Castro, Christi-Anne. 2001/2002. "*Dularawan*: Composing the Filipino Nation." *Pacific Review of Ethnomusicology* 10(1): 52–61.

———. 2001. "Music, Politics, and the Nation at the Cultural Center of the Philippines." Ph.D. dissertation. University of California, Los Angeles.

Cavan, Emilia. 1924. *Filipino Folk Songs*. Manila: Mission Press.

Chatterjee, Partha. 1998. "Beyond the Nation? Or Within?" *Social Text* 56: 57–69.

———. 1999. "Anderson's Utopia." *Diacritics* 29(24): 128–134.

Coloma, Roland Sintos. 2005. "Disidentifying Nationalism: Camilo Osias and Filipino Education in the Early 20th Century." In *Revolution and Pedagogy: Interdisciplinary and Transnational Perspectives on Educational Foundation*, edited by E. Thomas Ewing. New York: Palgrave Macmillan. pp. 19–38.

Constantino, Renato. 1964, 1997. *Julio Nakpil and the Philippine Revolution*. Manila: Academic Publishing.

———. 1975. *A History of the Philippines: From the Spanish Colonization to the Second World War*. New York: Monthly Review Press.

———. 1982. *The Miseducation of the Filipino*. Quezon City: Foundation for Nationalist Studies.

Coria, Joanquin de. 1872. *Nueva Gramática Tagalog Teórica-Práctica*. Madrid: J. Antonio García.

Corpuz, O. D. 1989. *Roots of the Filipino Nation*. Quezon City: AKLAHI Foundation.

Cortes, Rosario Mendoza, Celestina Puyal Boncan, and Ricardo T. José.[A] 2000. *The Filipino Saga: History as Social Change*. Quezon City: New Day.

Coseteng, Alice. 1965. "Interview with Imelda Marcos." *Graphic Magazine.* September.

Covar, Prospero. 1998. *Larangan: Seminal Essays on Philippine Culture*. Manila: National Commission for Culture and the Arts.

Cruz, Romeo V. 1989. "Nationalism in 19th Century Manila." In *Manila: History, People and Culture*. Manila: De La Salle University Press. pp. 57–70.

Cullather, Nick. 1993. "America's Boy? Magsaysay and the Illusion of Influence." *The Pacific Historical Review* 62(3): 305–338.

Cullinane, Michael. 1989. "*Ilustrado* Politics: The Response of the Filipino Educated Elite to American Colonial Rule, 1898–1907." Ph.D. dissertation. University of Michigan.

Cushman, Gregory T. 2005. "*¿De qué color es el oro?* Race, Environment, and the History of Cuban National Music, 1898–1958." *Latin American Music Review* 26(2): 164–187.

Dadap, Jerry A. 1986. "A Tale of Two Musicians." *Business Day* September 1: 25.

Dadap, Michael. 2000. Interview with author. April 15.

Daughtry, J. Martin. 2003. "Russia's New Anthem and the Negotiation of National Identity." *Ethnomusicology* 47(1): 42–67.

Davila, Arlene M. 1997. *Sponsored Identities: Cultural Politics in Puerto Rico*. Philadelphia: Temple University Press.

Davis, Fred. 1979. *Yearning for Yesterday: A Sociology of Nostalgia*. New York: Free Press.

Degirmenci, Koray. 2006. "On the Pursuit of a Nation: The Construction of Folk and Folk Music in the Founding Decades of the Turkish Republic." *International Review of the Aesthetics and Sociology of Music* 37(1): 47–65.

Delmendo, Sharon. 2004. *The Star-Entangled Banner: One Hundred Years of America in the Philippines*. New Brunswick, NJ: Rutgers University Press.

Demetrio, Francisco. 1978. *Myths and Symbols: Philippines*. Manila: Navotas Press.

Dolan, Ronald. 1993. *Philippines: A Country Study*. Washington, D.C.: Library of Congress.

Doronila, Amando. 1997. "President Macapagal's Many Wars." *Philippine Daily Inquirer* April 28: 9.

Doronila, Amando. 1992. *The State, Economic Transformation, and Political Change in the Philippines, 1946–1972*. Singapore: Oxford University Press.

Dube, Saurabh, and Ishita Banerjee-Dube, eds. 2006. *Unbecoming Modern: Colonialism, Modernity, Colonial Modernities*. Delhi: Berghahn Books.

Ebron, Paula. 2002. Performing Africa. Princeton, NJ: Princeton University Press.

Ellison, Katherine. 1988. *Imelda: Steel Butterfly of the Philippines*. New York: McGraw-Hill.

Enriquez, Elizabeth L. 2003. *Radyo: An Essay on Philippine Radio*. Manila: CCP, NCCA.

Enriquez, Virgilio. 1984. *Neo-colonial Politics and Language Struggle in the Philippines: National Consciousness and Language in Philippine Psychology (1971–1983)*. Quezon City: Akademya ng Sikolohiyang Pilipino.

Epistola, Ernesto V. 1996. *Nicanor Abelardo: The Man and the Artist, A Biography*. Manila: Rex Book Store.

Escalante, Salvador, and J. Augustus Y. de la Paz. 2000. *The EDSA Uprising: The Five-Percent Revolution; EDSA in Retrospect; A Deconstruction*. Quezon City: Truth and Justice Foundation.

Evasco, Marjorie. 2001. *A Life Shaped by Music: Andrea Ofilada Veneracion and the Philippine Madrigal Singers*. Makati City: Bookmark.

Finin, Gerard A. 2005. *The Making of the Igorot: Contours of Cordillera Consciousness*. Manila: Ateneo de Manila University.

Florentino-Hofileña, Chay. 1998. *News for Sale: The Corruption of the Philippine Media*. Quezon City: Philippine Center for Investigative Journalism.

Frishkopf, Michael. 2008. "Nationalism, Nationalization, and the Egyptian Music Industry." *Asian Music* 39(2): 28–58.

Gaerlan, Barbara. 1998. "The Politics and Pedagogy of Language Use at the University of the Philippines: The History of English as the Medium of Instruction and the Challenge Mounted by Filipino." Ph.D. dissertation. University of California, Los Angeles.

———. 1999. "In the Court of the Sultan: Orientalism, Nationalism, and Modernity in Philippine and Filipino American Dance." *Journal of Asian American Studies* 2(3): 251–287.

García-Canclini, Néstor. 1995. *Hybrid Cultures: Strategies for Entering and Leaving Modernity*. Minneapolis and London: University of Minnesota Press.

Geertz, Clifford, ed. 1963. *Old Societies and New States: The Quest for Modernity in Asia and Africa*. New York: Free Press.

Gellner, Ernest. 1983. *Nations and Nationalism*. Ithaca: Cornell University Press.

Giddens, Anthony. 1985. *A Contemporary Critique of Historical Materialism, Vol. 2: The Nation-State and Violence*. Cambridge: Polity Press.

Gilroy, Paul 1993. *The Black Atlantic: Modernity and Double-Consciousness*. Cambridge: Harvard University Press.

Greenberg, Clement. 1971. "Necessity of 'Formalism.'" *New Literary History* 3(1): 171–175.

Guzman, Leticia Perez de. 1987. "The Bayanihan Story." In *Bayanihan*, edited by José Lardizabal et al. Manila: Bayanihan Folk Arts Center. pp. 78–94.

Hagedorn, Katherine. 2001. *Divine Utterances: The Performance of Afro-Cuban Santeria*. Washington, DC: Smithsonian Institution Press.

Hall, Stuart. 1997. "Old and New Identities, Old and New Ethnicities." In *Culture, Globalization and the World System: Contemporary Conditions for the Representation of Identity*, edited by Anthony King. Minneapolis: University of Minnesota Press. pp. 41–68.

Hamilton-Paterson, James. 1998. *America's Boy: A Century of Colonialism in the Philippines*. New York: Henry Hold.

Hemley, Robin. 2003. *Invented Eden: The Elusive, Disputed History of the Tasaday*. New York: Farrar, Straus and Giroux.

Hernandez, Edith L. 1969. "*Mir-i-nisa*: Distinctly Filipino." *Manila Times* December 1: 21A.

Hila, Antonio. 1992. *Musika: An Essay on Philippine Ethnic Music*. Manila: Sentrong Pangkultura ng Pilipinas.

———. 1998. "Lucio San Pedro: The Creative Nationalist." In *The National Artists of the Philippines*. Manila: Anvil. pp. 307–318.

———. 2004. *Music in History, History in Music*. Manila: University of Santo Tomas.

Hobsbawm, Eric, and Terence Ranger, eds. 1983, 1992. *The Invention of Tradition*. Cambridge: Cambridge University Press.

Hosillos, Lucila. 1970. "Cultural Nationalism and World Traditions."
Diliman Review 18(4): 306–317.

Hutchinson, John. 1987. *The Dynamics of Cultural Nationalism*. London:
Allen and Unwin.

Ileto, Reynaldo. 1997. *Pasyon and Revolution: Popular Movements in the
Philippines, 1840–1910*. Quezon City: Ateneo de Manila University
Press.

———. 2005. "Philippine Wars and the Politics of Memory." *Positions*
13(1): 215–234.

Isleta, Pat D. 1986. "I Won't Be Home Tonight." In *We Were There*, edited
by Lourdes Angulo. Manila: Staff Members of Asian Development Bank,
Pasay City. pp. 51–63.

Jameson, Fredric. 1991. *Postmodernism, Or, The Cultural Logic of Late
Capitalism*. Durham, NC: Duke University Press.

Japitana, Norma L. 1982. *The Superstars of Pop*. Manila: Makati Trade
Times.

Jenkins, Shirley. 1954. *American Economic Policy Toward the Philippines*.
Stanford, CA: Stanford University Press.

Joaquin, Nick. 1996. *One Woman's Liberating: The Life and Career of Estefania
Aldaba-Lim*. Pasig City, Philippines: Anvil.

———. 2001. "Culture as History & Culture and History: The Filipino's
Becoming." In *Philippine Cultural and Artistic Landmarks of the Past
Millennium* (Proceedings of). Manila: NCCA. pp. 125–168.

Johnson, Bryan. 1987. *The Four Days of Courage: The Untold Story of the
People Who Brought Marcos Down*. New York: Free Press.

Jose, Regalado. 2007. Correspondence with author. August 22.

———. 2008. Correspondence with author. March 11.

Kahn, Joel. 1998. "Southeast Asian Identities: Introduction." In *Southeast
Asian Identities*, edited by Joel Kahn. London: Institute of Southeast
Asian Studies. pp. 1–27.

Kalanduyan, Danongan. 1996. "Magindanaon Kulintang Music:
Instruments, Repertoire, Performance Contexts, and Social Functions."
Asian Music 27(2): 3–18.

Kalayaan: Sandaang Taong Pag-Gunita (Various Artists). 1998. Dypro
Record DYP-316-2.

Karnow, Stanley. 1989. *In Our Image: America's Empire in the Philippines*.
New York: Random House.

Kasilag, Lucrecia. 1967. "Asian Music in Education." *Music Educators
Journal* 53(9): 71–73.

———. 1977. "Music in a New Era." In *Filipino Heritage: The Making of a
Nation*, edited by Alfredo Roces. Manila: Lahing Pilipino.
pp. 2583–2589.

———. 1998. Interview with author. Manila: September 2.

————. 2009. "Philippines: Spanish Period, 1521–1896." *Grove Music Online*. November 30, 2009. http://www.oxfordmusiconline.com.proxy. lib.umich.edu/subscriber/article/grove/music/48467.

Kerkvliet, Benedict J., and Resil B. Mojares. 1991. *From Marcos to Aquino: Local Perspectives on Political Transition in the Philippines*. Manila: Ateneo de Manila University Press.

Kong, Lily. 1995. "Music and Cultural Politics: Ideology and Resistance in Singapore." *Transactions of the Institute of British Geographers* 20(4): 447–459.

Kramer, Paul. 2006. The Blood of Government: Race, Empire, the United States, and the Philippines. Chapel Hill: University of North Carolina Press.

Lanot, Marra Pl. 1969. "A Center for Whom?" *Daily Mirror* November 18: 20.

Lardizabal, Amparo. 1976. "Our Customs, Beliefs, and Superstitions." In *Readings on Philippine Culture and Social Life*. Manila: Rex Book Store. pp. 104–123

Lardizabal, Amparo, and Felicitas Tensuan-Leogardo, eds. 1976. *Readings on Philippine Culture and Social Life*. Manila: Rex Book Store.

Laurel, José, Jr. (1956), 1974. "The Resurgence of Philippine Nationalism." In *Filipino Nationalism: 1872–1970*, edited by Teodoro A. Agoncillo. Quezon City: R.P. Garcia Publishing Co., pp. 312–320.

Leon, Anna Leah de. 1986. "The CCP Secrets." *Manila Times* March 24: 13.

Leon, Felipe de. 1966, 1976. "Culture: A Solution to Our Problems." In *Readings on Philippine Culture and Social Life*, edited by Amparo Lardizabal and Felicitas Tensuan-Leogardo. Manila: Rex Book Store. pp. 254–259.

Leon, Felipe de, Jr. 1990. "The Filipino's Image in the '*Kundiman*.'" *Malaya*. June 28: 15–16.

Lico, Gerard. 2003. *Edifice Complex: Power, Myth, and Marcos State Architecture*. Manila: Ateneo de Manila University Press.

Lim, Fides. 2006. "Jim Paredes: 'We Should Awaken Memory.' In *20 Filipinos 20 Years After People Power: Special EDSA 20th Anniversary Issue*. Philippine Center for Investigative Journalism.

Lipsitz, George. 1994. *Dangerous Crossroads: Popular Music, Postmodernism and the Focus of Place*. London, New York: Verso.

Long Live the Philippines! Mabuhay ang Pilipinas! (Various Artists). 1998. Ivory Records IRC-K-7073.

Lopez, Salvador. 1968. "Maria Clara—Paragon or Caricature?" In *Rizal: Contrary Essays*, edited by Petronilo Daroy and Dolores Feria. Quezon City: Guro Books. pp. 81–84.

Lopez, Zenaida. 2006. Correspondence with author. September 20.

Lumbera, Bienvenido. 1980, 1996. "The Nationalist Literary Tradition." In *Nationalist Literature: A Centennial Forum*, edited by Elmer Ordoñez. Quezon City: University of the Philippines Press and the Philippine Writers' Academy. pp. 1–16.

Maceda, José. 1963. "The Music of the Magindanao in the Philippines." Ph.D. dissertation. University of California, Los Angeles.

———. 1992. "Acculturation and Internationalization: The Philippine Situation." In *World Music-Musics of the World*, edited by Max Peter Baumann. Wilhelmshaven: Florian Noetzel Versa.

———. 1998a. "Upland Peoples of the Philippines." In *The Garland Encyclopedia of World Music, Volume 4, Southeast Asia*. New York: Garland. pp. 913–928.

———. 1998b. *Gongs and Bamboo: A Panorama of Philippine Musical Instruments*. Quezon City: University of Philippines Press.

Maceda, José, et al. "Philippines." *Grove Music Online.* [B] Available: http://www.oxfordmusiconline.com.proxy.lib.umich.edu/subscriber/article/grove/music/48467. [July 30, 2009].

Maceda, José, Lucrecia Kasilag, et al. 1980. "Philippines." In the *New Grove Dictionary of Music and Musicians*, edited by Stanley Sadie. London: Macmillan, pp. 631–652.

Maceda, Teresita. 1998. "The Singing Huks." *Kasaysayan: The Story of the Filipino People*, Volume 8, edited by José Y. Dalisay. Pleasantville, NY: Reader's Digest. pp. 132–133.

Majul, Cesar Adib. 1988. "The Moro Struggle in the Philippines." *Third World Quarterly*, Islam & Politics 10(2): 897–922.

Mananquil, Millet Martinez. 1979. "Lucresia R. Kasilag: Come to the CCP—Whether in Your Oldest T-Shirt or Finest Jewelry—But Please Come." *Expressweek* August 2: 16–17.

Manuel, Arsenio. 1997. *Francisco Santiago: Composer, Pianist, Virtuoso*. Quezon City: Valerio.

Manuel, Peter. 1987. "Marxism, Nationalism and Popular Music in Revolutionary Cuba." *Popular Music* 6(2): 161–178.

———. 2009. *The Horse-Head Fiddle and the Cosmopolitan Reimagination of Tradition in Mongolia*. New York and London: Routledge.

Martin, Dalmacio, ed. 1980. *A Century of Education in the Philippines, 1861–1961*. Manila: Philippine Historical Association.

Mascarinas, Leo. 2007. Correspondence with author. August 18.

———. 2008. Correspondence with author. February 28, March 2, March 8.

May, Glenn A. 1983. "Why the United States Won the Philippine-American War, 1899–1902." *Pacific Historical Review* 52(4): 353–377.

McGuire, Charles Edward. 2006. "Music and Morality: John Curwen's Tonic Sol-fa, the Temperance Movement, and the Oratorios of Edward

Elgar." In *Chorus and Community*, edited by Karen Ahlquist. Urbana and Chicago: University of Illinois Press. pp. 111–138.

Melencio, Cherie. 1986. "I Forgot All about My Groceries." In *We Were There*, edited by Lourdes Angulo. Manila: Staff Members of Asian Development Bank, Pasay City. pp. 49-50.

Mga Awit Sa Bagong Lipunan. 1974. Manila: ERA4.

Miller, Stuart Creighton. 1982. *"Benevolent Assimilation": The American Conquest of the Philippines, 1899–1903*. New Haven: Yale University Press.

Mirano, Elena Rivera 1992. *Musika: An Essay on the Spanish Influence on Philippine Music*. Manila: Sentrong Pangkultura ng Pilipinas.

———. 2008. Correspondence with author. September 6.

———. 2009. *The Life and Works of Marcelo Adonay, Volume 1*. Quezon City: University of Philippines Press.

Molina, Antonio. 1977. "The Sentiments of…*Kundiman*." In *Filipino Heritage: The Making of a Nation*. Manila: Lahing Pilipino. pp. 2026–2029.

Montañez, Kris. 1988. *The New Mass Art and Literature*. Quezon City: Kalikasan Press.

Muego, Benjamin N. "The Philippine Student Movement of the 1970's and the 'New Society.'" Paper presented at the Midwest Conference on Asian Affairs, November 1, 1974, at the University of Kansas.

Mulder, Niels. 1997. *Inside Philippine Society: Interpretations of Everyday Life*. Quezon City: New Day.

Mundo, Clodualdo del, Jr. 2003. *Telebisyon: An Essay on Philippine Television*. Manila: CCP, NCCA.

"Music Promotion Foundation of the Philippines: Its Birth and Evolution." 1966. *Music of Asia: Program for the Symposium of the National Music Council of the Philippines*.

Nakpil, Carmen Guerrero. 1968. "Maria Clara." In *Rizal: Contrary Essays*, edited by Petronilo Daroy and Dolores Feria. Quezon City: Guro Books. pp. 85–90.

———. 1997. "Kundiman and Intermezzo." *Malaya* March 21: 5.

Nance, John. 1975. *The Gentle Tasaday: A Stone Age People in the Philippine Rain Forest*. New York: Harcourt Brace Jovanovich.

Nettl, Paul. 1952. *National Anthems*. New York: Storm Publishers.

Noble, Lela Garner. 1973. "The National Interest and the National Image: Philippine Policy in Asia." *Asian Survey* 13(6): 560–576.

Obusan, Ramón. 2000. Interview with author. Parañaque: March 14.

Ocampo, Ambeth. 1998. *The Centennial Countdown*. Pasig City: Anvil.

———. 2005. "Looking Back: The Right Way to Sing the National Anthem." *Philippine Daily Inquirer* May 25: A15.

Osborne, Milton. 1997. *Southeast Asia: An Introductory History*, 7th ed. N.p.: Allen & Unwin.

Osit, Jorge. 1984. *Felipe de Leon: A Filipino Nationalist and His Music*. N.p.: Author.

Paauw, Douglas S. 1963. "Economic Progress in Southeast Asia." *The Journal of Asian Studies* 23(1): 69–92.

Pájaro, Eliseo. 1957. "Nationalism and Folk Music." *Comment* 2nd quarter: 34–35.

————. 1966. "Nationalism in Music." *Musical Journal of the Philippines* 1(2): 7–11.

————. 1976. *The Filipino Composer and His Role in the New Society*. Quezon City: University of the Philippines Press.

Pajaron, Ding. 2000. Interview with author. New York: May 25.

Paredes, Jim. 2007. Correspondence with author. July 13, July 20.

Pedelty, Mark. 2004. *Musical Ritual in Mexico City*. Austin: University of Texas Press.

Pelaez-Marfori, Berry. 1986. "In the Cultural Scene, 1986 Was a Year of Upheaval and Homecomings." *Manila Chronicle* December 30: N.p.

Pfeiffer, William. 1976. *Filipino Music: Indigenious [sic], Folk, Modern*. Dumaguete City, Philippines: Silliman Music Foundation

Philippine Madrigal Singers. 1998. *Bayan Ko, Aawitan Kita (My Country, I Will Sing to You): A Centennial Celebration*. BMG Records (Pilipinas). MRCD 133.

Philippine Music Festival, Program Notes. 1974. "The League of Filipino Composers."

Pickett, Terry. 1996. *Inventing Nations: Justifications of Authority in the Modern World*. Westport and London: Greenwood Press.

Program for the Inauguration of the Cultural Center of the Philippines. 1969.

Quiambao, Jacob S. 1976. "The Filipino Family and Society." In *Readings on Philippine Culture and Social Life*, edited by Amparo Lardizabal and Felicitas Tensuan-Leogardo. Manila: Rex Book Store. pp. 82–103.

Quibuyen, Floro C. 1999. *A Nation Aborted: Rizal, American Hegemony, and Philippine Nationalism*. Quezon City: Ateneo de Manila University Press.

Quirino, José A. 1956. "How Our Flag Flew Again." *Philippines Free Press*, June 9. Available: http://www.crwflags.com/fotw/flags/ph-reint.html. [October 12, 2008].

R.C. 1966. "Often Mispronounced Names of Foreign Musicians." *Musical Journal of the Philippines* 1(1): 40.

Rafael, Vicente. 1990a. "Nationalism, Imagery, and the Filipino Intelligentsia in the Nineteenth Century." *Critical Inquiry* 16(3): 591–611.

————. 1990b. "Patronage and Pornography: Ideology and Spectatorship in the Early Marcos Years." *Comparative Studies in Society and History* 32(2): 282–304.

————. 1993. *Contracting Colonialism: Translation and Christian Conversion in Tagalog Society Under Early Spanish Rule*. Ithaca: Cornell University Press.

————. 2000. *White Love and Other Events in Filipino History*. Durham and London: Duke University Press.

Rances, Teresa. 2000. Interview with author. Manila: February 29.

Regev, Motti, and Edwin Seroussi. 2004. *Popular Music and National Culture in Israel*. Berkeley, Los Angeles, and London: University of California Press.

Rengger, N. J. 1995. Political *Theory, Modernity and Postmodernity: Beyond Enlightenment and Critique*. Oxford: Blackwell.

Retana, Wenceslao. 1888. *El Indio Batangueño: (estudio etnográfico)*, 3rd ed. Manila: Tipo-Litografia de Chofre y Cia.

Rivera, Juan. 1978. *The Father of the First Brown Race Civil Code*. Quezon City: UP Law Center.

Rizal, José. 1887. *Noli Me Tangere*. Berlin: Setzerinnenschule des Lette-Vereins.

Roa, Malou C. 1986. "God Was Not Sleeping After All." In *We Were There*, edited by Lourdes Angulo. Manila: Staff Members of Asian Development Bank, Pasay City. pp. 29–32.

Romulo, Carlos P. 1943. *Mother America: A Living Story of Democracy*. Garden City, NY: Doubleday.

Rosaldo, Renato. 1989, 1993. *Culture and Truth: The Remaking of Social Analysis*. Boston: Beacon Press.

Rouland, Michael. 2005. "Creating a Cultural Nation: Aleksandr Zataevich in Kazakhstan." *Comparative Studies of South Asia, Africa and the Middle East* 25(3): 533–553.

Rubio, Hilarion. 1941. "Native Music." *Philippine Collegian* March 25: 61.

Salanga, Alfredo Navarro. 1986. "The New CCP." *Manila Times* July 18: 14.

Salazar, José S. 1969. "'Not Where It's At': Cultural Center is Anti-revolutionary Instrument of Establishment and Therefore Not Truly Cultural, Says Author." *Philippines Free Press* November 15: 14.

Samson, Helen F. 1976. *Contemporary Filipino Composers: Biographical Interviews*. Quezon City: Manlapaz.

Santiago, Francisco. 1928. "Why I Composed the Music for 'Philippines My Philippines.'" *Philippine Collegian* November 30: 21.

————. 1957. *The Development of Music in the Philippine Islands*. Quezon City: University of the Philippines.

Santiago-Felipe, Vilma R. 1969. "Symphony Concert 1: Revealing and Encouraging Outgrowths." *Daily Mirror* October 24: N.p.

———. 1977. "Pulse of the Music Makers." In *Filipino Heritage: The Making of a Nation*, edited by Alfredo R. Roces. Manila: Lahing Pilipino. pp. 2499–2505.

———. 1998. "Lucrecia R. Kasilag: A Gem of a Person, a Jewel of an Artist." In *The National Artists of the Philippines*, edited by Nestor Jardin et al. Pasig City: Anvil. pp. 209–218.

Santos, Bienvenido. 1967. *The Day the Dancers Came: Selected Prose Works*. Manila: Bookmark.

Santos, Isabel A. 2004. Bayanihan—*The National Folk Dance Company of the Philippines: A Memory of Six Continents*. Manila: Anvil.

Santos, Ramón. 1991. "The Philippines." In *New Music in the Orient: Essays on Composition in Asia since World War II*, edited by Harrison Ryker. The Netherlands: Fritz Knuf.

———. 1998. "Art Music of the Philippines in the Twentieth Century." In *The Garland Encyclopedia of World Music, Volume 4: Southeast Asia*. New York and London: Garland. pp. 868–882.

———. 1999. "Traditional Expressive Cultures in Modern Society: An Issue of Survival in Change." In *1998 Philippine International Dance Conference: Dance in Revolution, Revolution in Dance*, edited by Basilio Esteban Villaruz and Leonila Bondoy. Manila: CCP, NCCA. pp. 113–118.

———. 2001. "Constructing a National Identity through Music." *Bulawan: Journal of Philippines Arts and Culture* 2: 20–31.

———. 2002. "Revivalism and Modernism in Asian Music." *Bulawan: Journal of Philippines Arts and Culture* 7: 34–61.

———. 2005. "José Montserrat Maceda: Rebellion, Non-conformity, and Alternatives." In *Tunugan: Four Essays on Filipino Music*. Quezon City: University of the Philippines Press. pp. 125–178.

Schumacher, John. 1981. *Revolutionary Clergy: The Filipino Clergy and the Nationalist Movement, 1850–1903*. Quezon City: Ateneo de Manila University Press.

Scott, James. 1990. *Domination and the Arts of Resistance: Hidden Transcripts*. New Haven: Yale University Press.

Scott, William Henry. 1985. *Cracks in the Parchment Curtain*. Quezon City: New Day.

———. 1994. *Barangay: Sixteenth-Century Philippine Culture and Society*. Manila: Ateneo de Manila University Press.

Seagrave, Sterling. 1988. *The Marcos Dynasty*. New York: Harper & Row.

Shafer, Boyd. 1982. *Nationalism and Internationalism: Belonging*. Malabar, FL: Robert E. Krieger.

Shay, Anthony. 1999a. "Choreographic Politics: The State Folk Ensemble, Representation, and Power." In 1998 *Philippine International Dance Conference: Dance in Revolution, Revolution in Dance*, edited by Basilio Esteban S. Villaruz and Leonila Bondoy. Manila: CCP, NCCA. pp. 28–45.

———. 1999b. "Parallel Traditions: State Folk Dance Ensembles and Folk Dance in 'the Field.'" *Dance Research Journal* 31(1): 29–56.

Shrine of Mary, Queen of Peace (Our Lady of EDSA) website. Available: http://www.edsashrine.com/v2/aboutus.php. [May 12, 2008].

Smith, Anthony. 1998. *Nationalism and Modernism: A Critical Survey of Recent Nations and Nationalism*. London: Routledge.

"Songs in the Key of Politics." 2004. Philippine Center for Investigative Journalism. Available: http://www.pcij.org/imag/2004Elections/ Campaign/songs2.hmtl. [November 11, 2008].

Starner, Frances. 1963. "The Philippines: Politics of the 'New Era.'" *Asian Survey* 3(1): 41–47.

Stone, Christopher. 2008. *Popular Culture and Nationalism in Lebanon: The Fairouz and Rahbani Nation*. London and New York: Routledge.

"Suits against Center, 4 Gov't Firms Dropped." 1969. *Manila Chronicle* December 9: 13.

Tadiar, Neferti X. M. 2002. "Himala (Miracle): The Heretical Potential of Nora Aunor's Star Power." *Signs* 27(3): 703–741.

Tariman, Pablo. 1992. "PPO Program Foreign-Oriented: Filipino Works in the Dark." *Malaya* February 9: 9.

Tarling, Nicholas, ed. 1992, 1999. *The Cambridge History of Southeast Asia, Volume Two, Part Two: From World War II to the Present*. Cambridge: Cambridge University Press.

Taruskin, Richard. "Nationalism." *Grove Music Online*. Available: http://www.oxfordmusiconline.com.proxy.lib.umich.edu/subscriber/ article/grove/music/50846. [October 1, 2008].

Tiongson, Nicanor G. 1992. *Dulaan: An Essay on the Spanish Influence on Philippine Theater*. Manila: Cultural Center of the Philippines Special Publications Office.

Tokita, Alison McAueen and David Hugues, eds. 2008. *The Ashgate Research Companion to Japanese Music*. Hampshire, England: Ashgate.

Torre, Visitacion de la. 1984. *The Cultural Center of the Philippines: Crystal Years*. Manila: Cultural Center of the Philippines.

———. 1985. *Lucrecia R. Kasilag: An Artist for the World*. N.p.: Vera-Reyes.

Trimillos, Ricardo. 1999. "Gender in Dance Performance: Constructions and Paradigms from the Asia-Pacific Region." In 1998 *Philippine International Dance Conference: Dance in Revolution, Revolution in Dance,* edited by Basilio Esteban Villaruz and Leonila Bondoy. Manila: CCP, NCCA. pp. 145–154.

Tuohy, Sue. 2001. "The Sonic Dimensions of Nationalism in Modern China: Musical Representation and Transformation." *Ethnomusicology* 45(1): 107–131.

Turino, Thomas. 2000. *Nationalists, Cosmopolitans, and Popular Music in Zimbabwe*. Chicago: University of Chicago Press.

Urlanda, Randy V. 1998. "Come Dance, at the Ball of the Century." In *Kalayaan: Philippine Centennial Issue*. Manila: Manila Bulletin. pp. 77–79.

Urtula, Lucrecia. 1987. "Keeping in Step with Yesterday: The Choreography." In *Bayanihan*, edited by José Lardizabal et al. Manila: Bayanihan Folk Arts Center. pp. 117–129.

Veneracion, Andrea. 2000. Interview with author. Quezon City: April 4.

Viana, Augusto V. de. 2006. *The I Stories: The Events in the Philippine Revolution and the Filipino-American War as Told by Its Eyewitnesses and Participants*. España, Manila: University of Santo Tomas.

Villa, Maricor de. 1984. "The Cultural Center: A Grand Folly or a Home for the Arts." *Philippine Panorama* 13(36): 32–37.

Villa, Rodrigo L. 1967, 1976. "Filipino Identity in Folk Dances." In *Readings on Philippine Culture and Social Life*, edited by Amparo Lardizabal and Felicitas Tensuan-Leogardo. Manila: Rex Book Store. pp. 163–168.

Villaluz, Dina F. 1986. "The Tanks Stopped on the Fourth Hymn." In *We Were There*, edited by Lourdes Angulo. Manila: Staff Members of Asian Development Bank, Pasay City. pp. 97–98.

Villanueva, Paz. 2007 Correspondence with author. August 4.

Wendt, Reinhard. 1998. "Philippine Fiesta and Colonial Culture," *Philippine Studies* 46(1): 3–23.

Wurfel, David. 1988. *Filipino Politics: Development and Decay*. Ithaca, NY: Cornell University Press.

Yano, Christine. 2003. *Tears of Longing: Nostalgia and the Nation in Japanese Popular Song*. Cambridge: Harvard University Asia Center.

Yusah, Patricia. 2000. Personal correspondence with author, August 16.
———. 2006. Interview with author. Lexington, MA: August 6.

Zaide, Sonia. 1999. *The Philippines: A Unique Nation*, 2nd ed. Quezon City: All-Nations.

Loboc Children's Choir, 139
Locsin, Leandro, 109, 119
Lopez, Zen, 91
Lucila, 184
Lucrecia Kasilag, 21–22, 23, 32, 45, 46, 51–57
Lupang Hinirang (*see* National Anthem of the Philippines)

Mabuhay (song), 199
Mabuhay Singers, 143–144
Macapagal, Diosdado, 77–78, 112, 195, 212
Macapagal-Arroyo, Gloria, 110, 212
MacArthur, Douglas, 40
Maceda, José, 22, 53–54, 72, 103, 202, 203, 206
madrigal (genre), 145–146
Magellan, Ferdinand, 17
maglalatik, 98–100
Magsaysay, Ramon, 40–41, 174, 195, 205
Malacañan (Malacañang) Palace, 120, 122, 149, 163, 171
Mambo Magsaysay, 40, 174
Manila Sound, 152–152
Manila Symphony Orchestra, 48
MAPHILINDO, 78
Maragtas epic, 123
March of the New Society (*see Bagong Pagsilang*)
Marcha Nacional Filipina, 28, 29
Mascarinas, Leo, 139, 146, 149, 161, 163
McKinley, William, 28, 93
mestizo,17, 38, 91, 154, 212
Metropop Music Festival, 153
Mga Awit sa Bagong Lipunan, 129, 162
military bases (U.S.), 19, 77, 120, 199, 200
Mirano, Elena Rivera, 27, 142, 148, 163, 173, 174, 213
Mirinisa, 124, 125
Misang Pilipino, 57
Miss Universe, 117, 198–199
Molina, Antonio, 32, 34, 35, 36, 45, 46, 52, 182, 203, 212
Moran, Maria, 198
moro (*see* Muslim)
Mulder, Niels, 3, 19
Muslim, 17, 45, 53, 57, 62, 63, 82, 85, 93, 98, 99;
Muslim Suite, 92–96

Nacionalista, 30
Nakpil,Julio, 28, 32, 204
NAMCYA (*see* National Music Competitions for Young Artists)
nation (definition of), 10–11;
   nation vs. nation-state, 11
national anthem of the Philippines, 28–32, 36, 41, 131, 168, 193–194, 195
National Artist Award (*see Gawad Artista ng Bayan*)
National Music Competitions for Young Artists, 133, 134
nationalism (definition of), 11
nationalization, 23–24
Navarro, Leah, 153
Nixon, Richard, 120
Noli Me Tangere, 49, 88
nostalgia, 19, 49, 62, 76, 79, 80–82, 90, 92, 94, 96, 138, 181, 207

Obusan, Ramón, 86, 94;
   Folkloric Group, 86, 103, 199, 207
Onward Christian Soldiers, 174
OPM (Original Pilipino Music), 151–153, 174, 188
Osias, Camilo, 31–32

Pájaro, Eliseo, 43, 44, 45, 145, 203, 206
Pajaron, Ding, 59–60, 126
Palma, José, 29
Pambansang Awit ng Pilipinas (*see* national anthem)
Papin, Imelda, 153
Paredes, Jim, 172, 173, 174, 188, 190, 196, 213
paso doble, 47, 202, 208
Pearl of the Orient, 42, 198
Pedero, Nonong, 153
Philippine American Cultural Foundation, 108
Philippine Military Academy, 174
Philippine Music Festivals, 125, 133
Philippine Philharmonic Orchestra, 21–22
Philippine Scenes, 22
Philippine Women's University, 51, 55, 72, 73, 74, 116, 203
Pilipinas Kong Mahal, 33
Pilipinolohiya, 203
Pinpin, Tomas, 17
Pobreng Alindahaw (song), 34